EVOLUTION, COGNITION, AND PERFORMANCE

Culture and cognition work together dynamically every time a spectator interprets meaning during a performance. In this study Bruce McConachie examines the biocultural basis of all performance, from its origins, and the cognitive processes that facilitate it, to what keeps us coming back for more. To effect this major reorientation, McConachie works within the scientific paradigm of enaction, which explains all human activities, including performances, as the interactions of mental, bodily, and ecological networks. He goes on to use our biocultural proclivity for altruism, as revealed in performance, to explore our species' gradual ethical progress on such matters as the changing norms of religious sacrifice, slavery, and LGBT rights. Along the way, the book engages with a wide range of performances, including Richard Pryor's stand-up, the film *Titanic*, aerialist performances, American football, and the stage and film versions of *A Streetcar Named Desire*.

BRUCE MCCONACHIE is a professor in the Department of Theatre Arts at the University of Pittsburgh. A past president of the American Society for Theatre Research (ASTR), he has also held visiting professorships at Northwestern University, University of Warsaw, University of Helskini, and Queen's University Belfast. His publications include *Performance and Cognition: Theatre Studies and the Cognitive Turn* (with Elizabeth Hart, 2006), *Engaging Audiences: A Cognitive Approach to Spectating in the Theatre* (2008), and *Theatre and Mind* (2013). He is the recipient of the Barnard Hewitt Award in Theatre History and the Distinguished Scholar Award, ASTR.

EVOLUTION, COGNITION, AND PERFORMANCE

BRUCE McCONACHIE

CAMBRIDGE
UNIVERSITY PRESS

University Printing House, Cambridge CB2 8BS, United Kingdom

Cambridge University Press is part of the University of Cambridge.

It furthers the University's mission by disseminating knowledge in the pursuit of education, learning and research at the highest international levels of excellence.

www.cambridge.org
Information on this title: www.cambridge.org/9781107091399

© Bruce McConachie 2015

This publication is in copyright. Subject to statutory exception and to the provisions of relevant collective licensing agreements, no reproduction of any part may take place without the written permission of Cambridge University Press.

First published 2015

Printed in the United States of America by Sheridan Books, Inc.

A catalogue record for this publication is available from the British Library

ISBN 978-1-107-09139-9 Hardback

Cambridge University Press has no responsibility for the persistence or accuracy of URLs for external or third-party internet websites referred to in this publication, and does not guarantee that any content on such websites is, or will remain, accurate or appropriate.

This book is dedicated to
All of the friends, students, and colleagues
who have helped me to travel this road,
Especially my graduate students at the University of Pittsburgh and
The Members of the ASTR Working Group
in Cognitive Science, Theatre, Dance, and Performance

Contents

Acknowledgments		*page* viii
	Introduction: toward a biocultural performance studies	1
1	Enaction, evolution, and performance	29
2	Rituals, image schemas, and cultural-cognitive ecosystems	65
3	Sociality, emotions, and empathy	98
4	The dynamics of making meanings	131
5	A Deweyan ethics for performance studies	168
Bibliography		202
Index		216

Acknowledgments

For their permissions or protocols that allow for the republishing of material that I have written, I thank the following publishers for: parts of "Doing Things with Image Schemas: The Cognitive Turn in Theatre Studies and the Problem of Experience for Historians" and "Falsifiable Theories for Theatre and Performance Studies" published in *Theatre Journal*, used by permission of the Johns Hopkins University Press; parts of *Engaging Audiences: A Cognitive Approach to Spectating in the Theatre*, "Ethics, Evolution, Ecology, and Performance," in *Readings in Performance and Ecology*, "Moving Spectators Toward Progressive Politics by Combining Brechtian Theory with Cognitive Science," in *Playing with Theory in Theatre Practice, Theatre and Mind*, and "Empathetic Engagement," in *Performance Studies: Key Words, Concepts, and Theories*, used by permission of Palgrave Macmillan; parts of "An Evolutionary Perspective on Play, Performance, and Ritual," published in *TDR: The Journal of Performance Studies*, used by permission of The MIT Press; and parts of "All in the Timing: The Meanings of *Streetcar* in 1947 and 1951," in *The Theatre of Tennessee Williams*, used by permission of Bloomsbury Publishing Plc. Full citations for these books, anthologies, and articles are available in my Bibliography.

Introduction
Toward a biocultural performance studies

> ... [O]nce most people really come to understand what an embodied conception of mind entails, they are going to be upset about it. Much of what they hold dear is at stake – their view of mind, meaning, thought, knowledge, science, morality, religion, and politics.
>
> Mark Johnson, *The Meaning of the Body*, 15

Deceptive categories

There is no longer any doubt – the performing arts are good for learners! Several studies in the 1990s demonstrated that students K-12 who engage in music, theater, and other performance activities in school score higher on academic tests than students who did not have this benefit. Most of these early studies were conducted before the experimenters could begin to explain why and how, from a neurocognitive point of view, the performing arts had such apparent effects on the minds and actions of school children. The 2008 longitudinal study, *Learning, Arts, and the Brain: The Dana Consortium Report on Arts and Cognition*, organized by the celebrated neuroscientist Michael Gazzaniga, however, went further by opening up the complex cognitive processes involved in learning through the arts. Gazzaniga and his thirteen associates, working at neuroscientific labs in major US universities, deployed recent findings about learning and fMRI (functional magnetic resonance imaging) studies of the brain to investigate correlations among learning through the arts, skills in other areas of knowledge, and changes in the brains of learners. *Learning, Arts, and the Brain* confirmed the earlier findings from the 1990s and began to chart the still murky territory of brain plasticity and performance.

Among Gazzaniga's and his team's more impressive results, these stand out: "An interest in a performing art leads to a high state of motivation that produces the sustained attention necessary to improve performance ... in other domains of cognition"; "Specific links exist between high levels of music training and the ability to manipulate information in both working- and long-term memory"; "Training in acting appears to lead to memory improvement through the learning of general skills for manipulating semantic information"; and "Learning to dance by effective observation is closely related to learning by physical practice, both in the level of achievement and also the neural substrates that support the organization of complex actions" (Gazzaniga 2008a: vi). Although training in all of the arts motivates and improves learning in a range of tasks, one study compared performing arts students in music and theater to visual arts students and found that the former were "more likely to be engaged in symbolic retrieval (i.e., the recollection of words and other symbols) than non-performing arts students" (2008: 90). In his overview of the findings, Gazzaniga concludes that "the consortium's accomplishments to date have included bringing together some of the leading cognitive neuroscientists in the world to sort out correlative observations on the arts and cognition, and to begin the analysis of whether these relationships are causal" (2008: vii–viii). On the basis of the pathbreaking Dana Consortium Report, testing for such causal relationships has been ongoing and productive in the last several years. Recent studies and results are available in *Art for Art's Sake? The Impact of Arts Education* (2012), by Ellen Winner, Thalia Goldstein, and Stephan Vincent-Lancrin.

This is welcome news and should prompt those of us in performance studies to probe its implications for our work. At the very least, the current belief that only certain kinds of performances can be fully "performative" – that is, effect actual changes in our lives – should be questioned. Now it appears that all kinds of experiences in planning, rehearsing, and performing music, theater, and dance events reshape our brains. This is important because how neuronal networks interact with the rest of our minds, as well as with our bodies and environments, is arguably at the root of who we are and what we can do. Further, the reality and effectiveness of all performance touches on a distinction that most academics make between the arts, as a general area of experience, and what usually get called the "applied arts," in which music, theater, and other arts are applied in therapeutic and/or social arenas to produce practical results. If artistic experience always changes our minds in material ways, however, is there really a fundamental difference between "aesthetic" and "practical" results? Despite these far-reaching implications, most academics in performance studies have been reluctant to engage with the science that has been transforming our area of study and that is legitimating (if not yet producing) increased spending in arts education.

In this Introduction, I will suggest several reasons for the refusal of most arts and humanities academics to use scientific knowledge in their work. One of the most important of these causes is that artists, teachers, and researchers in the performing arts have been socialized to believe that their work is distinct from other areas of human endeavor. Our present divisions among schools and departments in most universities in the West – including the distinctions that set schools and departments of the arts apart from other areas of learning – are based on principles that we inherited from the Enlightenment, primarily from John Locke and Immanuel Kant. Many universities divide education in the arts from learning in the sciences on the basis of what Enlightenment thinkers understood as psychological "faculties," a term that retains some of its double meaning for academics today. Following Kant, educators in the arts believed they were teaching students how to use the faculties of their senses and feelings, while institutional arrangements featuring instruction in science and math involved what those teachers took to be the "faculties" of imagination and understanding.

As cognitive philosopher Mark Johnson points out, Kant and other Enlightenment philosophers relegated the arts to the realm of feeling and emotion, separating performance from cognition and practice. As a result, most Enlightenment aestheticians came to believe that artistic experience could play no role in shaping the self or the world. States Johnson, "[Faculty psychology] reinforced a pervasive mind/body dualism and generated a series of foundational dichotomies between the 'higher' faculties and functions and the 'lower' ones – understanding versus sensation, cognition versus feeling, reason versus emotion" (Johnson 2007: 210). From this perspective, the emotional delights of the arts relegated so-called aesthetic experience to the 'lower' side of each of these dichotomies. Performance and the visual arts could inspire the disinterested contemplation of beauty and passion, but such judgment need have nothing to do with one's practical, ethical, and political commitments. Even though most of us no longer accept Kantian aesthetics and the Enlightenment dichotomies on which such formalism is based, we live in academic institutions that continue to separate the arts from other "faculties" of knowledge, including the neuroscience of Gazzaniga and his colleagues. Our institutional arrangements reinforce our parochialism.

One could argue, however, that Gazzaniga and his neuroscientists are also perpetuating a kind of "faculty" psychology deriving from the Enlightenment in the way they have framed many of their questions about the arts and education. Summaries of their work suggest that the performing arts – the kind of learning that students do when they practice a musical instrument or rehearse a play – are indeed separable from other areas of learning. Further, it seems that such artistic experience is especially praiseworthy when the skills learned in rehearsal and performance can be transferred to other areas of education. One of their studies, for instance, found that "there appear to be specific links between the practice of music and skills in geometrical representation" (Gazzaniga 2008a: vi). While we might want to join the neuroscientists in applauding the discovery of this correlation, we should also pause to consider its implications. Are the arts only "good" for children when experiencing them facilitates the transfer of skills from a 'lower' activity such as music to a 'higher' one like geometry? Turning this assumption on its head, we might also want to know whether the improvement of a child's skills in geometrical representation will help that person to become a better trumpet player. Gazzaniga and his colleagues did not pursue answers to that question, however. Neuroscientists also live in academia; the remnants of "faculty" psychology partly shape their assumptions and questions as well as our own.

There is another way to approach this problem, however – one that will open a path to the thesis of this book. Instead of using such categories as "the arts," "geometry," and others that derive from Enlightenment faculty psychology, we need to move beyond these deceptive categories to get at what actually happens in interactions among the brain, the body, and the environment when people learn, practice, and enjoy performances and similar kinds of events. Because the Dana Consortium sought to influence the public debate about the arts in education, Gazzaniga and his colleagues framed their questions and investigations in terms and values that politicians, educators, and parents could understand, appreciate, and perhaps act upon. In the West, reading and math skills are valued more highly than training in singing and dancing; it is no surprise, then, that the question of transference from the arts to higher-valued areas in the curriculum should arise. But the current curriculum of western schools and universities cannot be mapped onto specific areas and functions of the brain. There is no single place in the mind where reading happens. Doing a math problem draws on many distinct mental functions, including human emotion. And when students act a role in a play, they engage in memory, attention, empathy, executive control, and a host of other skills, several of which overlap with the brain functions that animate reading and mathematics. In short, the psychological faculties isolated by Enlightenment thinkers – faculties that continue to shape our categories of schooling and thinking at all levels – have little to do with the actual interactions of brains, bodies, and environments, as biologists, neuroscientists, linguists, anthropologists, and others shaped by the "cognitive turn" are beginning to understand. Our common-sense categories to denote different kinds of learning do not align with cognitive realities.

Of course the neuroscientists who contributed to *Learning, Arts, and the Brain* understood many of these complexities, even though they fashioned their findings in accord with public expectations. In the case of the music and geometry study, for example, chief investigator Elizabeth Spelke and her associates at Harvard based their investigations on their prior knowledge of three core cognitive systems that lie at the foundation of numerical reasoning. These systems, which emerge in infancy and retain enough plasticity to enable learning into adulthood, undergird and animate specific kinds of skills in both music and geometry. Spelke's hypothesis, that training in music might enhance certain skills in mathematics and geometry, was based on her knowledge of these three foundational systems and her hunch that improving their operations through musical training would enhance skills in other areas of the curriculum supported by these systems. In other words, Spelke's contribution to the Consortium Report was not based on a simple notion of "transference" from instruction in the arts to the sciences. Notice that no transfer – in the sense of taking skills from the "music" area of the brain and transferring them into the "geometry" part – actually took place. Rather, as she emphasized in her conclusion, "our findings underscore both the importance and the feasibility of breaking down children's complex learning capacities into component systems at the foundations of human knowledge" (2008: 47). Children's skills in both music and geometry benefitted when the core "component systems" that support both areas of learning were stimulated and enhanced.

Spelke's approach prompts a larger question that will inform much of this book: What are the foundational "component systems" that shape the practice and enjoyment of human performance? While we should suppose that these systems support many areas of human activity – that none of them is specific to performance, *per se* – we do want to know how these component systems bring shape and purpose to making and experiencing the broad range of activities that we generally include as performances. As Gazzaniga's scientists knew, they would have to ignore the institutional organization of knowledge and brush aside conventional categories and understandings in several disciplines to get at the answers to a similar question about learning and the performing arts.

The problem with institutional categories for areas of learning also relates to the general definition of performance. Given the public purposes of their funding, Gazzaniga and his colleagues were looking primarily for links between "the arts" and learning in other areas of the curriculum. Nearly all definitions of performance, however, have encompassed areas of human activity that are not usually included in "the arts" and many of them are not taught in schools. These range from stand-up comedy and horror movies to tribal rituals and campaigning for political office. Richard Schechner and others began including these kinds of activities under the umbrella term of "performance" in the 1970s, and any book or article that attempts to define the general parameters of the category must include them or explain the reasons for their absence. From my perspective, these activities are indeed "performance," but it is clear that conventional approaches to "the arts" or any other faculty psychology still informing school curricula will not take us very far in understanding their operations.

The neuroscientific investigations of Gazzaniga and others point us toward a way of resolving this problem. If we can determine most of the underlying component systems that support and enhance the practice and enjoyment of "performance," broadly conceived, we are on our way to defining the scope and attributes of performance as a category of human activity. Just as there is no single area of the brain for "geometry," there is certainly no "performance module" that controls how our minds and bodies create and respond to the full range of performances. The cognitive sciences have advanced far enough, though, to enable us to identify several of the core systems that work together to support performance activities. The results of *Learning, Arts, and the Brain* confront us with a major problem to investigate: What are the common component systems that are necessary to generate and support all performances, from grand opera to krump dancing?

Beyond the "Two Cultures"

Before trying to answer this question directly, however, it is necessary to sketch the wider context of the "cognitive turn" in the humanities and its implications for the production of knowledge in our culture. The cognitive sciences have not only undermined our institutional categories and arrangements for investigating the performing arts and other areas of school curricula, they have also destabilized the traditional foundations and assumptions of knowledge across the humanities and the sciences. Artists and scholars in performance studies – that is, my colleagues in musicology, theater arts, sports, anthropology, film studies, religion, history, communication, as well as in specific performance studies programs – need to understand that they are not alone in questioning what counts as knowledge in our field. But we also need to confront the immensity of the problem before we can begin to chart a way out of the epistemological straightjacket that we in performance studies have helped to create. An introduction to our difficulties properly begins by recalling a lecture given at Cambridge University by British novelist and scientist C.P. Snow in 1959, entitled, "The Two Cultures." Snow later published an expanded version of his talk entitled *The Two Cultures and the Scientific Revolution*. As we will see, the ability to maintain clear divisions between the cultures of science and the humanities, although a no-brainer in 1959, is fast eroding.

Until about twenty years ago, scientists in linguistics, psychology, neuroscience, and biology had little to say to us humanists that seemed relevant to our work. Floating in our separate academic bubbles, humanists and scientists played out Snow's dance of the "two cultures" for most of the twentieth century. We recognized that we had distinctive kinds of truths, used different methods to pursue them, and supported our claims through separable types of evidence and argumentation. Near the end of the century, however, some scholars challenged what was for most of us a generally benign division of labor. A few humanists, convinced by one or another theory of poststructuralism, stated that "science" was a Relativistic discourse like any other and denounced as a power-grab scientific ideas that claimed some possibility for Objectivity. Despite the Sokal hoax and other revelations of the hollowness of such arguments, more humanists followed them into the anti-science trenches, believing the fight was ethically and epistemologically worthwhile. Most scientists ignored the skirmish, but some dug their own trenches to plant the flag of Objectivity and fight back against humanist foolishness and envy.

Although this contest continues among some scientific and (post)humanist warriors, most of us can see that the old epistemological battle lines have shifted, partly dissolved, and in some areas, even melted away completely. The fights in the 1990s about the validity of experimentation versus experience, the importance of nature over nurture, or the superiority of objective to subjective truths have dissipated, as both sides are beginning to realize that they can justifiably claim neither position as their own. The evolutionary and cognitive sciences have been at the center of this epistemological sea change. While philosophers attentive to these disciplines now understand that the sciences have the empirical tools to turn age-old philosophical dilemmas into relatively straightforward scientific problems, they also know that solving these problems will not deliver Objective Scientific Truth.

This is because our evolutionary inheritance and cognitive abilities, however marvelous, also prevent us from acquiring a God's-eye view of ourselves and our world. As cognitive literary critic Ellen Spolsky notes, "Precisely because the human species and its ways of knowing evolved by the accumulation of random mutations in interactions with changing environments rather than genetically engineered for the task of knowing, it is not at all surprising that they are unstable... The evolutionary success of the species would actually be compromised by an entirely rigid, that is, dependable, way of knowing" (Spolsky 2001: 52). Just because Objectivity is impossible, however, does not doom us to the epistemological chaos of Relativism. I agree with most pragmatists that such binaries set up false oppositions and expectations. With the collapse of the old poles of Relativity and Objectivity, however, it is clear that humanists and scientists are now standing on much the same spongy epistemological ground; neither can retreat to the previously rock-solid knoll of one or the other academic culture. This may be the first time since such Enlightenment academics as Descartes, Newton, Locke, Diderot, and Kant began dividing the sciences from the humanities that new knowledge is forcing us back together again. This is frightening but also salutary. We have much to learn from each other and it's important that we do so; there is a lot of work to be done.

Regarding another old dichotomy, Experience versus Experimentation, some scientists are now finding that both approaches are necessary. Cognitive scientists Varela, Thompson, and Rosch, for example, warned their colleagues back in 1991 that "to deny the truth of our own experience in the scientific study of ourselves is not only unsatisfactory; it is to render the scientific study of ourselves without a subject matter" (Varela, Thompson, and Rosch 1991: 13–14). These scientists have found that the rigorous first-person perspective of phenomenology can be an important corrective to the attempt to maintain a third-person aloofness, which remains the norm for most scientific investigation. As we will see, several more cognitive scientists working within the paradigm of Enaction are also discovering that their truth claims can be enhanced through phenomenology.

Perhaps the primary reason for the collapse of an Enlightenment approach to epistemology is the assumption that the mind is a "blank slate." Most academic disciplines in the humanities subscribed to the notion that social learning was more important than inherited nature – a belief that had been prevalent in the West since the dominance of Lockean psychology underwrote much of the Enlightenment. This view may be epitomized in a remark made by the former president of the Modern Language Association,

Robert Scholes: "Yes, we were natural for eons before we were cultural – before we were human even – but so what? We are cultural now and culture is the domain of the humanities" (Scholes quoted in Fromm 2009: 263). This Lockean belief also provided humanists with a moral agenda. For if *Homo sapiens* as a species has no inherent qualities, if culture is entirely learned, our political and social systems are fully contingent and changeable. In such a world, humanists could help to expose the depredations of power, propose possible alternatives, and bring about a fairer society. But evidence from the biological and cognitive sciences is rapidly piling up that our species is born with an elaborate cognitive architecture, which includes a surprising number of psychological predilections as well as genetic constraints. Like other animals, we were born with certain mental and physical capabilities acquired through evolution that help us to survive. While it's true that human cultures vary widely, that may have more to do with our cognitive flexibility in adapting to different ecologies than with any learned behaviors metaphorically inscribed on a Lockean mind without innate content.

The arbitrary separation between nature and nurture encouraged many social scientists to believe that they could rule out biology and genetically derived cognitive dynamics as having anything to do with things social or cultural. From the point of view of much current cognitive science, however, this view is seriously incomplete. The social constructivist accounts of Erving Goffman, Michel Foucault, Victor Turner, and many other sociologists, historians, and anthropologists who have influenced performance studies fit comfortably within what John Barkow, Leda Cosmides, and John Tooby attacked as the "Standard Social Science Model" (SSSM) of the human mind. Barkow, Cosmides, and Tooby first questioned this model in *The Adapted Mind: Evolutionary Psychology and the Generation of Culture*, a paradigm-shattering book at its appearance in 1992. In their introductory essay, they stated:

> The Standard Social Science Model requires an impossible psychology. Results out of cognitive psychology, evolutionary biology, artificial intelligence, developmental psychology, linguistics and philosophy converge on the same conclusion: A psychological architecture that consisted of nothing but equipotential, general-purpose content-independent, or content free [cognitive] mechanisms could not successfully perform the tasks the human mind is known to perform or solve the adaptive problems humans evolved to solve – from seeing, to learning a language, to recognizing an emotional expression, to selecting a mate, to the many disparate activities aggregated under the term "learning culture." (Barkow, Cosmides, and Tooby 1992: 34)

Barkow, Cosmides, and Tooby recognized that leading social scientists had assumed the SSSM model of human cognition and behavior for much of the twentieth century. The once firm divide between Nature and Nurture has dissolved, as have the other two dichotomies, and we are only beginning to make a different kind of sense of who we are and what we can know and do in the world. This recognition of new realities undermining old certainties has already destabilized the sciences and is spreading into the social sciences and humanities.

The shifting fault lines among the epistemological plates upon which our old disciplines rest have begun to shake things up in theater and performance studies. As occurs at the beginning of any paradigm change, however, these rumblings have mostly been felt at the margins of our field. Most performance academics, like most humanists and scientists, have ignored these cracks in what still seems like solid ontological and epistemological ground. Nonetheless, several of us have successfully demonstrated that the assumptions of Saussurian semiotics are ill-founded, that the poststructuralism of Derrida and others does not accord well with cognitive realities, and that the psychoanalytic tradition, from Freud to Lacan to Butler and Zizek, is inadequate and misleading from a scientific point of view. On the other hand, many of the new realities revealed by evolutionary and cognitive studies do jibe with aspects of phenomenology and varieties of materialism. In addition to posing challenges to still-current theories, those of us working in cognition and performance have successfully questioned assumptions about the willing suspension of disbelief, the attribution of meanings to performances, the rationalism behind *Verfremdungseffekt*, and many other conventional ideas and strategies in our field.

For many scholars in performance studies, however, epistemology and methodology have always been less important than morality. Pick up any journal in the field, and our rhetoric of ethical earnestness practically jumps off its pages. Partly because the performance events we study have so often been dismissed as mere entertainment, we have felt the need to insist that our scholarly "interventions" weigh in on the side of the angels. In retrospect, the putative fight between "performance studies" and "theater arts" in the 1990s was mostly about moral positioning, as each side claimed that it was better equipped to deliver politically progressive purity and radical change. Given the cultural habitus of our academic tribe, we tend to grab for handy definitions of racism, objectification, and identity, for example, regardless of their ontological and epistemological baggage.

My point is not that we should abandon our ethical concerns. Some performances, such as gladiatorial contests and racist lynchings, certainly deserve to be condemned. Others can indeed lead to ethical and political progress, as this book will show. But we need to understand how and why this is so, instead of putting the ethical cart before the scientific horse. Unless one is pulling the other, our attempts to change things will come to naught or perhaps even reverse our (always) unsteady course. On the whole, scientists have a better means than humanists of validating their ideas over time. This is not to say that science produces objective knowledge, and it is certainly not to claim that humanistic studies can be reduced to hard science. At least since Galileo, however, international protocols concerning empirical truth claims have produced reliable knowledge about our bodies and our world that has altered how we live. In the area of performance alone, scientific knowledge about electricity, optics, acoustics, and disease – not to mention gravity – has revolutionized what and where we perform, how we can meet at conferences to talk about it, and what we might say in print and digital forms of communication about performance continuities and innovations. It would be foolish to deny our significant debt to the scientific past. Nonetheless, many theater and performance scholars would prefer to ignore scientific findings if they appear to undermine what they take to be their ethical standards.

Because some neuroscientists affirmed the importance of the performing arts for general education, it was easy to feel good about our ethical and scientific credentials in the first part of my Introduction. A recent essay in *The Chronicle of Higher Education* by philosopher Stephen Asma, however, undermines one of our usual claims about occupying the moral high ground. Asma laments the fact that many humanists continue to ignore or resist the conclusions from the biological and cognitive sciences that nature and nurture are thoroughly entangled. His chief example is current scientific and humanistic discourse about sex and gender. In the last ten years, many scientists have come to understand that there are actually several sexes in our species, from male and female bodies with male and female brains to male bodies with female brains, female bodies with male brains, and many combinations in between. States Asma, "Biology now recognizes the immense domain of external triggers and influences (from intrauterine environment to social structures) that shape phenotype expression of genetic possibilities. Biology has become dialectical" (Asma 2011: B7).

In contrast, the thinking of most humanists on this matter has changed little since the 1970s, when some feminist theorists drew (what was then) an important distinction between sex and gender on the basis of differences between nature and nurture. Foucault's theories helped to harden this distinction, and soon other social constructionists argued that society sorted people into arbitrary gender categories on the basis of powerful discourses. After Queer and LGBT Studies built many of its own ideas upon this assumption in the 1980s and 1990s, many humanists believed they had an ethical stake in defending conventional sex–gender theory. Consequently, when scientists began to collapse the nature–nurture divide, insisting on the biological complexity of sexuality, some humanists rallied to the ethical battlements and damned scientific discourse. From Asma's perspective, moral panic in the humanities trumped scientific evidence and logic.

Asma recognizes that the humanists' sex–gender distinction in the 1970s rightly rejected a long history of sexual essentialism, but he notes that there is nothing inherently conservative or repressive about current biological approaches and categories. Thankfully, he also finds that "increasing numbers of humanities scholars ... are slowly getting over biophobia" (2011: B9). Asma concludes by summarizing the findings of a recent book, *The Mirage of a Space between Nature and Nurture*, by Evelyn Fox Keller, who had defended the sex–gender dichotomy early in her career but is now firmly on the other side of the argument. The basic question about sexual identity, says Asma, is, "Which traits are malleable, and to what degree?" He concludes that "the answers will come from a prudent marriage of biocultural analysis, because developmental pathways don't recognize academic divisions" (2011: B9). We should not be surprised; present "academic divisions" derive from a faculty psychology put in place 300 years ago.

It is significant that Asma ends with a question. While the old certainties are gone, scientists willingly concede that they are a long way from clarifying such problems as the "biocultural" basis – the inevitable mix of nature and nurture – of sexual identity. The same might be said about many other areas of human behavior where biology and sociology intertwine. Sorting out the probable degree of malleability regarding the many traits that make up the range of human possibility will take decades and perhaps another century. Humanists need to get over their biophobia and give the scientists time for their experiments before jumping to conclusions. Or we might join the scientists to help all of us in academia figure it out. At the very least, we need to question the epistemological and moral "certainties" that varieties of social constructivism have backed us into during the last thirty years.

Social constructivism and changes in cognitive science

So how can scholars in performance studies begin to incorporate the findings of the evolutionary and cognitive sciences in order to reformulate the foundations of our discipline? As a first step, we need to recognize the extent to which social constructivism, with its "blank-slate" assumptions, has pervaded our dominant theories and methods. The cognitive revolution forces a radical reevaluation of performances studies – radical in the sense of going to the roots. While this discussion is taken up throughout this book, an introduction is in order now to give us a sense of the enormity of the task.

To begin with, social constructivism, especially when joined with scholarly guilt about ascribing western "universals" to all cultures in the past, has scared performance studies scholars away from the recognition that there are likely to be a fair number of biocultural universals for performance that are shared by all peoples. As members of the same species, our bodies and minds share massive similarities, and many of these are based in evolutionary genetics. For every other species on earth, genetics significantly shape an animal's behavior and action; why should we be significantly different? Among cognitive humanists, Patrick Colm Hogan has mounted a strong defense for the scholarly exploration of universals in the arts. Hogan points out that politically correct quibbles that denigrate universalism as "reactionary" actually get the problem backwards: "[N]o racist ever justified the enslavement of Africans or colonial rule in India on the basis of a claim that whites and nonwhites share universal human properties" (Hogan 2010: 38). He cites Kwame Appiah on the need to distinguish between the "pseudouniversalism" of past European hegemony and the search for universals based in our common human inheritance. Hogan endorses Lalita Pandit's notion of empathic universalism, which he adumbrates as "based on the assumption that all people share ethical and experiential subjectivity and that universality must both derive from and contribute to this sense of shared subjectivity, with all that it entails in terms of allowing each set of subjective experiences equal weight" (2010: 39).

Cognitive universals and social constructivism are two of the topics taken up in *Arguing About Human Nature: Contemporary Debates* (2013), an anthology of essays edited by Stephen M. Downes and Edouard Machery. As Machery argues in "A Plea for Human Nature," advances in the evolutionary and cognitive sciences invite us to step away from essentialist conceptions of human nature toward a notion based on evolutionary realities. For Aristotle and most other western philosophers, this essentialist notion supposes that "human nature is the set of properties that are separately necessary and jointly sufficient for being a human. Furthermore, the properties that are a part of human nature are typically thought to be distinctive of humans" (Machery 2013: 65). In sharp contrast, Machery proposes that "human nature is the set of properties that humans tend to possess as the result of the evolution of their species" (2013: 65). Machery includes such properties as bipedalism, biparental investment in child rearing, and the capacity to speak. Although evolution has clearly endowed our species with these physical, behavioral, and cognitive abilities, not all humans possess them. This is primarily because evolution leads to substantial diversity in all species, not uniformity. The fact that some *Homo sapiens* are born without legs, do not learn how to speak, and cannot love their children does not exclude them from our biological species, however. It simply invites us to understand these humans as atypical – but not abnormal; evolution does not generate norms – as indeed they are. States Machery, "What is required of the properties that are a part of human nature is that they be shared by *most* humans as a result of a specific causal process – the evolution of humans. Relatedly, the properties that are a part of human nature do not have to be possessed *only* by humans" (ital. in original) (2013: 66).

Defining human nature in terms of evolution also leads Machery to reject explanations for common human traits that rely solely on social constructivism. He gives "outgroup bias," the tendency to reject others not in your "ingroup," as an example. Any explanation that the occurrence of outgroup bias is "exclusively due to enculturation or to social learning" should be rejected, says Machery (2013: 68). "Exclusively" is important here; Machery is not saying that evolution alone is the cause of such beliefs and behaviors as racism and classism. His point is that both nature and nurture are implicated in the human proclivity to divide "us" from "them." Where humans are concerned, biology and culture are thoroughly entangled and have been for the last million years.

The false divide between nature and nurture continues to be a major epistemological problem for performance studies. Marvin Carlson's second edition of *Performance: A Critical Introduction* (2004) remains a useful guide to the diverse theoretical investments of most performance studies scholarship. According to Carlson, semiotics, deconstruction, and discourse theory have provided important ideas for linguistic approaches to performance studies. I have already noted the general shortcomings of the first two of these social constructivist theories when measured against the new scientific insights. Regarding discourse theory, its Lockean "blank-slatism" runs deep in performance studies and humanistic scholarship, generally. Commenting on the prevalent modes of doing literary analysis, the four (self-named) "literary Darwinists" who wrote *Graphing Jane Austin: The Evolutionary Basis of Literary Meaning*, note correctly that "the dominant theoretical framework for current literary study is Foucauldian cultural critique. The central concept of this school is 'power'" (Carroll et al., 2012: 160). The authors, Joseph Carroll, Jonathan Gottschall, John A. Johnson, and Daniel J. Kruger, go on to state that a range of scholars, from feminists and Marxists to postcolonial and ethnic critics in the humanities, tend to measure the exercise of Foucauldian power against a "utopian norm" in which "the differential exercise of force in social relations" might no longer exist. The literary Darwinists point out, though, that "from an evolutionary perspective, conflicting interests are an endemic and ineradicable feature of human social interaction" (2012: 160). If this is so – if orientations toward social power are a hardwired part of our nature as well as a learned part of our nurture – it makes little sense to link all power to discourse and to investigate it as a wholly social–historical problem that might be made to go away.

Not surprisingly, much of Carlson's overview of the theoretical traditions informing performance studies is devoted to the social sciences. Carlson discusses the broad impact of cultural anthropology, ethnography, and sociology, with particular attention to the ideas of Clifford Geertz, Victor Turner, Johan Huizinga, and Erving Goffman, in his summary. In general, each of these theorists and their social scientific disciplines relied on the 300-year-old Lockean tradition that divides nature from nurture in the study of humankind. This is not to say that all of their conclusions should be thrown out, but it does mean that their founding assumptions must be examined in the light of the massive evidence now available in the evolutionary and cognitive sciences. Scholars in the social sciences have already begun to tackle this important work, and we can learn from their insights.

Carlson also notes three traditions in performance studies with roots in the biological sciences – psychoanalysis, physical anthropology, and ethology, the study of animal morphology and behavior. Although Freud built psychoanalysis on turn-of-the-century biology, Lacanian versions of the field (which merged it with semiotics in the 1950s) have shifted the ground of psychoanalysis to social constructivism. Nonetheless, Freud's ideas might have provided some footing for current scholarship if they could claim scientific validity; unfortunately, the truth claims of psychoanalysis cannot be falsified, as many have already explained. This leaves physical anthropology and ethology, with its interest in the rocks, tools, and skulls of the past along with animal behavior in the present. Schechner and others mined these veins of scholarship in the 1970s in an effort to explore the evolutionary bases of human rituals and came up with conclusions that made good sense then in terms of the science of the time. Better scientific ideas based in new experiments and insights, however, have replaced the assumptions and findings upon which Schechner based his work; the roots of ritual need to be revisited.

Although Carlson does not explore behaviorism, which dominated the general discipline of psychology in the middle decades of the last century, this discipline also drew on "blank-slate" assumptions. In brief, the behaviorists believed that the brain, in addition to controlling the internal workings of the body, was set up to generate individual and social behavior by responding to external stimuli. From a behaviorist perspective, people had little control over their goals and intentions; they could be conditioned to do all sorts of things and there was very little in the genetic and neurological constitution of the brain to constrain such responses. Because stimulus-response operations were assumed to be at the base of much social behavior, further knowledge about the cognitive operations of the mind and body was deemed relatively unimportant when it came to predicting how someone would act in a given situation. The assumptions of behaviorist psychology moved beyond experiments with lab rats in mazes and inflected the work of many scholars in the social sciences; now sociologists could add a psychological explanation to reinforce their findings at the social level of behavior. Behaviorism also influenced significant theories in theater studies, from Meyerhold's Biomechanics, to Method acting, to the notion of a "passive audience" primed for conditioning.

In response to behaviorism (as well as too many unresolved questions in early neuroscience), cognitive approaches to human behavior emerged in the 1960s. The digital computer became the first general model for the human brain, and that model continues to provide some insights into human cognition. At first, this model primarily mapped the stimulus-in, behavior-out assumption of behaviorism onto brain operations. When the brain-as-computer could not explain a growing range of cognitive phenomena, a second generation of cognitive scientists turned to "Connectionism," a paradigm that focuses on rapidly shifting neuronal networks to explain the speed and flexibility of our minds. Connectionism helped to account for a wider range of mental phenomena, but it continued to rely on notions of symbols in the brain representing external realities, much as digital combinations work in computing. Faced with problems concerning mental representation and the apparent off-loading of cognitive operations onto our environments, a third generation of cognitive science is now exploring paradigms variously termed "dynamic systems theory," "situated cognition," and "Enaction theory."

In biology, the theory of evolution has not undergone the same kinds of paradigmatic shifts, primarily because many biologists continue to believe that Darwin got most of it right. There has been a new emphasis, however, on "continuity theory," the insistence that there can be no ontological breaks between all living beings and the "higher" group of animals we call humans. These changes in emphasis at the paradigm level of the sciences have been motivated by rapid advances in experimental findings and mid-theory levels, as thousands of cognitive and evolutionary scientists continue to push the boundaries of our knowledge.

The general thrust of this work over the last fifty years, however, is indisputable. "Minding," to adopt the verb form of cognition, has morphed from a compliant manager of external stimuli in behaviorism and early neuroscience into a facilitator of our individual consciousness, embodied awareness, and social interaction in Enaction theory. As cognitive and evolutionary scientists have shared the results of their work, minding has also become a proactive protector of our individual survival. The former "blank slate" of the brain is not only overflowing with organic processing. It has moved beyond the head into full cooperation with the body, and is now colonizing its surrounding environment. If this sounds like a horror movie (perhaps "Invasion of the Hungry Brain"), it is only horrible for those who continue to hold on to nature–nurture distinctions and social constructivist assumptions. The question, then, is how to step away from the "blank slateism" of most of our theories, return to the basics of performance that got us interested in this field in the first place, and reconstruct our scholarship on a new, more scientifically valid foundation.

Given the speed of new discoveries and the elaboration of new paradigms in the evolutionary and cognitive sciences, there can be no guarantee that any new epistemology based in scientific investigation will survive for very long. But that recognition is part of the price we pay for joining the knowledge revolution of the twenty-first century. The alternative, however, is worse. If we stay with most of the orthodoxies of High Theory from the 1980s, biophobe reactionaries will welcome us in the trenches, but our "knowledge" will become increasingly irrelevant. The result will likely be the further marginalization of performance studies within the academy and perhaps its eventual demise. The most relevant historical precedent for our situation is probably the transition from the late medieval period to the renaissance. Before Galileo, the preference for groundless theory over experimental evidence led to many web-spinning niches for medieval monks in the short term, but also to the eventual collapse of the medieval world view (and to the disappearance of many of its monastic jobs). Given the increasing pressure on humanistic education throughout the West, those programs that ignore the merging of the former "two cultures" to hold on to an antiscientific scholasticism face bleak prospects in the twenty-first century. Even more alarming, perhaps, performance studies scholars will be promoting an ethical agenda with no clear procedures or standards to enable us to know how performances actually shape ourselves and the world.

Nonetheless, one might question whether the wholesale reconstruction of the field is really possible, especially at this early stage in the transition from the "two cultures" of academia to some new, still inchoate culture that joins together the humanities and sciences on the basis of a different epistemological foundation. Those who understand performance studies as an interdiscipline that brings together insights from the disciplines of music, anthropology, theater, religion, and related areas of study might caution that we should not get ahead of our academic allies; we should wait until our partners in the traditional disciplines in the arts, humanities, and social sciences have embraced the cognitive turn and then work for some synthesis of these new approaches. Unfortunately, this is not a real option. As I have explained, the current disciplines of academia are built upon misleading categories of "faculty" knowledge with little basis in evolutionary and cognitive realities. If we understand performance studies as an interdiscipline, an ingenious synthesis of related, but separable disciplines, we doom ourselves to even more incoherence and irrelevance than we face today.

In *Evolution, Cognition, and Performance*, I will argue that "performance" is the foundational activity from which theater, rituals, sports, and other performative activities emerged in the course of our biocultural evolution and upon which a coherent performance studies should be built. From its founding in the 1970s, Richard Schechner, Dwight Conquergood, and others tried to arrive at insights and terminology that could work at a level of generalization below the scholarly understandings of the traditional performance disciplines. I believe that goal, though only partly achieved in the past, may be approached through the opportunities opened up by the collapse of the two cultures. Even if we do not reach this goal in the next ten years, it should continue to command our attention. Performance studies scholars need commonly accepted definitions, frameworks, terminologies, and procedures that can be deployed to understand nineteenth-century minstrel shows in Sydney, last year's Rose Bowl parade in Los Angeles, the royal entry of the king into medieval Paris, multiple performances of Beethoven's Ninth Symphony in Tokyo, ritual initiations among gang members in the slums of Baltimore, performances for tourists at the Polynesian Cultural Center in Oahu, and the Pan-African Historical Theatre Festivals in Ghana between 1992 and 2010. Although scholars from music, theater, anthropology, and elsewhere might take up one or another of these investigations, none of the conventional performance disciplines has a stake in demonstrating how all of these activities are related and why their commonalities are important for understanding and interpreting each of the thousands of separate instances of performance that occur every day. Once celebrated as an anti-discipline and sometimes approached as an interdiscipline, performance studies needs to emerge as its own discipline, if it is to have relevance and influence in this century. Establishing the foundation of all performance activities remains a necessary challenge for performance studies, one that cannot be met by yet more monographs on gamelan music in Java or avant-garde theater in New York, as important as such work may be.

Toward a naturalistic epistemology

Several of the scientists I will be borrowing from in the following pages call themselves naturalists, a philosophical position associated with the ideas of Charles Darwin and John Dewey. Among these is Peter Godfrey-Smith, whose justification of Deweyan naturalism in philosophy provides a suitable preface to my own reasons for adopting this orientation for performance studies:

> Naturalism in philosophy requires that we begin our philosophical investigations from the standpoint provided by our best current scientific picture of human beings and their place in the universe... The science we rely on is not completely certain, of course, and may eventually change. The questions we try to answer, however, need not be derived from the sciences; our questions will often be rather traditional philosophical questions about the nature of belief, justification, and knowledge. Science is a resource for settling philosophical questions, rather than a replacement for philosophy or the source of philosophy's agenda. (Godfrey-Smith 2003: 154)

Replace "philosophy" with "performance studies" in the above quotation, and the general aim of my project becomes clear. I am asking "traditional" questions about performance studies and using science as a "resource" to settle them. Rather than "belief, justification, and knowledge," my questions concern such performance fundamentals as role-playing, event perception, emotional engagement, and memory. Like Godfrey-Smith, my naturalistic orientation will permit me to use science as a resource without allowing it to set my agenda.

The protocols of naturalism impose significant limitations on this study. In the chapters to follow, I will work with up-to-date scientific ideas on matters that concern the foundational component systems of performance, even though there is no general agreement among evolutionary and cognitive scientists as to what constitutes "our best current scientific picture," as Godfrey-Smith would require. Some experimental conclusions that I will use have not survived as many empirical challenges as others, but they remain open to continuing rounds of confirmation in the future. For instance, in the next chapter I will draw on Didier Bottineau's explanations of how language and memory work together – ideas that offer a relatively new explanation of these mutually supporting phenomena. While most of the theories I will use come from the sciences, several derive from empirical work in the humanities and social sciences. In their *Graphing Jane Austen* (2012), for example, the authors discuss the method and results of an experiment they put together using an on-line survey to test their hypothesis about whether the "agonistic structure" of several nineteenth-century novels helped readers to ascribe meaning to their experience, primarily through an evaluation of the novels' major characters. Like biological scientists, the authors recognize that their study, though empirically responsible, cannot be definitive, and they invite further investigations to test their results.

Philosophical naturalists are aware that scientists investigate truth claims at many levels. Although most scientists effectively work "in the trenches," seeking better validation for one or another hypothesis located in their own corner of a fairly well-established paradigm, others seek to test broader claims, and a few ask questions about accepted paradigms and begin to chart possible new explanatory syntheses. As already noted, cognitive psychologists raised substantial objections to behavioral psychology in the middle of the last century and gradually established more robust explanations to account for much of human behavior. In this case, as occurs when any new paradigm is challenging an older one, it was important for scientists and philosophers to posit "big picture" theories to guide new research questions and hypotheses, even though such pictures must be based on as yet slim empirical evidence. While no new theory ever springs fully tested from the head of Zeus, scientists must figure out how their new ideas may achieve provisional validity through programs of empirical work and explanatory logic and then begin to pursue them.

For *Evolution, Cognition, and Performance*, I am relying on what philosopher of science John Stewart calls the "proto-paradigm" of Enaction (Stewart 2010: 1), which is challenging standard cognitive science. Enaction theory began in the 1980s and first flowered in 1991 with a publication that was paradigm-shifting in its implications: *The Embodied Mind: Cognitive Science and Human Experience*, by Francisco Varela, Evan Thompson, and Eleanor Rosch. In the twenty-four years since then, scientists have found increasing experimental validation for many of the authors' positions. The emerging Enaction paradigm is replacing "Connectionism" and other computational models as the paradigm of choice for many cognitive scientists. A broad research program with many branches, Enaction now encompasses varieties of evolutionary psychology, embodied cognition (which locates the dynamics of the body in the brain to understand meaning-making), linguistics, situated cognition (which extends cognition from the brain and body into the environment), and several naturalistic philosophical orientations. Versions of phenomenology, materialism, and pragmatism, for example, may be aligned with the main principles of Enaction. By understanding action in the brain, the body, and the social and the material surround as the motive power of cognition, the Enactivists extend the arena of cognition from learning, memory, language, and behavior to include historical as well as psychological phenomena. In general, Enaction provides a broader basis for investigating the range and significance of all kinds of performances than does conventional cognitive science.

The Enactivists challenge what has come to be called representationalism, one of the central ontological premises of the standard approach to cognition. For most cognitive scientists, cognition involves algorithmic processes in an individual's brain that center on symbolic representations of the internal and external world. This Computational Theory of Mind (CTM), however, has no clear explanation for how the senses and the brain translate the world into a series of representational symbols for mental manipulation and then retranslate those symbolic calculations into signals for action. This leads Enactivists to question why the brain would require such symbolic representations at all. If the animal is "active, embodied, [and] environmentally situated," asks philosopher Alva Noë, why would it need "to act as if the world were not immediately present" (Noë 2004: 22)? This problem prompts phenomenological psychologist Benny Shanon to speculate that the representational-like patterns that currently fascinate most cognitive scientists today are actually "the product of cognitive activity, not its substrate or source" (Shanon 2010: 388).

Instead, according to ecological psychologist Tim Ingold, "the human emerges not as a creature whose evolved capacities are filled up with structures that represent the world, but rather as a center of awareness and agency whose processes resonate with those of the environment" (Ingold 2000: 289). Consequently, notes Stewart, one of the editors of *Enaction: Toward a New Paradigm for Cognitive Science*, "[E]very living organism *enacts*... or *brings forth* the world in which it exists. This has important ontological consequences, as it means that 'reality' is not pre-given but co-constructed by the organism" (Stewart 2010: 3). From an Enactive perspective, "meaning is inseparable from the whole of context-dependent, life-motivated, embodied activity, without being at all a hazy concept beyond the reach of scientific understanding" (2010: 36). In addition to representationalism, Enactivists point to other problems that undermine the conventional view of cognition, such as its refusal to consider the limitations it places on perception, emotions, and intentionality and its disinterest in the dynamic systems of the body as the location for higher-level cognitive processing.

Evolution, Cognition, and Performance will deploy the ideas of several scientists and philosophers who embrace Enaction, as well as others whose ideas are generally congruent with this orientation. While several theater and performance scholars have productively deployed one or another research program within the emerging paradigm of Enaction, much of the work in our field – as, indeed, in cognitive-oriented scholarship in music, film, sports, ritual studies, and elsewhere – has been more ad hoc in nature. This is not surprising. Because scholarly publishing always benefits from buzz, scholars new to the field have tended to gravitate to those areas of cognitive research in the arts and humanities that have been grabbing headlines. The flurry of activity around "mirror neurons" a few years ago is a case in point. Initial claims from some scholars in the arts about the importance of the mirror neuron system (MNS) had little to say about the complexities of empathy and so-called Theory of Mind and generally ignored the fact that scientists were still struggling to validate the existence of mirror neurons in humans.

The larger problem here is that scientists and humanists – despite the general convergence of both areas of scholarship – continue to pursue what they take to be significant knowledge in different ways. Scientists need to divide human cognition into a variety of subcategories to be able to isolate variables, engage in a series of discrete experiments, and incrementally advance verifiable knowledge. Many neuroscientists, for example, are now working on the molecular chemistry of neural networking in the brain, a series of complex processes that has implications for the workings of memory, emotions, and much else in cognition. While such small advances help to shape our understanding of how the mind makes meaning, humanists cannot operate at the molecular level when asking questions about, say, the actions of a stand-up comic and the meanings that a spectator might put together from watching that performance. It is now clear that many cognitive operations connecting a comic to an audience member occur nearly simultaneously, in a matter of seconds and even milliseconds, in the telling of a joke. And those operations, in turn, rest upon and within larger contexts concerning bodies, environments, and cultural-cognitive networks. Those of us interested in cognition and performance can follow the science to parse many of those operations separately, but finally we want and need to know how all of these operations fit together. Why the spectator laughed is never simply the result of mirror neurons or a specific type of memory, much less the kind of specific chemical bonding that has occurred among some networked neurons in the brain. When it comes to brains, bodies, and ecologies, scientists must dive into the details and humanists must work at a level of synthesis before they can ask larger questions about performance, culture, and history. Concerned to make sense of what they are finding for their colleagues on one of another side of the sciences–humanities divide, both pull against the others' protocols for truth claims and relevance. This ongoing tension is probably inevitable for another twenty years or so, especially because much of the experimental evidence is still relatively new and a genuine scientific synthesis that might be satisfactory to many remains far off.

Recognizing that humanists require a level of synthesis to do their work, I have adopted the Enaction paradigm as a productive roadmap for performance studies. Because the option of taking the "cognitive turn" has only recently become available to many scholars, driving into the vastness of "cognitive territory" without some kind of GPS opens up research choices that can be as much bewildering as they are inviting. I hope that *Evolution, Cognition, and Performance* will provide one such framework for this kind of exploration. While no single book can answer all of the questions that will interest performance studies scholars, the approach offered here does aim to provide broad principles that may guide scholars toward one set of ideas and methods for addressing them. I believe the Enaction highway that I describe will at least illuminate one major orientation that can provide coherence, direction, and discipline for our work. This is as true for future scientists working in theater and performance studies as it will be for future humanists. Empirical work cannot proceed without relying on some basic definitions and a general framework of assumptions.

Because the proto-paradigm of Enaction will guide my steps, the organization of this book departs from most of the other work that has enriched the emerging field of cognitive science and performance in the recent past. Given the need to establish firm links between cognitive processes and performance activities – between embodied image schemas and ballet dancing or between empathy and spectating at a football game, for example – our investigations have usually moved from specific scientific explanations to discrete performance practices. In the best cases, this strategy has allowed us to establish the empirical foundations and alternative interpretations of the science before applying it to one or another element of a specific performance. Because I must offer a big picture of the Enaction paradigm if it is to provide a possible anchor for the discipline of performance studies, I cannot adopt this strategy; to do so would require an 800-page tome.

Instead, my approach to linking the science to performances will necessarily be more deductive and top-down than I and most of my colleagues have used for our books and articles in the past. Even though Stewart and several others I have cited concede that Enaction rests partly on probabilities and justifiable hunches, in addition to many wide-ranging empirical confirmations, I will begin with the assumption that the proto-paradigm of Enaction is largely correct. Further, I will assume that the scientists working within its parameters will discover many more ways of confirming Enaction's major claims over the next twenty years. This assumption will allow me to present summaries of the Enaction-based science that are relevant to performance studies now without delving into the details of the experiments that lie behind those scientific conclusions. I will, however, try to indicate when one or another conclusion still needs further experimental validation.

Presuming that the main outlines of Enaction are valid may seem like an unstable premise on which to rest *Evolution, Cognition, and Performance* until one realizes that no single overarching paradigm that integrates these concerns can claim that its truths have a better purchase on such realities. This is because all scientists working in the areas that are relevant to the dynamics of performance concede that the field is still in its youth; it is too early to judge CTM, Enaction, or other possible options as the "right" approach. As neuroscientist Gary Marcus and two of his colleagues noted recently, "[N]obody yet has a plausible, fully articulated hypothesis about how most brain functions occur, or how the interplay of those functions yields our minds and personalities" (Marcus 2014: B12). Nor, I would add, about how performances function, either. This recognition must modify Godfrey-Smith's statement that pragmatic naturalism requires "our best current scientific picture of human beings and their place in the universe." If there is no "best," investigators in the arts and humanities eager to ground their generalizations in some confirmable empirical realities have a hard choice to make. Accepting the results of all experiments and logical arguments among all scientists is not an option because different groups of scientists do not agree on the ontological and epistemological foundations and implications of their work. Nor can we wait for some consensus to emerge because that will likely be a long time coming, if it ever truly arrives. Godfrey-Smith's "best current scientific picture" works well enough for some areas of science – genetics, molecular chemistry, and perhaps astronomy – but it presents too high a bar for the current controversies in cognitive science.

Many of us working in the emerging field of cognition and performance studies, however, have found that Enaction is a much better fit with our knowledge of performance than is the computational approach. If Enaction had little empirical support, our professional bias would not matter. But insider knowledge that joins experience to experimentation has already been an important source of curiosity and insight in the fields of literature, music, and film studies, where evolutionary and cognitive studies are further along. By confirming and building upon our pre-scientific, mostly phenomenological, historical, and pragmatic insights, the many experiments that already validate significant parts of Enaction theory also encourage us to extend our empirical investigations of performance in this direction.

In addition, and perhaps more crucially, Enaction offers performance studies the kind of ontological and epistemological rigor that it has lacked since its origins. A general definition of performance that borrowed from competing ideas and moved carelessly among several paradigms of knowledge could not be coherent; in the end, it could not be confirmed. I hope that *Evolution, Cognition, and Performance* will spark new experiments that can eventually validate performance studies as a coherent discipline and, perhaps along the way, move the proto-paradigm of Enaction toward a greater degree of justifiable acceptance. Exploring the many dimensions and dynamics of performances within Enaction promises to open up an enormous number of investigations that this book can only gesture toward. Rather than constructing yet another pet theory with its own terminology and methodology that is unconnected to any empirical protocols for confirmation, we performance studies scholars should be working within a common set of ontological assumptions and epistemological procedures that pull away from the ongoing fragmentations of our field and actually allow us to make some long-term progress.

I am also interested in the short-term goal of cleaning up our scholarly acts. Enaction forces important choices that performance studies scholars have largely fudged or avoided, often in an attempt to broaden the definition of performance to please all comers. This occurred recently at the American Society for Theatre Research conference in 2014, for example, when the planners posed the question, "What Performs?" as the conference theme. Because the "what" in "what performs" assumed that inanimate objects could actually perform without any human agency to facilitate the action, most speakers simply avoided the ontological foolishness of the conference theme. For the record, I saw no performing objects unguided by human minds and bodies at ASTR in Baltimore – no costumes performed by themselves and no computerized dummies told fortunes that ranged beyond their human programming. As will be clear, Enaction theory draws an unambiguous distinction between animate life forms and inanimate objects. In this book, "What performs?" is simply a non-starter.

A few caveats

When I began this book project, I had hoped to build upon my conclusions concerning the biocultural basis of performance to forge specific methods as models for writing history and criticism within the Enaction paradigm. Realizing those goals within the confines of this monograph has proven impossible, however. While I deploy several methods of critical analysis and historical explanation to advance my arguments, I am not advocating these approaches alone as the only ways to manage this kind of work. Nonetheless, I do believe that future evolutionary and cognitive approaches should include an emphasis on spectators as the co-makers of "meaning" in performance criticism and that historians must venture into "deep" evolutionary history if they are to discover how performances work. On the whole, though, it is too early in the development of this new paradigm to settle on preferred methods to follow in the future. Instead, I would encourage others to extend some of the approaches I am using and to try out others that may help us to elaborate the promise of Enaction for scholarly work in performance studies. I do believe, though, that this book provides a solid foundation upon which many projects in the history and/or criticism of performance, large scale and small, might be imagined, researched, and written, and I happily invite other scholars to embark on those journeys.

Due to the complexities of the science and my generally philosophical goals, I have also used examples that I expect will be easily understood by many readers. In order to demonstrate that our universal biocultural proclivities can support many different kinds of performances, I have drawn on both popular and elite examples from a wide range of performance types and genres. Occasionally I will note non-western instances to emphasize what I take to be the universality of the foundations of performance for all *Homo sapiens*. For the most part, though, I stay with examples that I expect will be familiar to most of my readers, whom I take to be generally western, if not by birth than through enculturation. While no performance can ever "work" for all peoples in all biocultures, this truism does not undermine the naturalistic basis of my arguments. More non-western examples might have helped to support my claim of universality, but by themselves they could not validate it; only the scientific side of my argument can do that. Because non-western examples always require more explanation for western readers, however, their proliferation would necessitate a much longer book.

In the epigraph at the top of this introduction, I quote Mark Johnson to the effect that most people "are going to be upset" when they understand the philosophical ramifications of embodiment. The gist of Johnson's warning was echoed recently by philosopher Rebecca Goldstein, who drew from her *Plato at the Googleplex: Why Philosophy Won't Go Away* (2014) to note that philosophy is really about rendering "our human points of view ever more coherent... We lead conceptually compartmentalized lives, our points of view balkanized so that we can live happily with our internal tensions and contradictions, many of the borders fortified by unexamined presumptions. It is the job of philosophy to undermine that happiness..." (Goldstein 2014: B11). Following Goldstein, I aim to counter the balkanization of performance studies by presenting a coherent understanding of performance. In the succeeding pages, I will "undermine the happiness" of most of the present camps within our field in my search for an overarching unity that can provide an Enactive and empirical basis for performance studies. Among other tasks, this will mean challenging some of the extensions of current notions of performance into areas of non-human activity that are not warranted by the evidence. It will also mean applying our emerging definition of performance to areas where it has occasionally been unwelcome, such as mediated narrative fictions that involve images of human action on film, television, and computer screens.

In the course of exploring the latter issue, I will dip into the mediated versus live debate that continues to trouble some of the scholarly discourse in our field. I will also touch on a few other debates insofar as they are related to the understanding of performance I am constructing. For the most part, however, I will not be addressing the similarities and differences between my Enactive approach to performance and other major subfields and theories within performance studies. There is much to say in this regard, but not enough space to say it in. I should note, though, that it would not be too difficult to repurpose for deployment within the Enaction orientation some of the terms and ideas from approaches that are based primarily in phenomenological, metaphorical, and/or materialist approaches to performance. These would include, in no particular order, Kenneth Burke's dramatism, Victor Turner on liminality, Erving Goffman's framing theory, Joseph Roach on surrogation and "it," Marshall McLuhan and Walter Ong on the influence of modes of communication, Richard Schechner's restored behavior, Clifford Geertz on the power of ritual, John MacAloon's notion of cultural performance, Scott Magelssen's "simmings," Jill Dolan and Josè Muñoz on the possible utopian reach of some performances, and Dwight Conquergood's ethical understanding of a critical cultural politics. Several other approaches and insights might be included as well.

On the other hand, terms and ideas deriving from Lacanian, Foucauldian, and Saussurean premises and traditions will simply not fit in Enactivism. This is primarily because these orientations understand human language rather than mindful bodies as the foundation of biocultures and meanings. These and other poststructuralisms hang on among humanists despite the fact that our ancestors were making meanings long before they learned to communicate through spoken language, as the next chapter will show. So I end this Introduction with the same warning that began it: Beware the deceptions of language.

CHAPTER I

Enaction, evolution, and performance

Although this chapter focuses on key cognitive systems that facilitated the eventual ability of evolving *Homo sapiens* to practice and enjoy performances, my inclusion of "evolution" in the title should not suggest that a single chapter will exhaust the importance of species variation and changing ecologies for the overall project of this book. Evolution constituted and continues to facilitate the biological basis of all human action, including the development of myriad human biocultures and their performances; erase evolution and performances simply vanish from the earth. While I will primarily discuss the likely evolution of event perception, conceptual blending, psychological projection, and language in this chapter, evolution must be a recurrent theme throughout the book. Before turning to these matters, however, I want to underline the importance of intentional action for the evolution of life. From an Enaction perspective, all species – before they can flourish, play, and procreate – must survive. The main cognitive implication of this simple but massive truth is that the human brain was primarily built for action, because only action could enable the survival of our own (or any other) animal species.

Action in enaction and evolution

In a recent article, "Horizons for the Enactive Mind: Values, Social Interaction, and Play," authors Ezequiel A. Di Paolo and others review and reaffirm the major principles of Enaction articulated in Varela, Thompson, and Rosch's *The Embodied Mind*. As they note, "five highly intertwined ideas" constitute the enaction approach: "autonomy, sense-making, emergence, embodiment, and experience" (DiPaulo 2010: 37). Each of these pillars of the proto-paradigm may be applied to all living things and all rest upon intentional action. (1) Autonomy refers to the ability of a living system to build an identity for itself, which enables some level of freedom of action within internal and external constraints. Living beings do not simply respond to external stimuli or internal demands. (Humans and elephants, for example, can act with the knowledge that their bodies and brains are autonomous and, to some extent, self-motivating.) (2) Enactive agents also interact with and make sense of their social and physical environments. Engagement with the world is proactive; agents do not simply seek information, but use their bodies and minds to perceive a world that makes sense for their actions. (Dogs primarily perceive through their noses and ears; we mostly use our eyes to make meanings.)

Further, (3) Meaning emerges for animals in the course of taking action. As the authors state, "Meaning is not to be found in elements belonging to the environment or in the internal dynamics of the agent, but belongs to the relational domain established between the two" (2010: 40). (Because meaning is relational, a mound of grass will mean one thing to an African elephant and a very different thing to a nearby villager.) (4) For Enactivists, the body is the ultimate source of meaning, not simply a functional way of taking action in the world: "[E]mbodiment means that mind is inherent in the precarious, active, normative, and worldful process of animation, that the body is not a puppet controlled by the brain, but a whole animate system with many autonomous layers of self-constitution, self-coordination, and self-organization, and varying degrees of openness to the world that create its sense-making activity" (2010: 42). (Although the minds of dogs are like ours in many ways, they use consciousness differently than we do because evolution has shaped their bodies and minds for different relations of openness to the world.) Finally, (5) Regarding experience, Enactivists emphasize that experiences transform our bodies and brains over time. In younger animals especially, new experiences can activate memory and learning to enable new capabilities, interactions, and identities. (Humans, elephants, and even old dogs really can learn new tricks.)

Although these five principles are intertwined and mutually supporting, the first principle, autonomy, is a necessary prerequisite for the rest. As Enactivist philosopher–biologist Evan Thompson explains, all animals possess an "autonomous agency" (Thompson 2007: 13) that facilitates modes of self-organization and interaction with their social and material environment. Unlike an ATM machine at a bank, for instance, amoebas, insects, and human beings are autonomous creatures whose dynamics are determined internally, by genetics, learning, and other processes, rather than externally, by manufacturing and programming. When ATMs begin to malfunction, someone from the outside must fix them. When living creatures experience internal problems, they have the capability to fix themselves and readjust to their environment, unless their problems overwhelm them and they die. This generalization holds true for all biological life. The result of these life processes for human beings, says Thompson, is a mode of being and cognition that "unfolds as the continuous coevolution of acting, perceiving, imagining, feeling, and thinking" (2007: 43). The general term to describe such autonomy in living systems is "autopoiesis"; when life forms strive to maintain their autopoiesis, they involve the other four foundational components of the Enaction paradigm – sense making, emergence, embodiment, and experience. In this fundamental sense, action is simply part of what it takes to stay alive.

We might pause here to underline some of the stark differences between most of the theories that dominate performance studies now and the possibilities available within the orientation of Enaction. First, some level of agency is possible in the world. Human animals are neither the playthings of internal drives and repressions (à la psychoanalysis) nor are they wholly manipulated by external demands (social conditioning) or arrangements of power (Foucauldian discourses). Second, human animals seek to make meaning in the world primarily for action and survival, not for objective understanding. Embodied meanings emerge for individual agents in moments of interaction with animate and inanimate elements in situations and environments; "meaning" is not available for discovery in internal subjectivities (conditioned identity formations) or in either stable or unstable external representations, such as language (Saussurean semiotics and deconstruction). Third, culture is both institutional and cognitive; it is an intertwined and mutually supportive network of habitual practices coupled with fairly stable cognitive structures for a group of people over several generations. Consequently, it cannot be reduced to objective social facts (the Durkheim tradition of sociology and anthropology) or to subjective interpretations (à la Geertz). Finally, historical change emerges from many factors, including the tensions within cultures and from human learning and memory. Given the kind of animals we are, the flow of history is not overdetermined from the past (the recursive mentalities of new historicism) nor is it predetermined by an inevitable future (orthodox Marxist materialism or, for that matter, apocalyptic Christianity).

Attentive to evolution and ecology, philosophers and scientists working within Enaction understand that animal action is never unconstrained. Internal and external realities will always limit what any animal can do. Regarding human action, cognitive philosopher Owen Flanagan discards the possibility of what he calls "libertarian action," which posits that we can do something without anything causing or limiting us in making it happen. Libertarian action assumes that humans can become prime movers, like the Judeo-Christian God, unmoved and unimpeded by anything else in our bodies or environments. Like Flanagan, other Enactivists understand that internal and external realities will always limit what any animal can do.

Apart from rejecting libertarian action, most philosophers and scientists who endorse Enaction go beyond Flanagan's position on the nature of action itself. Flanagan agrees with Donald Davidson's "standard theory" of human action. In brief, Davidson argued that propositional attitudes, such as beliefs and desires, cause human action. For example, if a person believes that someone might hurt him and if this person also has a desire for some object, this belief and desire could lead him, consequently, to avoiding the threat and the attempt to gain the object. As philosopher Frederick Stoutland explains, Davidson's understanding of action requires a kind of conscious intentionality, which begins in the brain and then controls the movement of the body. Conscious control, however, often has little to do with such intentional actions as walking across a street or shopping in a grocery store because there is a continual feedback loop involving the body, brain, and environment that facilitates such action in time. We don't need to be fully conscious of such habitual actions while they are occurring. Notes Stoutland, "The Davidsonian picture has its roots in the Cartesian revolution, which conceives of the physical world as consisting only of what plays a role in the new physics, physics purified of the teleological, intentional, and normative terms of Aristotelian physics" (Stoutland 2011: 30). In other words, while the Newtonian physics of Descartes is all about particles and forces, human beings need to discern meanings, establish teleological ends, and enact intentions for themselves if they are to survive and flourish.

Instead, Stoutland turns to an understanding of intentional, practical action first articulated in the 1950s by Elizabeth Anscombe and recently revisited by pragmatists and Enactivists interested in an embodied approach to defining this problematic term. Disputing Donald Davidson's influential approach to action, advocates of Anscombe's position state that her notion of practical action, an Aristotelian term that joins the mind and body together through flows of intentionality, can actually be applied to a wide variety of actions. In his dissertation on the philosophy of action, University of Pittsburgh graduate David J. Wright points out that Anscombe's definition works very well in describing the action of a play, a musical improvisation, and other performance events. Anscombe separated intentionality from the psychological state of the human agent – from his or her beliefs and/or desires – to argue that intentionality is always inherent in practical action itself. Practical action for Anscombe, as for Aristotle, always involves an end point; an action is a series of parts that are the means toward some whole. In this sense, the activities it takes to build a house are the same as the notes of a song or the episodes of a dramatic action – all of these parts are the means toward a finished house, a whole song, or a complete drama. The straightforward answer to any question about intention directed toward the practical action of performing is teleological; "I'm competing in this sport to win the game," for example. There may be many other "answers" as well, but Anscombe's point is that the structure of all human actions (unlike, say, psychological states or reflex responses) necessarily involves intentionality working through time toward some end. An agent may consciously layer other intentions upon those actions, but these will be secondary to the intentionality that is already inherent in practical action itself. I will be using Anscombe's understanding of intentional action throughout this book.

Given the interest of Enaction theorists in intentional action, it is not surprising that they understand the evolution of forms of life as the development over time of cognition for action. As John Stewart points out in his "Foundational Issues in Enaction as a Paradigm for Cognitive Science," if cognition in the service of action is life itself, "it follows . . . that the historical evolution in forms of life, ever since its origin, *is* an evolution in forms of cognition" (ital. in original) (Stewart 2010: 4–5). Stewart traces the major phylogenetic events over the course of evolutionary time with cognition-for-action as his essay's theme. Stewart's story of animal evolution emphasizes its continuous and cumulative effects on increasing the range and effectiveness of animate actions. Regarding our own species, he singles out our ability to use language and make tools as cognitive-actional advantages that humans have over our primate relations on the evolutionary tree.

In particular, Stewart points to the importance of the work of neuroscientist and Nobel Prize winner Gerald Edelman, which distinguished between primary and higher-order consciousness in humans as a significant evolutionary development. Like the Enactivists, Edelman is also critical of computer-based models of cognition. As we have seen, intentionality is more foundational to all life than consciousness, but consciousness of ourselves and of our surroundings is important in helping us to shape integrated perceptions of the world. While all higher animals have a level of primary consciousness, only humans – and perhaps chimpanzees and bonobos to a minimal degree – are "conscious of being conscious," says Edelman (Edelman 2004: 8). According to him:

> Primary consciousness is the state of being mentally aware of things in the world, of having mental images in the present. It is possessed not only by humans but also by animals lacking semantic or linguistic capabilities whose brain organization is nevertheless similar to ours. Primary consciousness is not accompanied by any sense of a socially defined self with a concept of a past or a future... In contrast, higher-order consciousness involves the ability to be conscious of being conscious, and it allows the recognition by a thinking subject of his or her own acts and affections. It is accompanied in the waking state explicitly to recreate past episodes and to form future intentions. At a minimal level, it requires semantic ability, that is, the assignment of meaning to a symbol. (2004: 9)

As we will see, gaining higher-order consciousness was a lucky turn in our evolution; without it, humans could not know when they were performing and when they were not.

Edelman acknowledges, however, that higher-order consciousness has little to do with the general operations of our minds and bodies. Contemporary neuroscientists estimate that the human senses send about eleven million bits per second to the brain for processing, while the conscious mind is able to generate only about fifty bits per second. Most of this sensory information comes from the eyes, with the skin and the ears far behind. On the whole, it seems that good eyesight was much more important than higher-order consciousness for the survival of our ancestors. Indeed, as we will see, higher-order consciousness was a late evolutionary arrival for our emerging species.

Among other things, this means that knowing that we are conscious has not cut us off from our evolutionary roots. Pragmatic naturalist Mark Johnson underlines the significance of evolutionary continuity, initially emphasized by John Dewey, for understanding human actions. According to Johnson's *The Meaning of the Body*, scholars working within the orientation of continuity theory should follow three major guidelines when considering human evolution. First, "there must be an account of the connections between humans and others animals as regards the emergence and development of meaningful patterns of organism-environment interactions" (Johnson 2007: 123). Second, scholars should use a bottom-up approach, relating matters of thought and culture to our elementary "capacities for perception and motor response" (2007: 123). Finally, says Johnson, "Because judgments of value are essential to an organism's continued functioning, there must be an account of the central role of emotions and feelings in the constitution of an organism's world and its knowledge of it" (2007: 123). In sum:

> The principle of continuity entails that any explanation of the nature and workings of mind, even the most abstract conceptualization and reasoning, must have its roots in the embodied capacities of the organism for perception, feeling, object manipulation, and bodily movement... Furthermore, social and cultural forces are required to develop our cognitive capacities to their full potential, including language and symbolic reasoning. Infants do not speak or discover mathematical proofs at birth. Dewey's continuity thesis thus requires both evolutionary and developmental explanations. (2007: 122–23)

In terms of performance, the continuity hypothesis means, first of all, that we ought to be able to trace the roots of doing and watching performances to evolved abilities that we share with other animals. Johnson would not deny the importance of "social and cultural forces" and the need for "language and symbolic reasoning" in performances. Nonetheless, he insists that we focus on the more foundational capabilities that make culture, language, reasoning – and performance – possible. Second, says Johnson (following Dewey), we should be able to observe the ability to perform in developing infants, toddlers, and children.

The evolution of performance from play

What happens to our understanding of the evolution of performance if we take the advice of Flanagan, Anscombe, Stewart, Edelman, and Johnson? First, perhaps, we would need to reject earlier definitions of performance based upon so-called animal rituals. Examining physiology and behavior as indications of similar evolutionary functions, ethologists such as Konrad Lorenz in the 1960s charted a direct path between animal "rituals" (such as the "waggle dance" in bees to indicate the nearby presence of pollen to other bees) and the development of rituals and other performance arts in humans (Lorenz 1967). Although expressing some skepticism about Lorenz's conclusions, Richard Schechner followed the major outlines of 1960s' ethology in presenting a "ritual tree" that tracks the evolution of ritualization based in "expressive behavior" from genetically fixed forms in insects and fish to "religious" and "aesthetic" rituals in humans. His second edition of *Performance Studies: An Introduction* reprints the drawing (Schechner 2006: 61). Despite their evolutionary emphasis, Lorenz's and Schechner's approach to ritual and performance privileges physiology and behavior rather than perceptions, emotions, and other bottom-up cognitive dynamics.

Further, waggle dances and similar forms of communication among most animals do not require Edelman's higher-order consciousness. Many animals communicate by emitting signals that are received by other members of their species, leading to a coordination of actions among them; the waggle dance is a good example. But such communication is not the same as human language. Our species can intend to communicate with words and syntax, which may be combined in an enormous number of ways. Further, we know that we know we are communicating while such actions are occurring. There is no sense in which bees and other social insects understand what they are up to, however; waggle dances are stereotypical actions triggered by pheromones that fire in response to external stimuli, involving no self-knowledge of communication. While our chimpanzee cousins may be taught the rudiments of higher-order communication through language, they forget it easily and do not develop language in the wild. As Stewart states, "The general conclusion is that 'animal communication,' both the emission of signals and the behavior triggered by perception of them, are stereotyped reactions that are typical for all normal members of the species. As such, they can perfectly well be explained by natural selection, and do not necessarily imply 'understanding'" (Stewart 2010: 14–15). Deriving performance directly from the evolution of animal communication contradicts Edelman's focus on higher-order consciousness and Johnson's mandate that we investigate evolutionary origins and links with a bottom-up approach.

In contrast, Brian Boyd's *On the Origin of Stories: Evolution, Cognition, and Fiction*, follows Johnson's guidelines. Boyd's 2009 book provides a useful synthesis of much of the current knowledge relating evolution to play and play to the emergence of all of the arts, broadly conceived (Boyd 2009: 80–125). According to Boyd – and many others would agree – our impulse to craft performances and to engage with the performances of others comes from our evolutionary heritage of play. Because the scientific research on animal play far outweighs research focused solely on human play, most scholars, Boyd included, begin with characteristics that are widely shared among all playing animals. Boyd cites Robert Fagen, one of the celebrated researchers in the field, and his findings provide an important framework for the discussion that follows.

According to Fagen, "play occurs in only a small minority of the Earth's million or more species. Animal play is easy to recognize. Specific movement qualities and signal patterns characterize the familiar play behavior of cats, dogs, and human children as well as the play of other animals. Mammals and birds, and perhaps a few fishes and reptiles, are the only kinds of animals known to play" (Fagen 1995: 24). Fagen's categories of animal play include brief repetitive acts by groups of rodents, running and jumping performed singly by some mammals and birds, the sparring and wrestling of primates and carnivores, and more complex forms of social play, in which animals use objects or features of the landscape to play proto-human versions of hide-and-seek, tug-of-war, and follow-the-leader. Not surprisingly, young *Homo sapiens* play in all of these ways, too. Although Fagen includes an ethological examination of behavior, he is also attentive to animal psychology.

Fagen's examples point up several continuities between animal play and the play of *Homo sapiens*. Like human children, other playing animals recognize play as a semi-distinct event that is usually separate from other events in their lives. Young monkeys, like human infants, seem to know soon after birth that playing need not arouse a fight-or-flight response. Second, from Fagen's descriptions of these activities and from numerous experiments performed on playing animals, it is clear that animals enjoy their mutual play. Scientists know this because they have tracked chemical changes associated with joyful emotions in the brains of mammals during and after play. Consequently, play is emotionally self-reinforcing. Finally, these animals, especially the young of the species, will seek out opportunities to play when they perceive that they are in a safe environment. Rather than simply responding automatically to external stimuli, as occurs with much communication among adult animals, primates and others will take up play spontaneously. At some level, these mammals and birds "intend" to play. As the likely foundation of all performance, the activity of play in animals already entails emergent notions of event, enjoyment, and intentionality.

As a result of these findings, many scientists have concluded that play was probably a species-wide behavior in some animals that functioned in ways that ultimately helped and continues to facilitate their ability to survive. Although the evolutionary record is too sparse to fully substantiate this conclusion, Boyd summarizes the logic and evidence behind it:

> Play evolved through the advantages of flexibility; the amount of play in a species correlates with its flexibility of action. Behaviors like escape and pursuit, attack and defense, and social give-and-take can make life-or-death differences. Creatures with more motivation to practice such behaviors in situations of low urgency can fare better at moments of high urgency. Animals that play repeatedly and exuberantly refine skills, extend repertoires, and

sharpen sensitivities. Play therefore has evolved to be highly self-rewarding. Because it is compulsive, animals engage in it again and again, incrementally altering muscle tone and neural wiring, strengthening and increasing speed in synaptic pathways, improving their capacity and performance. (Boyd 2009: 14)

What apparently worked evolutionarily for rats, panthers, and kangaroos has also worked for us. It is likely that hominids (the anthropological term for species that directly preceded us) had been playing for a long time before our eventual species parted ways genetically from our near relations, the proto-chimpanzees, about six or seven million years ago.

Since that time, judging from the increasing size of hominid skulls and other clues, our ancestors survived as much by their wits as by their physical acumen. According to Boyd, playing allowed proto-humans to flourish because it increased their cognitive flexibility, especially their ability to recognize, repeat, and refine patterns. Boyd defines pattern broadly as any discernible arrangement of order or form; contemporary humans find patterns in a face, the night sky, and a narrative, for example. He particularly emphasizes the cognitive patterns – patterns of sound, design, words, and/or action – embedded in artistic creation and reception. Such patterns constitute his view of art as "a kind of cognitive *play*, the set of activities designed to engage human *attention* through their own appeal to our preference for inferentially rich and therefore *patterned* information" (ital. in original) (2009: 85). The arts helped evolving hominids to pattern their lives, coordinating curiosity, memory, attention, empathy, and other cognitive capabilities in socially engaged and open-ended ways. Boyd is clear that "even if it diverts energy away from immediate survival or reproductive needs, [art] can improve cooperation within a group enough for the group to compete successfully against others with less inclination to art." And when it comes to the arts, he adds, "We should think in the first place not of art galleries or concert halls..., but of chants, drums, dance, body-markings, costumes, banners and the like" (2009: 106). Boyd provides persuasive (if not fully confirmable) evidence that the arts, broadly conceived, increased the survivability of our species.

Assuming that Boyd and others are generally correct about the importance of play for human survival and the arts, does this logic simply reduce performance (along with literature and the visual arts) to a kind of play? Collapsing performance into play is a current trend in performance studies, evident in discourses that range from advice about acting technique to the apparent performances of animals. Holding that performance derives evolutionarily from play, however, is not the same as equating the two.

We may trace our ancestors to the same family of early primates that eventually led to chimps and bonobos, but that evolutionary heritage does not make all three species "the same."

One way of approaching this problem is through the sociology of play. The foremost sociologist on human playing is Brian Sutton-Smith, who lists about 300 types of activity that are conventionally described as playing. These include daydreaming, building models, running, reading, stamp collecting, photography, bicycling, playing tricks, practicing yoga, dancing, getting laid, gossiping, watching television, gambling, going to a folk festival, playing music, playing Iago, golfing, windsurfing, arm wrestling, and celebrating a birthday. Some activities in Sutton-Smith's catalogue of play involve what most other scholars would also term performances. Many academics in performance studies would likely agree that playing music, dancing, watching television, golfing, and playing Iago are kinds of play that share enough "family resemblances" to also be placed in the category of performance. Notice that all of these examples of performance engage human action in attending to patterned activities; they accord with Boyd's definition of art, even though some of them (watching television and golfing) fall outside of conventional definitions of "the arts." In this general sense, it is clear that performance fits within Boyd's definition of the arts and, following his logic, that human performance can be considered a subcategory of animal play. Tentatively, then, we can hypothesize that there could be several kinds of play, one of which is performing. In phylogenetic terms, the broad "genus" of play would include the "species" of performance.

With this genus–species perspective in mind, it is probable that our ability to perform derives evolutionarily from mammalian play. We have already seen that human play, including performance, involves some of the same cognitive abilities found in the playing of other higher mammals. Further, if play led to human performance, most of the evolutionary improvements in cognitive operations evident in humans should build upon those in chimps, dolphins, and elephants. From the evolutionary evidence available, this appears to be true. Take the mutual motor attunement that many mammals can achieve among each other through their "mirror neurons," for example. Networks of such neurons in the frontal lobe of the brain, evident in many higher mammals and likely in humans, respond to intentional motor action initiated by others. If an actor/character on stage in a murder melodrama grabs for a gun, the grabbing motion will be picked up by the mirror networks of those sitting in the auditorium; the spectators' mirror networks will fire in much the same way that they would have if each of them had done the grabbing. In contrast, if the actor/character on stage accidentally drops the gun – an unintentional mistake – the mirror networks of audience members would not respond. Although the experimental work on mirror networks in humans is far from complete, many scientists agree that these groups of neurons allow a viewer to process some information about social "others" by responding to muscles in their faces and other parts of their bodies. As we will explore in Chapter 3, mirror neurons probably provided a starting point for human empathy.

Many higher animals also have mirror networks that allow them to stay in tune with the intentional actions of conspecifics. If a group of chimps sees another one pick up a stick and use it to reach for a piece of food, the mirror neuron systems of the other chimps will respond much as the human spectators at the murder mystery responded to the actor grabbing the gun. But it is clear from experiments that the ability of the other chimps to begin to empathize with the intentions of the stick-wielding chimp is very limited, primarily because they cannot form concepts about what others of their kind generally do with sticks when food is out of reach. Nor could they likely deduce that their fellow chimp was hungry. Humans, in contrast, easily move from specific instances to general deductions, even though their conclusions are sometimes wrong. With regard to low-level empathy, then, our mirror networks appear to be similar to those of chimps, but they are connected to other parts of our brains that can exercise greater conceptual ability.

In other ways, too, our play is similar to but different from that of other animals. Dolphins may have some limited memory, but their performances at Sea World and similar venues cannot begin to approach our production and enjoyment of stand-up comedy, soccer matches, and theatrical farce in terms of their ambitious demands on attention and the complexity of patterned actions. Although we and other higher mammals share the same primary emotions, as we will see in Chapter 3, we can gain consciousness of some of our emotions and recognize them as feelings. While many spectators might prefer to let their sentimental emotions overtake them while listening to a romantic ballad, they will usually know that they are experiencing feelings during the song and can choose to moderate them. In contrast, anyone who has played with dogs knows that their emotions often overwhelm and control them; they may continue to rag a stuffed toy until their master intervenes or they tire of their play.

Although we share important continuities among our mirror networks, memories, and primary emotions with other mammals, other of our cognitive operations and abilities demonstrate significant differences from the rest of the animal kingdom. In his "Neuroscientific Approaches and Applications within Anthropology," James K. Rilling summarizes the recent research on four human capabilities that require Edelman's higher-order consciousness. The most striking of these is the human capacity for oral communication through language and, with it, symbolic expression and reasoning. Even chimpanzees trained to learn symbolic communication cannot approach the still-developing language ability of a normal two-year-old child. Second, chimps deploy simple tools such as twigs, but making complex tools – those requiring that several parts be joined together – is beyond them. In order to manufacture a Stone Age axe, our ancestors needed levels of mimetic and conceptual ability that were (and are) unique to hominids and *Homo sapiens*. The third difference, says Rilling, is altruism: "Although all primate species exhibit altruism toward genetic relatives, humans are exceptional in the extent to which we cooperate with non-relatives" (Rilling 2008: 19). As many scientists have noted, managing altruism in social relations requires several complex cognitive abilities, from trust to detecting non-reciprocators to instilling the social emotion of shame. Rilling's fourth area of discontinuity separating human cognition from that of other primates is mental self-projection. Although chimps may have some low-level skill in mental projection, humans "can simulate alternate worlds that are separate from the one being directly experienced," we can "project ourselves into the past to remember things that have happened to us, into the future to formulate and rehearse plans, and even into the minds of others . . . " (2008: 22). Clearly, all four of these uniquely human abilities are necessary parts of most performances. Rilling's fourth area of human uniqueness, however – the ability to simulate alternative, imaginary, and future worlds – provides performance's cognitive foundation.

Projecting the self into imaginary worlds appears early in the normal development of *Homo sapiens*. Research into pretend-play demonstrates that sometime after the age of two, nearly all children will spontaneously adopt and play roles within make-believe situations. According to child psychologist Paul Harris, who cites numerous experiments with young children, "When children engage in role play, they do not simply remain off-stage directors or puppeteers. They enter into the make-believe situation that they create and adopt the point of view of one of the protagonists within it. The real world recedes into the background and is replaced by the make-believe landscape and experience that would be available to that protagonist" (Harris 2000: 31). Further, says Harris, "A pretend episode includes causal chains with an unfolding structure much like a narrative" (2000: 10). During this improvised event, the child will often stay "in character," performing within the fictional situation and, in the process, validating the imagined reality of the make-believe world.

In a paper entitled "Toward a Theory of Play as Performance: An Analysis of Videotaped Episodes of a Toddler's Play Performance," John Gerstmyer related his year-long study of his two-year-old daughter's play activity, performed both solo and with friends of her own age. Sutton-Smith reports several significant conclusions from Gerstmyer's study:

1. [The toddler] used paralinguistically appropriate "in role" speech, such as "motherese" when she was pretending to be a mother. "Motherese" is the kind of high pitched, dramatically toned, but slow and emphatic speech that mothers use with their babies.
2. She used vocalized sound effects to identify and enhance a non-verbal enactment, for example "vroom vroom" when pushing a toy car.
3. She used "magicking," which is a play "shorthand" whereby, for example, a brief nonverbal play action, such as shaking a pot accompanied by the verbalization "cook cook," might be used to represent a relatively sizable time segment of ongoing food preparation. It is typical for play to be a highly condensed representation of whatever it is about...
4. She showed anticipatory and facilitative enactive behavior: for example, picking up the toy telephone before saying "hello."
5. There was, at times, brief out-of-role behavior that served the play action objective, as when she looked for a prop and retrieved it for ensuing action...
6. There were brief affiliative, out-of-role facial expressions or gestures, which served to touch base between partners, such as giggling and laughing during, say, a pretend action of violence.
7. She prepared the onlooker for forthcoming climactic events by lower-volume confidential cues of a more intense kind: head nodding, pursed lips, lip smacking, and swallowing" (qtd in Sutton-Smith 1997: 194).

As Sutton-Smith recognizes, Gerstmyer's toddler self-consciously stepped into and out of roles to create what he calls "actions about actions" (1997: 195).

Before a child can create and manipulate the doubleness of all performance situations – "the actions about actions" – she or he must recognize other humans as intentional beings who can cooperatively share with him or her a field of attention. This understanding usually emerges at about nine months of age with a cluster of other cognitive abilities that cognitive psychologist Michael Tomasello terms "shared intentionality." Shared intentionality builds upon the infant's emerging abilities to use adults as social reference points and to look where they are looking. Drawing on the insights of philosopher John Searle and a series of experiments, Tomasello concludes that shared intentionality entails: "(i) the cognitive skills for creating joint intentions and attention (and other forms of common conceptual ground) with others; and (ii) the social motivations for helping and sharing with others (and forming mutual expectations about these cooperative motives)" (Tomasello 2008: 73). While Tomasello's explanations about the implications of joint attention have been questioned, his general findings about the process have been confirmed. As a result of joint attention, infants create triadic structures involving self, adult, and shared object or event. Toddlers must have the ability to jointly attend with others before they can intentionally engage in make-believe play. If we were looking for the origin of theater and other kinds of performances in childhood development, the ability of an infant to act through "shared intentionality" is probably the best candidate. Already, before his or her first birthday and usually before the full emergence of language, the child can become a part of an audience with a significant other and watch a third person enact a separate event.

While shared intentionality and pretend-play are necessary first steps, what Radu Bogdan calls "imagination" must follow them before a child can fully engage in the possibilities of adult role-playing and spectating. Bogdan calls his 2013 book *Mindvaults* because his synthesis of much of the empirical evidence about evolution and developmental psychology encouraged him to celebrate the many ways that a child could use her or his mind to vault over present, quotidian reality to inhabit and manipulate imaginative possibilities. At roughly the age of four, the normally developing child experiences an expansion of her or his ability to build sequences of images and actions in the mind that are unconnected to ongoing present activities. According to Bogdan, these emerging executive abilities come with several new cognitive operations. The four-year old can now:

> SUSPEND the truth-value and even modal (possibility, probability, etc.) as well as doxastic (or belief-relevant) status of what is imagined; ADOPT THE PERSPECTIVE of an imaginative projection; use what is imagined from the adopted perspective SUPPOSITIONALLY as a basis or premise for further imaginative projections and inferences; DEPLOY such further projections in a thematically connected manner; [and develop] a METAREPRESENTATIONAL SENSE that one's own offline thoughts represent something imagined. (capitalization in quotation) (Bogdan 2013: 140)

With these abilities, the child can deliberately intend to build imaginative structures, project memories and perceptions into this mental "space," combine such images with new ones, and hold these combinations in working memory for active play or later recall. After watching a Spiderman cartoon or learning about Spiderman from a bedtime story book, the child can decide to create her or his own story about Spiderman, adopt the perspective of Spiderman himself, and then sling some imaginary webs to enable her/himself to "fly" around the backyard or bedroom. Two days later the child can return to that invented scenario and modify it so his/her friend, perhaps another four-year-old, can also play in Spiderman's world. Pretending to be "mommy" or another adult, Gerstmyer's toddler could imitate adult actions, but Bogdan's four-year-old can go beyond simple mimesis to invent roles and scenarios unconnected to everyday realities and later return to this imagined space to further elaborate a past situation. With these new imaginative abilities, four-year-olds can begin to think like filmmakers and to practice specific kinds of movements like athletes or dancers. As with pretend-play, evolution appears to have granted this kind of imaginative capability to our species alone.

This combination of imagination and pretend-play is what I will call performance. A higher-order form of play, performing can be understood as a "species" of the larger "genus" of general playing. As noted above, performance relies upon each of the four improvements that, says Rilling, separates us from (but keeps us linked to) other animals – languaging, complex tool-making, mental projecting, and (as we will see) treating others altruistically. Performance incorporates all the elements of animal play, but builds upon it in crucial ways.

Performance events and conceptual blending

Embodying, rehearsing, performing, and enjoying an imagined action as a part of play makes performance part of a larger cognitive category that has been termed subjunctive action. In English grammar, "subjunctive" designates a verb form expressing contingent or hypothetical action. Whenever people construct conditional phrases, consider alternative possibilities, fantasize about the past or the future, build models to explore how something might work, propose hypotheses about a scientific experiment, or perform a dramatic fiction for an audience, they are engaging in subjunctive action. For Edelman, only animals with higher-order consciousness can act subjunctively. The famous acting teacher Konstantin Stanislavsky was inviting actors to involve themselves in subjunctive possibility when he spoke of "the magic if." The question, "If I were this character in that situation, then what would I do?" – one understanding of Stanislavsky's meaning of "the magic if" – is the basis for the actor's imaginative investment in her or his character and, consequently, in the dramatic action of the play. Such theatrical subjunctive action may also be termed virtual action; the realities created by play performances and computer games are foundationally the same. Thinking with virtual, "as if" realities pervades science, the arts, the law, and all forms of planning for the future. Without subjunctive thought, culture as we know it would be impossible.

Subjunctive action depends on the cognitive capability of conceptual integration, also known as blending. In *The Way We Think: Conceptual Blending and The Mind's Hidden Complexities*, Gilles Fauconnier and Mark Turner (F&T) demonstrate that this cognitive operation is a necessary prerequisite for all subjunctive performances – and, as we will see, for much more. Without it, as F&T relate, humans would not be able to "fantasize, deceive, delude, consider alternatives, simulate, make models, and propose hypotheses" (Fauconnier and Turner 2002: 217). Surprisingly, perhaps, Bogdan does not integrate conceptual blending into his understanding of imagination, even though the terms "blending" and "imagining" cover much of the same territory. Looking at childhood development rather than the linguistic abilities of adults (F&T's focus), Bogdan was apparently unaware that F&T had described very similar processes about ten years earlier. Although Bogdan's "imagination" is a broader term than F&T's "blending," it is also clear that the imagining that four-year-olds can do brings with it a few other abilities that enhance the performing available to four-year-olds through blending. I will primarily use F&T's "conceptual integration" or "blending" rather than Bogdan's "imagination" in the discussions to come because "imagination" has too many other connotations for users of English.

Elephants and dolphins may approach the subjunctive performance activity of blending, but we seem to be the only animals on the planet that can fully accomplish these kinds of tasks. "The great evolutionary change that produced cognitively modern human beings," state F&T, "was a matter of evolving an organism that could run off-line cognitive simulations so that evolution did not have to undertake the tedious process of natural selection every time a choice was to be made" (2002: 217). Consequently, states Turner, "over the last fifty thousand years, give or take (the dating is still being worked out in the archaeological record) human beings have demonstrated a remarkable ability to create new conceptual diversity" (2002: 95). Our ability to imagine and perform as-if simulations enormously extended our potential for action and performance.

Among its other advantages, blending allows humans to compress what might otherwise be perceived as a diverse range of behaviors into a single, subjunctive event. Other animals watching lawyers in a court of law or actors on a stage cannot see the activity in front of them as part of a whole trial or play performance; lacking conceptual integration, they cannot blend such multifarious activities into the subjunctive concept of a single event. Humans, in contrast, find pattern and regularity in the apparent confusion of existence all the time, mostly without thinking about it. The gradual evolution of conceptual blending among our ancestors eventually led them to perceive complex events as isolable and significant durations in time.

What is an event? In their *Philosophy in the Flesh*, cognitive linguist George Lakoff and Mark Johnson borrow from the work of others to sketch what they call a "skeleton" of the human structure of an event. As they point out, this structure is based in how we initiate and complete any movement of our bodies through space:

Initial State: Whatever is required for the event is satisfied
Start: The starting-up process for the event
End of Start: The end of the starting-up process and the beginning of the main process
Main Process: The central aspects of the event
Possible Interruptions: Disruptions of the main process
Possible Continuation or Iteration: The perpetuation or repetition of the main process
Resultant State: The state resulting from the main process. (Lakoff and Johnson 1999: 176)

This outline of an action could describe both the path of a woman who begins in a standing position, walks across a room, swerves to avoid another person, and sits in a chair, as well as a week-long presidential nominating convention of the U.S. Republican Party. Both are events, albeit of very different magnitudes. Both concepts of meaningful duration rest upon the physical process of moving from one location to another, although the "locations" at a nominating convention are metaphorical; "We started here, without a candidate, and now look where we are – we just nominated Mitt Romney!"

As this example suggests, the compression of many actions into the larger action of a coherent event is as much an achievement of culture as it is of evolution; like most human practices, blending to create events is inherently biocultural. Take a three-year-old to a soccer game to watch his older sister play and afterwards ask him what he saw. Unless someone has carefully explained what soccer is all about, the child will not see the parts of the game as a whole event. More likely, he will see it as a series of discrete activities – running, kicking, chasing a ball, etc. – that might be intermittently fun, but have no part–whole relation to each other. Three-year-olds are already blending to create many events in their everyday lives, from "breakfast time" to "getting ready for bed," but understanding complex biocultural performances as whole events usually takes more time and learning. Comprehending and enjoying the various pieces of the Wimbledon championship tennis playoffs, for example – from the rules of the game, to the force and finesse of tennis playing, to the procedures of seeding and elimination, etc. – require knowledge about an enormous number of actions, metaphors, and blends. Complex performance events involve compressing thousands of cognitive operations so that we can understand the moment-by-moment play of the game (or drama, or concert, etc.) in directly human terms.

How event perception evolved among our hominid ancestors cannot be known with any certainty, but some speculation about its origins and emergence is useful because its likely development suggests the value of sociality for human evolution. Cognitive scientist Merlin Donald pulls together much suggestive evidence to hypothesize that the harsh realities of early hominid life put evolutionary pressure on our ancestors to expand their cognitive, affective, and social capacities to enable them to cooperate and compete as a group for survival. From skull sizes, primitive tools, ecological changes, and other factors, it is clear that our precursors on the family tree slowly arrived at moments in the past when their cognitive abilities facilitated the kinds of learning that helped them to transform their physical and social environments through emerging human culture. In other words, genetics and culture worked together to shape our emerging species. Tomasello compares the gradual evolution of culture among groups of hominids to a car jack; as an automobile is gradually elevated, ratchets in the jack keep the car from slipping back down. "Ratchet culture" allowed accumulated knowledge to be passed down from one generation of hominids to the next (Tomasello 1999: 203–17). In contrast, a group of chimpanzees might figure out a better way of hunting for food, but without intergenerational teaching and learning, which chimps cannot manage, the group had no way of maintaining their higher level of hunting and gathering over time.

Our hominid ancestor *Homo erectus*, who lived between roughly one hundred and eighty and half a million years ago, learned early on to ratchet up her culture through tool-making and fire-using. According to Donald in his *A Mind So Rare: The Evolution of Human Consciousness* (2001), the axes, spears, and cooking implements of this era suggest that *Homo erectus* hominids spent much of their time imitating each other to craft tools that could ensure their survival. Donald terms this the "mimetic era" and assumes that our ancestors found a variety of ways to imitate each other, including attention-grabbing and pattern-making events that might be called proto-performances. Whether some level of performing was happening or not – whether their mimetic pretend-play was enhanced by conceptual blending – it is clear that *Homo erectus* needed to set aside significant times when learning through imitation could occur, so that their primitive tools could be replaced and the band of hominids could maintain their tool-making knowledge from one (short-lived) generation to the next. The era of *Homo erectus*, in other words, probably practiced some of the complexities of event-integration and -perception, an achievement that would culminate later in advanced conceptual blending. Donald celebrates this early achievement of hominid tool-making as an example of networking: "Human cultures can be regarded as massive distributed cognitive networks, involving the linking of many minds . . . that guide the flow of ideas, memories, knowledge" (Donald 2006: 4). He adds, "The canonical example of this kind of integration is event-perception, which can unify a blur of millions of individual sensations of sight, sound, touch, taste, smell and emotions into unitary event-percepts" (2006: 4).

Although the neuroscience behind conceptual integration is not yet conclusive, it appears that blending is not simply an option for performance; it is a cognitive necessity for the role-playing that performing involves. Fauconnier and Turner explain blending by inviting readers to imagine two input spaces containing different kinds of concepts. During the performance of a role, some of the concepts from each of the two input spaces get combined in a third space, the space of the blend. As we have seen, the four-year-old playing Spiderman might be able to "run" and "talk" like the famous web-slinger, but he would leave behind aspects of the superhero that were physically impossible, such as actually clinging to the side of walls, to become a self/Spiderman. Like adult actors who can momentarily step out of role to adjust a costume piece or improvise a bit of business when a fellow actor misses a line, the four-year-old Spiderman could also unblend his actor/character concepts to make adjustments should circumstances demand it. While the executive brain initiates blending, its cognitive processes occur below the level of consciousness.

Blending and memory

The dynamic of "conceptual" integration rests on an understanding of the mind, common among cognitive scientists of many persuasions, in which "concepts" are necessary prerequisites for many cognitive operations. Essentially rough categories in memory, concepts may include agents, locations, objects, times, roles, events, and actions. In the brain, neural networks constitute each concept, and millions of these networks compose the individual's knowledge about the world. "Concept" means something different within the paradigm of Enaction, however, than it does for those neuroscientists who follow a more traditional orientation to cognition. In the traditional view, conceptual neural networks are understood as abstract codes that are not context specific, much like the os and 1s of a computer code, and these codes represent entities in the world that remain fairly stable over time. Those advocating a computational model of the brain usually term such a conceptual system "semantic memory," because the codes are arbitrary symbols (like one aspect of language) that represent entities in a person's experience of the world. Semantic memory is said to be a part of "explicit" or "declarative" memory, in the sense that it is directly available to consciousness and involves the ability to "declare" what something is. "Procedural" memory, in contrast, helps people remember how to do something. For traditional neuroscientists, for example, when a person sees an animal in a backyard and seeks to identify it, the neural network in the individual's brain that represents the category of "dog" (or "squirrel" or "bird," etc.) will instantly and unconsciously activate and the person will recognize the animal. Semantic memory works much like a huge dictionary, in which individual entries stand for discrete categories that are separated from each other in the networks of the brain.

There is increasing evidence, however, that the brain does not work like this. In this discussion, I will follow Lawrence Barsalou's essay, "Situating Concepts," which proposes an Enactive account of concepts and memory. To simplify his explanation, Barsalou focuses on visual images and their counterparts in brain networks and recollected memories, not on the other senses, although he suggests that his conclusions about visuality may be generalized to include the entire conceptual–memorial system. First, Barsalou demonstrates that people initially perceive situations, not individual entities, when they interact with the world. For example, a person may experience dogs in many situations, some involving positive emotions that come with petting and feeding and others centered on negative emotions, perhaps concerning the fear of attack. Second, when these visual images arrive at the brain, there is no mental operation that strips these images of their context to arrive at the abstract, dictionary-like category of "dog." Instead, says Barsalou, the brain creates a "simulator" (Barsalou 2009: 239) that integrates all visual (as well as auditory, somatosensory, affective, etc.) information about dogs from these networks and this simulator helps individuals to interact with dogs in different contexts in the present. Concepts are fundamentally simulators containing many examples, in Barsalou's understanding. As he explains, "A potentially infinite number of simulators can become established in the cognitive system. Simulators can develop for all aspects of experience, including agents, objects, properties, settings, events, actions, interoceptions, and so forth. In general a simulator develops for a component of experience that attention selects repeatedly" (2009: 240). Third, each new experience with a dog creates a new situational memory and that memory will alter the simulator for dogs in some contexts, but not others. Someone who has loved dogs all his life may be attacked by a dog, and the memory of that painful situation could significantly alter some parts of the dog simulation in his mind. Barsalou emphasizes that simulators prepare the body and mind for action:

> From this perspective, a concept is neither a static database nor a single abstraction. Instead, it is an ability or competence to produce specialized category representations that support goal pursuit in the current setting, where each specialized representation is akin to an instruction manual for interacting with a particular category member.... [A concept] is the ability to construct a wide variety of situated conceptualizations that support goal achievement in diverse contexts. (2009: 244)

Barsalou's simulations eliminate the need for the category of "semantic memory." The general category of declarative memory, however, as groups of simulations that can be quickly retrieved for use to name what something is, remains and retains its importance. Lacking a single concept in memory for "dog," humans have no need to shift mental gears from a generalized, dictionary-like definition to a concrete situation to know that they should approach a whimpering puppy differently than a growling guard dog. Instead, they retrieve one or a few simulations concerning whimpering puppies that assist them in framing the belief that this is a puppy that is seeking help or affection and is not to be feared. Then they may or may not act accordingly. Concepts-as-simulations accords with Mark Johnson's view, which notes that concepts should be understood "as the various possible patterns of activation by which we can mark significant characteristics of our experience" (2007: 160).

Because the simulators for "dog" (or anything else) in our minds are fundamentally about strategies for action and not about stable codes (or signs) of representation, language itself must be understood as pragmatic and enactive. In his essay, "Language and Enaction," cognitive linguist Didier Bottineau builds on the work of more than fifty other linguists to unpack the implications of what he terms "the experience of languaging" (Bottineau 2010: 267). As Bottineau emphasizes, an Enactive approach to languaging undermines the traditional categories of linguistics – langue, parole, grammar, the lexicon, etc. – because these categories "cannot be taken as scientific objects of scrutiny as long as they have not been redefined in terms of dynamic sensorimotor experience" (2010: 270). Two people conversing are not using language to "*refer* to the world," notes Bottineau; rather, their conversation "*causes an experience* that happens to coincide or not with the narrow situation or the larger reality" of these two people (2010: 278, emphasis in original).

Consequently, "to speak is to command vocally the connection between the immediate and recorded experiences by reproducing the controllable sensorimotor experience, the word, used as a token or common denominator (rather than *symbol*)" (2010: 278). As Bottineau explains, this means that "the lexicon has to be reconstructed from a phenomenological point of view, and is connotational rather than denotational" (2010: 281). Echoing Barsalou, it also means that communication through language involves procedural rather than declarative memory. The classic example for procedural memory is learning and recalling how to ride a bike, which involves the coordination of perception, muscles, prior knowledge, and other phenomena. Communicating "dog" to another person demands similar acts of brain, body, and extended cognition and action in an appropriate environment that draw on biological and cultural capabilities. Following Barsalou, then, Bottineau would understand the word "dog" used in conversation as a simulator for many experiences with dogs; this token sound, uttered by one and heard by another, would be somewhat differently interpreted by each of the two people in conversation. As Bottineau realizes, an Enactive approach to linguistics eliminates semiotics as a viable approach to language and "destabilizes what Foucault (1966) called the epistemological basis of our knowledge" (2010: 267). Because it upends semiotics and challenges Foucauldian premises, language as nonsymbolic token and connotation also undercuts the linguistic assumptions of poststructuralism.

Bottineau follows in the footsteps of George Lakoff's work on metaphors in the 1970s and 1980s. Lakoff's linguistics abandoned a correspondence theory of language, in which truth might be ascertained in the relationship between words and an objectively real world. Rather, Lakoff found that languaging emerged from our embodied experiences. The metaphor "life is a journey," for example, derives from human action in the world, as when an infant crawls from a source along a path toward a goal. After she has crawled across a room a few times to, say, get a toy or see daddy, she builds up a mental schema that charts this experience in her brain. Later, when the infant gains the ability to talk, she can understand and express this metaphor because she has lived a foundational version of it. For Lakoff, "life is a journey" is one of many metaphors that derive from the SOURCE–PATH–GOAL schema, or PATH for short. Together with Mark Johnson, Lakoff identified many of these schemas, from which spring thousands of specific metaphors. As we will see in the next chapter, image schemas give expressive order to all performances and are a chief means for communicating meanings to spectators.

Turner worked with Lakoff and adopted much of his orientation to linguistics. Turner recognized, however, that many linguistic constructions could not be understood as metaphors. While a metaphor maps the connotations of one word onto another, a blend takes two words and the concepts implicit in each and fuses parts of them together. The concepts to be blended, however, under an Enactive approach to language and conceptual cognition generally, must be understood as a range of simulators. Our four-year-old Spiderman, for example, probably had several simulators for Spiderman in his memory when he blended a few of them with other concepts about himself to create a self/Spiderman blend. Enactive cognition appears to fit nicely within F&T's understanding of conceptual integration.

I have focused on role-playing because of its obvious importance in acting. Blending also occurs in performances involving puppets and marionettes. A live human being blends her agency – typically, her physical and vocal expressiveness – with the inanimate properties of a hand puppet or a wooden figure on strings to create a dramatic character. Sometimes several actors are needed to animate a puppet character, as when five facilitators create and move the character of "Uncle Fatso," one of Bread and Puppet Theatre's oversized figures. This is not to reduce conceptual integration to a "tool" of acting; actors need not think about blending at all for it to occur. But, of course, actors can decide to adopt a certain walk, a different accent, or a possible psychology for their characters, and blending will help them to accomplish this unconsciously at the level of concepts and neurons. Engaging in imaginary characterization through conceptual integration involves yet another step away from the rest of the animal kingdom; to perform a subjunctive role is far beyond the reach of all higher mammals except humans.

Conceptual integration also makes subjunctive role-playing continuous with the social roles that all people necessarily assume in their daily lives. The same person may be a mother, professor, home-maker, wife, friend, co-worker, and twenty other social types, each role more or less freely chosen or assigned by society. Depending on the person and the circumstances, the social role-player may blend some fictitious, subjunctive elements into presentations of herself and interactions with others in many of the social roles she plays every day. Blending for role-playing may allow people to shake up their habits and inject some fun into their daily lives. Some cultures set aside times in which everybody has license to play in these ways; Latin American Carnival season is a good example. Outside of these occasions, however, a person's temporary role-playing might not rise to the status of an event. It may not even be noticed by other people as a riff on "normal" reality. Role-playing in everyday life is always a possibility, but it is not always perceived by possible spectators as a performance.

From languaging to the High Paleolithic

No one is sure how or when hominids began to use language. Direct evidence for this in the fossil record has been very difficult to find. Among *Homo sapiens* today, the neural center for "languaging" is in the frontal lobes of the brain. Producing sounds also involves the vocal chords, trachea, tongue, mouth, and facial mask. And hearing their subtleties involves the fine-tuned biology of the human ear. According to some physical anthropologists, our predecessor, *Homo erectus*, may have had a large enough skull to house frontal lobes that facilitated some kind of vocal communication around a million and a half years ago. The development of an adequate speaking and hearing apparatus to produce and distinguish among a range of distinctive sounds, however, probably took another million years of evolution.

At whatever time in the past that hominid voicings began to approach languaging, it is clear that the production and comprehension of early words and syntax relied on accompanying gestures. We know this because spoken language today cannot be separated from the gestures that accompany most utterances. Although earlier studies of the relations between gesture and speech in everyday life had suggested that gestures were a separate system of communication, recent experimental evidence strongly underlines their complementary, co-expressive relationship. In his *Gesture and Thought* (2005), David McNeill synthesizes much of this evidence to argue for a single-system approach. "It is profoundly an error to think of gesture as a code or 'body language,' separate from spoken language," he asserts. "Gestures are *part* of language" (emphasis in original) (McNeill 2005: 4).

Of course our ancestors had been gesturing and making noises among members of their bands for millennia, much as chimps do today, before they began to utter communicative speech. Given the findings of McNeill and others, it is probable that early languaging, from an evolutionary point of view, was a supplement to gesturing. Speech probably evolved gradually, as our species gained the ability to construct co-expressive gestural–vocal actions from more random packages of movements and sounds. While estimates vary, many experts put the evolution of symbolic language within most groups of *Homo sapiens* at about 200,000 years ago. And the link between speech and gesturing continues strong today.

Early proto-languaging probably reinforced what social psychologist Jonathan Haidt, in his *The Righteous Mind* (2012), calls "groupishness." As distinct from the usual selfishness facilitated by evolution for most mammals, including our own species, "groupish" behavior, says Haidt, makes us "adept at promoting our group's interests, in competition with other groups" (Haidt 2012: 221). As generations of primitive bands gradually built up their own means of communicating, they forged closer links with each other that distinguished their band from external "others." Separate gesture-languages plus acts of altruism within those language groups primarily consolidated trust and expectations of cooperation within these "in-groups," a process that continues today. Haidt points to the probable early evolution of Tomasello's "shared intentionality" as another reason for our species' groupishness. The ability of humans to work together on such common projects as food gathering and hunting created common ties.

By the time our ancestors began developing proto-languaging and groupishness – perhaps a million and a half years ago, or so – it is likely that genetics and culture were reinforcing one another in our evolution. That is, some bands of *Homo erectus* hominids built upon their biological advantages of gesture–speech, shared intentionality, and other inherited traits to shape a more cooperative culture that, in turn, facilitated the evolution of more genes that gave their group further advantages in the competition with other animals for land and resources. Darwin had discussed the probability of group (as distinct from individual) evolution, but the idea had fallen into disfavor among evolutionary scientists until the 1984 publication of *Not In Our Genes*, by Richard Lewontin, Steven Rose, and Leon J. Kamin. By positing a "dialectical" relationship between culture and genetics, notes evolutionary musicologist Gary Tomlinson, *Not in Our Genes* "knocks down the firewall between nature and nurture that remains even today a thoughtless stumbling block in vernacular discussions of evolution" (Tomlinson 2015: 36).

In *Not by Genes Alone* (2005), anthropologists Peter J. Richerson and Robert Boyd provided substantial empirical and theoretical support for the coevolution of genes and culture. This allowed them to state that with the evolution of *Homo erectus*, "culture must have increased the reproductive success of our ancestors: otherwise, the features of our brain that make culture possible would not have evolved. The operational products of this evolution are innate predispositions and organic constraints that influence the ideas that we find attractive, the skills that we can learn, the emotions that we can experience, and the very way we see the world" (Richerson and Boyd 2005: 265). By the time of *Homo heidelbergensis*, the common ancestor of both us and the Neanderthals that flourished around 700,000 years ago, the confluence of genes, culture, and the environment "favored the evolution of a suite of new social instincts suited to life in such groups, including a psychology which 'expects' life to be structured by moral norms...; new emotions such as shame and guilt...and a psychology which 'expects' the social world to be divided into symbolically marked groups" (2005: 214).

Recent evidence from the human genome project suggests that the speed of biocultural evolution can increase when *Homo sapiens* are pressed by difficult ecological circumstances. Between about 140,000 and 10,000 years ago, the pace of genetic and cultural evolution quickened, apparently in response to climate swings that forced sometimes rapid changes in food sources and cultural habits. A volcanic eruption 74,000 years ago, for example, apparently blanketed the earth with ash, killing off many species of plants and animals. At some point around this time, a similar calamity exterminated most of emerging humanity; our entire species today is descended from only a few thousand ancestors. Evidently, those bands of hunter-gatherers that survived had to rely on each other even more so than before. By 50,000 years ago, however, bands of humans in Africa and elsewhere were not only perpetuating in-group languages, but crafting rituals, complex tools, and permanent dwellings. By this point, too – conventionally designated the "High Paleolithic" period of evolution – *Homo sapiens* had added music and numeracy to languaging as a means of symbolic communication.

Basic numeracy and what Tomlinson and others call "musicking" are typical, hardwired capabilities of our species. Even in hunter-gatherer societies today where their words for numbers end at "five" or "three," the members of those cultures can readily distinguish among smaller and larger groups of items that far exceed a total of five. Children in these societies are genetically primed to learn the basics of addition and subtraction as they acquire the culture of their elders. Musicking, like languaging and numeracy, requires higher-order, symbol-manipulating consciousness, but departs from both in significant ways. Specifically, says Tomlinson, "The communicative functions of vocalization that preceded musicking and language helped to determine both deep connections and deep differences between them. Hierarchic and combinatorial cognition of several sorts [e.g., high and low notes, not words; a melody, not a sentence] preceded the musicking and language that today embody it" (Tomlinson 2015: 49). As with numeracy, infants are not born with these abilities, but they learn them quickly as children. Moreover, as in other genres of performance, "The information comprised in musicking... was tightly bound up with experiences of motion and emotion. The deep heritage of musical information lies in a set of mainly emotive communicative acts" (2015: 49). Finally, says Tomlinson, "Musicking is implicated deeply in *thinking-at-a-distance*. It developed alongside a 'release from proximity' whereby humans gradually gained the capacity to imagine things not present to the senses" (2015: 50). While Tomlinson does not use the term "subjunctive," his notion of release from proximate realities into imaginative possibilities implies the same idea.

Regarding languaging, Merlin Donald concludes that it demanded more working and long-term memory, sharpened attention, led to greater neural plasticity, and vastly extended the executive functions of our brains. From Donald's perspective, languaging encouraged *Homo sapiens* to develop "a narrative mind-set" and launched us into what he terms an "oral-mythic culture" that lasted into the Common Era (2001: 295). In traditional oral cultures, says Donald, "we are dominated by our stories, whether of magic, witches, devils, demons, great heroes, or genesis" (2001: 295). "Narrative traditions ruled the minds not only of poets and artists, but of emperors and foot soldiers. Local narratives ruled every tribe and village, through their elders, chiefs, shamans, and bards" (2001: 296).

From languaging to the High Paleolithic 57

With the addition and gradual refinement of language, numeracy, music, and other capabilities in their cultures, bands of *Homo sapiens* flourished during the "High Paleolithic" period between 50,000 and 13,000 years ago. The High Paleolithic ended with the gradual shift from an economy of hunting and gathering to agriculture among some of those bands. These biocultures featured more complex tools, built living sites, the long-distance transportation of raw materials, and the rapid expansion of their populations into new territories. Cave painting, burials, and weaving were also a part of High Paleolithic practices. And performing. There is evidence that our ancestors decorated their bodies with ocher at least 120,000 years ago; probably it was in use much longer than that. Early *Homo sapiens* also fashioned flutes for music making whose finger holes fixed what the players evidently recognized as exact pitches.

With the invention of language and music, our species could engage in storytelling and elaborate these tales through dance, mime, and song. Conceptual and actual event-building through blending probably encouraged our ancestors to elaborate longer and more complex performances. Mental projection gave them the ability to enact the animals they hunted and those that hunted them – and to impersonate any other animal they could see or hear. Much better than could their hominid precursors, the new species on the block could use blending to plan ahead; their complex tool creations, living sites, and extensive networks attest to their ability to envision and act on future possibilities. Further, these humans likely enjoyed most of the performances done for each other; their experiences of joint attention probably produced trust and solidarity within their bands. Overall, these performances must have broadened and deepened the communicative cognitive networks of their cultures. Performances helped bands of *Homo sapiens* to "ratchet up" their culture, especially since languaging provided a good way to pass on what they had learned to the next generation and a metacognitive tool for reflecting on and changing their performance events. We can never know what these performances looked and sounded like, of course, but the evidence is sufficient to know how and what these early peoples were capable of performing.

Human performances changed with the introduction of literacy and writing among the elite during the agricultural era, and kept changing in response to the many communication, economic, and biocultural shifts that have accelerated rapidly over the past 500 years. Nonetheless, we must distinguish between foundational modes of human action together with the basic kinds of performance activities they could generate and those instances of performance throughout history that could not have occurred at all unless such evolutionary foundations were already in place. Otherwise, humanists will continue to confuse the universal elements present in the biocultural constitution of our species with causal factors resulting from changing historical circumstances. In this regard, all of the major elements necessary for humans to imagine, create, and respond to performances seem to have been in place since the High Paleolithic era, roughly 50,000 years ago.

From the High Paleolithic to *Hamlet*

With this contrast in mind, I want to consider various performances of *Hamlet*, from the initial production in 1600 or so to a recent film of Shakespeare's tragedy in 2000. First, however, I must acknowledge one substantial (though not foundational) difference between performances in the High Paleolithic era and Elizabethan England: the invention and proliferation of reading and writing. Before writing, which initially emerged during the agricultural era as a means of keeping track of stores of grain, there could be no playwrights. In fact, theater as we know it today does not emerge until ancient playwrights in the Greek city-states and the Indus valley began crafting written narratives for several performers that could benefit from the complex organizational mandates of a script or at least of a scenario with the outline of an action. Instead, the performing modes of choice for most oral cultures seem to have been storytelling by a single narrator, sporting contests, and religious rituals with music, none of which require writing to be produced (although all would benefit from writing after it was introduced). Preliterate performers may have staged short pantomimes and improvised scenes as well, although there is no evidence for such early efforts. Nonetheless, as we will discover in more detail in the next chapter, these early performances in oral cultures, like theater at a later time, rested upon the same evolutionary and cognitive foundations that were present in the High Paleolithic. Reading and writing provided another ratchet effect for human cultures, but did not require the biological evolution of new cognitive and physical capabilities. So, while no literate troupe of caveman players could have produced *Hamlet* 30,000 years ago (had Shakespeare's script somehow fallen into their hands), this historical difference should not prevent us from considering the basics for the conception, production, and reception of the play.

This look at performances of *Hamlet* is not intended to be exhaustive. I say little about the training and rehearsal process, and omit substantive discussion of the importance of empathy and emotion in productions of the tragedy. Entirely excluded is any examination of the dynamic system that organizes all of the major elements of the performance for the actors and spectators. These must await the synthesizing discussion of Chapter 4. Rather, I am primarily interested in tracking the consequences of the major abilities that our species had acquired through the coevolution of genetics and culture in making and understanding performances of a single play. I will pay particular attention to event perception and conceptual integration.

First of all, any performance of *Hamlet* must proceed as an event. Recall that all events have an important "starting-up process" that must occur before the main activity can get underway. According to Lakoff and Johnson, starting consists of an "initial state" and concludes with "end of start." As noted, this "starting-up process" metaphorically extends the process of a person initiating movement in space. Just as people will only begin moving when they decide to go somewhere, play performances can only begin when one or several people conceive of an action that they decide to present to others. The "initial state" of the starting-up phase, in other words, is tied to human agency and bioculture. Performances require the actions of people who can envision a possible production process that may lead to a future event of patterned subjunctive activity that will attract the attention of other people in their culture. With regard to dramatic performance, the "end of start" arrives when an actual audience has gathered to watch the actors perform the play. The main event of *Hamlet* could only begin in 1600 ACE after evolution, Elizabethan culture, and William Shakespeare and the rest of the Lord Chamberlain's Men had done their preparatory work.

At its first performance, then, *Hamlet*, like other performance events, proceeded as a series of nested, part–whole actions from its beginning to its end. The action of the mousetrap scene, for example, required a whole series of subsidiary actions before that larger action could come to fruition. And the mousetrap scene, in turn, was only one of a series of actions that constituted the completed, teleological action of the entire event. As the realization of a simulated world, the success of *Hamlet* on stage usually depends for most spectators upon the coherence of its causal and performance elements more so than it does upon its correspondences between the actual world and the subjunctive world of the play's actions. That was probably as true in 1600 as it would be for a performance today.

Performing *Hamlet* requires actors who can mentally project themselves into a blend of self and character; the actor playing Hamlet will unconsciously blend a concept of himself (or herself, if a woman is cast) with a concept of the Prince of Denmark. Although experiments have yet to fully validate the process, the actor cast as Hamlet constructs a mental image, a concept of the Prince speaking and moving within the narrative constraints of the play, and then imitates it through the same mirroring neural circuits used for action observation in everyday life. Neuroscientist Vittorio Gallese has remarked on the importance of mirror neurons for the actor when s/he constructs the blend of characterization. As Gallese explained in a conversation with an actor: "Your relationship with a character you're supposed to play is intrinsically relational, so you try to enter into the... body of someone else. In the body, in the gesturing, in the mind. So more than a mirroring mechanism, it's an imagery mechanism which partly impinges upon the same neurocircuits which are involved in action observation" (cited in Kemp 2012: 116). As theater scholar and professional actor Richard Kemp observes, this notion of treating the character as "someone else," and not simply as a part of oneself, is found in several acting theories, mostly notably those of Michael Chekhov and Jacques Lecoq. Whether they understand it or not, all actors who attempt Hamlet probably begin with a concept of the Prince as "someone else." We can presume that Richard Burbage did this in 1600. Following this imaginary construct, the integration of Burbage/Hamlet occurred during rehearsals and performances.

When spectators perceive the blend of an actor and Hamlet, they perform a similar operation. Like the actors, they do not mix all of the information from each of the concepts into the final actor/character blend; they temporarily put aside their knowledge that the actors have other lives outside of their immediate role-playing and that the characters began initially as words on a page. If the spectator perceives the actor as a star, however, she or he may include the star's public persona in the final actor/character blend. For many spectators at the premiere of *Gone with the Wind* in 1939, for instance, the persona of Clark Gable was much more important to their enjoyment of the film than the Rhett Butler character as written by Margaret Mitchell in the novel and adapted by Hollywood script writers. While the extent to which Richard Burbage could ride on his public persona when he played Hamlet cannot be known, he certainly had some star appeal by 1600; he had been performing leading roles in London theaters for about ten years. In *The Haunted Stage: The Theatre as Memory Machine*, historian Marvin Carlson notes that early performances of influential actors often "ghost" their later ones and thereby shape spectator response. During performances of *Hamlet* at the Globe and elsewhere, many in the audience probably looked for and found similarities between Burbage's earlier tragic roles and his Prince of Denmark.

With the advent of media stars, "ghosting" has been more prevalent in the twentieth and twenty-first centuries than before. Given the longevity of media images, recent Hamlets have had to make sure that their performances did not appear to the public to be ghostly reflections of the Hamlets of previous stars. This was a problem especially for Kenneth Branagh, who sought to distinguish his 1996 film of *Hamlet* from Laurence Olivier's effort in 1948. Having filmed and starred in a version of *Henry V* a few years previously (like Olivier before him), Branagh was aware that he seemed to be following in Lord Olivier's footsteps; if the public desired to take him as the new Olivier, Branagh's unique *Hamlet* made it clear that they would at least have to take him on his own terms. Branagh chose to present his *Hamlet* in shallower focus, on a wider screen, and, crucially, with a script containing all of Shakespeare's words (mostly based on the second quarto edition of the play), so that his epic lasted over four hours, compared to Olivier's two. As Patrick J. Cook notes in his *Cinematic Hamlet*, "most often in [Branagh's] *Hamlet*, shallow focus will encourage scrutiny of a speaking or reacting face, scrutiny that is further encouraged by the format's high resolution... Branagh's well-chosen cast members have abundant opportunity to activate our facially responsive mirror neurons" (Cook 2011: 107).

Cook is referring here to the "facial actions coding system" that Paul Ekman and other cognitive psychologists have researched and codified since the 1970s. His *Cinematic Hamlet* draws on many of the evolutionary and cognitive theorists and critics who now populate film studies, including Carl Plantinga, Edward Branigan, and Torben Grodal. I will be discussing the ideas of several of these scholars in the next two chapters. Cook's comment refers to the fact that our mirror neuron systems, which help actors to get into character, also assist spectators in interpreting the actions that they perceive on the screen – as well as in live action on the stage, in sports arenas, and in assemblies for public speakers. Branagh was able to sustain his four-hour *Hamlet*, in part, because he could rely on spectators' mirror neuron systems responding to the medium and close-up shots of his actors' faces.

As we will see in detail in the next chapter, the emotional responses to performances activated by our mirror neurons and other cognitive mechanisms are closely related to the kinds of meanings that audiences will tend to discover in performances. The blending activities that spectators engage in will also shape the meanings that emerge from such experiences. Hollywood released Michael Almereyda's *Hamlet* in 2000, starring Ethan Hawke in the lead and Sam Shepard as the Ghost of Hamlet's father. Almereyda updated his version of *Hamlet* to the late twentieth century, figuring the old King as the CEO of a corporation and Hamlet as his disaffected son, no longer a Prince away at school but a Gen X videographer.

Amy E. Cook (no relation to Patrick J. Cook above) points out that spectator blending might have constructed multiple meanings from the Shepard/Ghost integration. In his initial appearance as the Ghost, Shepard is wearing a long leather trench coat and smoking a cigarette, an image probably meant to evoke television commercials from the 1960s and 1970s of the Marlboro man. Shepard usually played such a figure in his few film roles, including Chuck Yeagar in *The Right Stuff* (1983) – a lone cowboy, embodying individualistic, frontier values. Further, some film viewers would have known that Shepard was also an award-winning playwright. By 2000, when Almereyda's *Hamlet* premiered, however, Shepard had apparently given up writing difficult plays for small audiences. In short, concludes Cook, "As the ghost of Hamlet's father, Shepard is the death of theater... He is crying for revenge to a son who we know will only disappoint him. He is the old west and high art looking to a disaffected New York arty intellectual for salvation. He is the past left homeless by the apathetic, postmodern present" (Cook 2010: 112). The Shepard/Ghost blend encourages all of these interpretations, allowing spectators to choose any or all of them. The blending of all actors and characters usually opens up a similar variety of possible meanings, depending on the cultural memories, current concerns, and other interests of the spectators. For Almereyda's *Hamlet*, as for all other *Hamlet*s, audience blending makes the meanings of Shakespeare's tragedy contingent upon the spectator's negotiation with the performance. The possible meanings of a performance are not on the stage (or on the screen) nor are they in the minds of the spectators; they are present, fleetingly, in the negotiations between them. Blending for meaning is another one of our evolutionary legacies from the High Paleolithic era.

Given the importance of evolution in the workings of performance, we are now in a position to discard some of the activities that scholars have occasionally stretched their definitions of performance to accommodate. As we have seen, performance depends initially upon the mental projection of a subjunctive world, which occurs in all pretend-play, and it requires role-playing, spectating, and the duration of an event with a beginning and end. Due to human evolution and culture, most children reach this capability before they are five years old. If, as I have argued, these elements are a necessary part of all performances, some activities that do not include these features of higher-order consciousness but are occasionally included as examples of performance should be excluded from our definition.

Non-human animals, for example, cannot perform. There is no evidence that they can project themselves into subjunctive, as-if situations, constitute a complex series of actions as a whole event, or manage the kind of role-playing that involves conceptual integration. Among playing primates, only *Homo sapiens* can perform. Attributing human traits to animals is a long tradition in human cultures; it dates at least from the animism of our early religions (and probably before that). But anthropomorphizing other mammals is an unscientific strategy for performance studies, which should rest upon clear biocultural definitions and distinctions. Although non-human animals cannot perform, many animals can certainly play, and they have the ability to alter their behavior through learning. Consequently, we can train them to appear in performances organized and shaped by us, such as horse racing, dog shows, a variety of circus acts, and cat videos on YouTube. Certainly, too, just because humans can do a few things that other animals cannot does not mean that our species has some inherent right to slaughter or drive into extinction the other animals of the earth. Arguably, our continuities with the rest of the animal world as well as our singular ability to formulate conceptions about the rights of animals (which no other species can do) ought to move us toward empathy with other animals and ecological sanity, although it has yet to do so.

All animals also generate actions to maintain and advance their survival. Machines, on the other hand – from primitive spears to modern computers – can neither play nor act once they are detached from human agency; from an Enaction perspective, including the operation of machines as performances *per se* is simply wrong-headed. Machines lack autopoiesis. While humans may engage other animals and machines as a part of their performing, this human ability simply renders animals and machines extensions of human acts; it does not turn them into performers (or spectators). For similar reasons, objects do not perform, either. Even art objects, such as paintings and sculptures (which may share some aesthetic qualities with performances), are not embodied performances. An artist might invite others to watch her or him perform as a painter and that action could constitute a performance, but once the painting is displayed it becomes an inanimate object and is no longer a prop in a performance action. Nor is looking at a painting a performance event; there is nothing inherent in Picasso's "Guernica" that tells the viewer when to begin looking at it and when to stop. As blended human actions and events, performances are ontologically distinct from objects, machines, and the activities of other animals.

CHAPTER 2

Rituals, image schemas, and cultural-cognitive ecosystems

Chapter 1 noted the importance of patterned actions for generating performances and engaging the attention of spectators, primarily in the theater. Similar dynamics also occur in all other performances, including rituals, sports, and musical events. An important key to understanding how action works in all performances is through its crystallization in image schemas, the gestalt perception of recurrent biocultural patterns of action that play out in the brain, the body, and the networked ecosystem. As will be clear, these performed and perceived image schemas help to generate much of the conflict that is inherent in nearly all performances. Further, their repetitions over time lend coherence and perdurance to all cultural-cognitive ecosystems. The last chapter also ended with discussions of several films, on the assumption that movies of *Hamlet* should be considered within our definition of performance along with live concerts and stage plays. But should they be? What about other media, including computer games? Related to this question, as we will see, is the place of ritual events within performance studies. In this chapter, I will first look at ritual before discussing an Enactive approach to mediated performances.

Performance and ritual

In the 1970s, Richard Schechner braided play with ritual to create a definition of performance that remains influential today. In his understanding of the sequence of evolutionary events that led to the emergence of performance, Schechner placed play and ritual first, with their later synthesis resulting in performance. He continues to make this argument in his 2006 textbook, *Performance Studies: An Introduction*. "Playing, like ritual, is at the heart of performance," he states (Schechner 2006: 89). "In fact performance may be defined as ritualized behavior conditioned/permeated by play," Schechner concludes (2006: 89). As we saw in the last chapter, however, making play and ritual coequal partners in a definition of performance contradicts what Boyd, Donald, and others have been claiming about the likely evolution of performance from play. But if those claims are correct, where does this leave ritual?

Social scientists have defined "ritual" in many competing ways. As anthropologist Peter G. Stromberg remarks, "Ritual may refer to a Catholic Mass, a greeting routine, a formulaic courtship dance undertaken by a certain species of bird, the obsessive hand-washing of a person suffering from obsessive compulsive disorder, and so on. The potential application of the term is so broad and so open to interpretation that pinning down the essential nature of ritual is unlikely" (Stromberg 2009: 101). I will follow Stromberg and define ritual in what he admits is "a conservative and fairly restrictive sense"; ritual, for him, is "simply a religious ceremony of some sort" (2009: 102). This definition has the advantage of parsimony. Since nearly all social scientists would include religious ceremony within their definition of ritual (and many would point to it as a prototypical example), any generalization about ritual that is not true for religious ceremonies can count as mistaken in the subsequent discussion.

Are rituals performance events? Certainly many traditional rituals exceed the typical running time of theatrical and musical events. Performances of Korean *Kut* usually last for several days, for example. Enacted by female shamans to allow the dead to rest in peace, *Kut* may include consuming ritual food and drink, reciting stories, playing music, and dancing as though possessed by the spirit of the dead person. Over the course of this ritual event, there are many periods of time when everyday life is partly suspended and the performers and spectators are expected to remain in ritual readiness, even though no part of the *Kut* ritual is actually occurring. A rough parallel to this situation would be a contemporary theater festival at Edinburgh, Avignon, or similar sites, where visitors try to maintain their holiday mood even as they wait for the next production. In both instances, a mood of subjunctive possibility – ranging from the quest for spiritual transformation to the expectation of playful engagement – eases the transition from one part of the performance to the next. In evolutionary terms, the hopefulness of play pervades the entire event, surrounding and helping to establish the ambiance for the next section of the performance. This elasticity of ritual time may distinguish them from "Monopoly" and magic shows, but should not disqualify rituals as performances.

But do rituals allow their participants to take a subjunctive perspective on their play? Theatrical spectators know that they are participating in a convention-bound activity; they understand that they and the actors on stage are playing temporary roles in events that have been consciously separated from everyday culture. In contrast, ritual activities in religious events may be separate and convention-bound, but they are not usually understood as subjunctive experiences by their believing participants. A priest celebrating a Catholic Mass, for example, does not assume that he is playing the role of a priest who believes in a God that only exists for the duration of the ritual performance. There is no "what if" from the point of view of participant-believers at a Eucharist. When the ritual of the Mass is complete and the church service is over, the priest remains in what Catholic theology assumes and teaches is a special relation to the Almighty. For the faithful of all religions, belief severely constrains the incursion of subjunctive possibility into ritual experience.

Is the seriousness of belief enough to separate ritual from other activities involving play and performance, however? Evolutionary examinations of ritual usually consider religious belief when exploring its possible origins and adaptive values. Several anthropologists attuned to the insights of cognitive science have taken a fresh look at the likely evolutionary roots of religion. Many of the contributors to *Religion, Anthropology, and Cognitive Science* emphasize the importance of what they call the "Hypersensitive Agency Detective Device" (HADD) in the minds of hominids and later *Homo sapiens* as a primary reason for our species' creation and worship of gods (Lanman 2007: 125–26). Like conceptual blending, HADD draws on the specifically human cognitive operation of projection. People often claim that they have detected supernatural agency in images, natural events, and accidents where none really exists. Believers think they can see the face of a deity in the embers of a fire, for example, or are able to perceive the workings of the gods in a thunderstorm. In these instances, they have projected their own notion of agency into a situation they cannot explain to enable them to understand it as the will of some superhuman power.

HADD builds on the assumption that evolution primed our species to be hypersensitive about invisible agents that might do them harm. Better to interpret that rustling behind the bush as a lurking tiger about to pounce than to ignore the signs of possible agency! On those few occasions when such interpretations were correct, the hunter-gatherer might survive. Lanman and his fellow authors presume that a belief in unseen higher powers often operated in the same ways in our past and probably continues to shape religious belief today. Better to believe, like the rest of the band, that the gods might curse your hunting or blight your berry-picking than to risk offending unseen but always lurking animate powers. Better still to try to propitiate such deities, even if the rituals that your tribe had formulated were seldom effective. According to anthropologists Jonathan A. Lanman, Justin L. Barrett, James Laidlaw, and Harvey Whitehouse, HADD, initially an evolutionary adaptation that sensitized our ancestors to the possibility of dangerous agency nearby, led to the secondary cognitive effect of helping them to invent and perpetuate religious deities with superhuman agency. In prehistoric times, our hypersensitivity about agency facilitated the extension of performance into religious ritual.

As sociologist Robert A. Scott explains, HADD works cognitively through blending. Scott focuses on the attribution of divine intervention to medieval Christian saints as an example. "In a sense, the 'job' of a saint," he notes, "is to supply a mechanism by which it becomes possible for humans to connect to and gain the protection of heaven" (Scott 2006: 217). To create the blend of a saint, worshippers project characteristics from three sources – a concept of a corpse (because all historical saints are dead), a concept of a live person with human agency, and a concept of the divine – and integrate them into a fourth space. A blend of attributes from each of these spaces, the saint becomes a body with superhuman, divine agency that can influence God on behalf of a worshipper. Scott concludes that "this transference of divine powers also makes possible the potential for intercession and healing that humans consider the acid test of whether a dead human being is or is not a saint" (2006: 218).

Whitehouse, Scott, and several anthropologists underline what other investigators of religion have emphasized: Belief in supernatural agency derives evolutionarily from our ancestors' search for causal explanations. Trying to figure out how the world works, especially in matters of life and death, has always had survival value for our species and their precursors. In his *Religion Explained*, Pascal Boyer notes that religious representations throughout the world focus predominately on five related themes: agency, predation, mortality, morality, and social exchange. Agency ensures life, predation and mortality deal with the fear of individual death, and morality and social exchange center on the desire for future life and the success of the band, tribe, or nation. Boyer also points out that most religions tell stories about their central supernatural agents that render them semi-human and believable in terms of the causal constraints on their agency. Jesus may walk on water, Mohammed may perform a few miracles, and the Buddha may take some fantastic journeys, but in most respects these gods eat, sleep, breathe, and walk about the earth just like other mortals. If their superior abilities allowed them to avoid most of the causal realities of human life, such as gravity and the need for food and air, it would be difficult for people to understand, value, and remember their superhuman powers.

Scott Atran's study, *In Gods We Trust: The Evolutionary Landscape of Religion* (2002), generally confirms the insights of later scholars who emphasize the crucial role of HADD in the evolution of religion. Atran also notes that cultural religious expression presents what seems to be an evolutionary quandary: Why should cultures embrace practices that range from stopping work at specific times of the day, to sacrificing animals, to mutilating the body, and (in some instances) to killing relatives, simply to keep faith with an immaterial deity? According to Atran, most primitive religious rituals rehearsed situations of danger, stress, pain, and occasional death to enable humans to process traumatic experiences in their lives that have no logical or probable explanation or outcome. Such events played a much larger part in human history 50,000 years ago than they do today, when disease, starvation, and violent death were more frequent occurrences. Despite appearances, then, Atran shows that sacrifice, mutilation, and similar ritual practices sanctioned by religious belief helped *Homo sapiens* to deal with life-threatening events and to bind individuals more tightly to their group. Primarily for this reason, most religious rituals encouraged "groupishness."

Some religious rituals, both today and probably during the High Paleolithic, also involved trance states that had social and restorative benefits. Recent neuroscientific experiments with hypnosis and other altered states of consciousness suggest that this psychological condition bypasses the executive functions of the brain that coordinate attention, implicit memory, intention, and voluntary action to induce "a sense of timelessness, denial of self, little if any self-reflection and analysis, little emotional content, little abstract thinking, no planning, and a sensation of unity," according to one scientist (Dietrich cited in Ott 2007: 262). In cases of hypnosis, the suggestions of an authority figure can lead the hypnotized individual to "involuntariness bordering on compulsion" (Woody and Szechtman 2007: 244). Letting go of a sense of self, agency, and emotional engagement through trance states, induced through drugs or other means, can help individuals to alleviate pain. Evolutionary psychologist William J. Ray adds that hypnotizability is also associated with "an ability to . . . modulate the immune system and achieve greater benefits [from] psychosocial therapies" (Ray 2007: 237). Groups of our ancestors that could practice such psychological medicine with each other in religious rituals or other kinds of performances probably increased their solidarity and gained an evolutionary advantage over other groups that did not.

If religious rituals are understood from these evolutionary perspectives, it is clear that they are an offshoot of other kinds of performances. Indeed, it is likely that performance activities in general preceded specifically religious rituals in our evolutionary past. Brian Boyd notes that while the earliest sketchy evidence for religious practice dates from funeral rites practiced 90,000 years ago, *Homo sapiens* were decorating themselves with ocher 30,000 years before that. Taking on temporary subjunctive roles and enacting discrete events for each other around the campfire were probably not complex performances – singing a melody, juggling some branches of firewood, dancing to rhythmic drumming, for example – but they were performances as I have been defining them. Boyd reasons that our species, already habituated to dancing and singing for each other, likely presumed that their gods would perceive and enjoy their performances in the same ways. Religious belief and ritual, then, probably emerged during the High Paleolithic era, when religion was also able to draw on the thousands of years in which HADD was operative for hominids. Since, as Atran notes, belief plus ritual performances reinforce social cohesion, those early bands that began performing and worshipping together also thrived together.

Consequently, there is some evidence to reverse the assumption of many theorists that performance and the arts grew out of religion. Rather, rituals tied to religious beliefs are the evolutionary offspring of play and performance. Boyd is clear that patterning and attention in the arts had to precede religious rituals:

> Indeed, those who claim that art derives from religion do not explain how it could do so. If a group of early humans had begun to believe in supernatural forces, why *would* and how *could* they then have invented art to serve the purposes of religion? Why would they have thought of art as a next step, if there had not *already* been ways of embellishing surfaces and altering shapes and producing sounds and movements that elicited a deep response in human eyes and minds? Religion, on the other hand, needs art as a precursor. Without the existence of stories that diverge from the true . . . religion could not have arisen. (ital. in original) (Boyd 2009: 113–14)

The evidence and logic of evolution do not support those priests and congregants who believe that their faith has nothing to do with subjunctive experience, who place their earnest rituals in opposition to play and performance. Nonetheless, those religious fundamentalists throughout history who sought to distance their worship services from theater and other performances were perhaps right to worry; conceptual blending in one area of life can prompt the pursuit of subjunctive play in another.

Of course there are many believers across the world who understand their religious rituals as a kind of performance and take great joy in marrying theater to faith. In his *Theatre and Religion on Krishna's Stage: Performing in Vrindavan*, David Mason investigates a large group of Hindus who stage plays with child actors to worship Lord Krishna. A major goal of *ras lila* performances, as their religious theater is called, is to celebrate the embodiment of Krishna's playful spirit in the performances of selected boys in the town of Vrindavan, located south of New Delhi. Lightly rehearsed, the boys stumble through many roles in scenes from the early life of Krishna, but the spectator-worshippers for this theater are not disturbed by their lack of professionalism because they see the playfulness of the young Krishna in the boys' antics and glory in their fun. As Mason explains, *ras lila* combines both the doubleness of theatrical representation and the goal of honoring a god. "*Ras lila* theatre, then, is not only theatre, but a worship service," states Mason. "The stage activity quite unselfconsciously crosses boundaries between ritual and theatre, and, in this way, *ras lila* theatre may demonstrate just how artificial those boundaries can be" (Mason 2009: 7). Indeed, *ras lila* exemplifies one culture's synthesis of play and ritual in performance. Conceptual blending anchors the role-playing and spectating that occurs in the event. HADD is evident in the agency of Lord Krishna, credited by all believers for the joy that the boy actors take in their performances and for the general success of the ritual. Finally, play separates this performance event from the workaday world and suffuses all of its artistic patterns and demands for attention with rapture and release.

Many peoples, including the Maori of New Zealand, believe that the bones of their ancestors, carved into a pendant or some other object, have agency in the world of the living. Performance historian Margaret Werry has taken the Maori example to argue that the epistemology of Polynesians and others who believe in the agency of ritual objects should form the basis of a performance history of everyday life. Objecting to the representationalism of current theory, she posits a new "vitalism" (Werry 2013: 228) in which the belief that objects may be infused with agency would provide an alternative to outworn semiotics and encourage a more ethical approach to non-western thinking. According to Werry, this approach means "believing that objects act with a will that is also a destiny" (2013: 222). Such historiographical projects that credit the mental projections of HADD as a mode of causation and conflate actual and subjunctive realities are unnecessary, however. The paradigm of Enaction both avoids the problem of representationalism and provides a naturalistic epistemology as an alternative to Werry's unscientific combination of vitalism and relativism.

Mental projection and modern media

From the perspective of Enaction, projecting agency onto objects or invisible deities involves the same cognitive operation as projecting agency onto the human images we watch on a film, television, or computer screen. Of course there is no doubt that many of the dynamics of producing, communicating, and responding to mediated events are different from the usual ways that live performances of rituals and other events generally occur. But the main problem for performance studies critics who seek to privilege live over mediated performances has typically been the latter's apparent diminishment of human agency. At stake is also the question of evolutionary continuity. Has the media changed us in fundamental ways, or are mediated performances an extension of the same kinds of basic evolutionary and cognitive abilities that our species has been using for over 50,000 years?

Theater theorist Peggy Phelan makes an ontological distinction between live performance and mediated communication. In *Unmarked: The Politics of Performance*, Phelan asserts, "Performance cannot be saved, recorded, documented, or otherwise participate in the circulation of representations of representations: once it does so, it becomes something other than performance. To the degree that performance attempts to enter the economy of reproduction, it betrays and lessens the promise of its own ontology" (Phelan 1993: 146). Phelan builds her ontological position primarily on psychoanalysis and the poststructuralism of Jacques Derrida. Because I have already noted the problem of confirmability with Freudian and Lacanian psychoanalysis, I will not delve into this side of Phelan's argument. Through an elegant and complex logic, Phelan uses Derridean notions of *différance* and iteration to conclude that "presence" is possible in live but not in mediated performance. Because performance is not repeatable, she says, it can escape the problem of iteration – that is, it can avoid the limitations of textuality – and thus remain "unmarked." She believes that the nonrepeatability of performance gives its agents more political power.

The problem with this argument for the paradigm of Enaction is not Phelan's logic, but the Derridean assumptions behind it. Like most poststructuralists, Derrida assumed that social-linguistic conditioning beyond human control determines what "subjects" will find meaningful in their lives. Following Derrida, Phelan maintained a strong version of this claim in *Unmarked* and continued to assert it in later books. "The body is not coherent," she noted in 1998; "[O]nly reading practices ... make [it] beautiful, sick, well, living, or dying" (Phelan 1998: 16). This statement, of course, positions language as ontologically prior to embodiment and contradicts nearly all of the empirical findings I have noted from cognitive psychology, biology, linguistics, and neuroscience. (It also has the awkward effect of denying that sickness and death could ever have occurred in evolutionary time before there were *Homo sapiens* around who could use language to declare that some animals were alive while others had died.) Further, as discussed in the last chapter, languaging and conceptual thinking are strategies for action, not overarching determinants of behavior. Language may play some role in "marking" individuals and groups through categorization, but not necessarily a determining one. Thus, for Phelan to assert that performance can somehow escape the trap of textuality is a claim of little consequence. If evolution, cognition, embodiment, and bioculture – not textuality – are the relevant contexts for understanding and defining performance, such poststructuralist positions are simply beside the point.

In rejecting Phelan's position, Philip Auslander disclaims any interest in proposing an ontological solution to the live-mediated problem. Nevertheless, he builds much of his case on Walter Benjamin's supposition that modernity initiated what could only be called an ontological break with the past. In his 1936 essay, "The Work of Art in the Age of Mechanical Reproduction," Benjamin argued that modernism, specifically mass production, had fundamentally altered the relationship between humanity and art. Traditional cultures had valued the arts as "auratic"; they found in artistic expression a source of authenticity and uniqueness, which increased the value of artistic agency. By the 1930s, however, Benjamin believed that the mechanical reproduction of art objects and the mass distribution of drama through films had trivialized the arts. Benjamin and his followers, however, have never produced convincing evidence that traditional arts produced an "aura" for earlier viewers that modern media had somehow destroyed. His position is yet another version of "blank slateism," the belief that cultural and historical forces alone can effectively erase and rewrite our evolutionary inheritance to alter the foundations of human psychology.

Auslander is certainly correct about the proliferation of microphones on stage, video screens in sports arenas and rock concerts, and the other, similar incursions that he cites, however. But a historian of performance could rightly complain that his, and Benjamin's, understanding of performance history is too short-sighted. The reproduction, if not the mass distribution, of several parts of performance had been going on for a long time before the industrial age. Scribes began copying the words and music for performances after the invention of writing, and this process accelerated with the printing press, which in turn hastened the mass distribution of the same scripts and musical scores for dances, plays, speeches, and other performances to audiences around the world. As we know from physical anthropology, such advances in tool-making and networking often lead to slow cultural changes, but these do not necessarily require or produce an increase or decrease in fundamental human capabilities. From this perspective, performances in the West had been losing their "aura," if they ever had one, since the death of Homer and the transition to cultures of reading and writing. Modernity forced no ontological break between live and mediated performances in the twentieth century.

If the case for the ontological distinctiveness of mediated communication in the twentieth century is problematic, how good is the case for continuity? In *Embodied Visions: Evolution, Emotion, Culture and Film*, Torben Grodal emphasizes the conservative and creative organization of the human mind. Our brains do not engage in new modes of operation when older capabilities can be called on to serve the same general purposes. In the case of film viewing, two of our most evolutionarily primitive cognitive mechanisms come into play, HADD, our hyperactive tendency to project agency onto inanimate objects, and visual representationalism. Regarding the latter, Grodal asserts, "The fundamental architecture of the brain was made at a time when incoming data were essentially true, so that reality status evaluation was a secondary process and the later cultural development of visual (and acoustic) simulations made it necessary to contain the impact of such simulations by higher-order cognitive processes" (Grodal 2009: 185). The primitive parts of our brain that control flight-or-fight and similar motoric responses necessary for survival process all visual and aural stimuli as accurate representations of the world. Better to believe in one's perception of a huge carnivore nearby, of course, than to be eaten.

Closely linked to this primitive mechanism is our tendency to project and attribute agency onto what we see, as already noted. Consequently, when we watch images of actors playing characters in a film narrative, our first tendency is to see them as real people capable of agency, not as photographic images incapable of interacting with us. Because our ability to evaluate the "reality status" of what we perceive evolved later, it takes an extra mental effort to step back from the immersive quality of a film to be able to understand it as a material, inanimate, and manufactured product. Even that understanding, however, is tempered by the fact that we know that real, embodied people did intentionally make the film we are watching, although we cannot directly experience their embodiedness while we enjoy it. Besides, spectators do not usually wish to step back from their immersion in a filmed fiction; frequently reminding themselves of the artificiality of a film would temporarily stop their pleasure in the flow of the experience.

Regarding the believability that spectators impute to staged and filmed fictions, Grodal points out that Coleridge's maxim about spectators needing to engage their "willing suspension of disbelief" in order to believe the illusion actually gets the process backward. Because evolution initially prepared us to believe what we see, spectators must willingly suspend their belief – not their disbelief – if they want to question the apparent reality and constructedness of a piece of fiction at the multiplex or playhouse. This includes sights that we "know" to be false, such as angels on stage or vampires and zombies at the movies. "The frontal brain needs to perform reality status evaluations... to qualify that what we see has no reference in real worlds" (Grodal 2009: 255), he says. Evaluating the reality status of a film (or any mediated event) is also the first step toward criticizing how it was made. This takes us back to the difference between actual and subjunctive realities and the necessary doubleness of all performances. What Grodal calls "reality status evaluation" is really the ability to perceive the differences between actual and subjunctive realities. In order to critique a film (or any other performance), we need to be able to suspend our belief in its complete actuality and approach the event as a work of art and craft. All spectators, even the most credulous among us, can make this distinction; unlike other mammals, we were born to be both crowd followers and critics.

Often, though, we prefer to suspend such cognitive evaluations. People who enjoy being frightened at horror films will usually go as far as their imaginations (and stomachs) can stand before pulling back from horrible sights to tell themselves that such visions cannot be true. This kind of reality check is similar to the cognitive operation we must use to remind ourselves that, despite "sunrises" and "sunsets," the earth actually moves around the sun and not the other way around. The fact that spectators will tend to believe in the actual reality of film performances for the same reasons that they believe in theatrical ones is a strong argument against an ontological break and for the evolutionary continuity of mediated performance events.

Another way of understanding what happens in films is through the actions of its artists and producers. When actors make a film, as when they perform a play, they still draw on themselves and the resources provided by writers, directors, costumers, and others to blend self and role to create an event for spectators, even though those spectators are not present for the initial performances of the actors in front of a camera. Nonetheless, while it may be said that the performance event resulting from their activities was delayed, the performance was not denied. Like what used to be called a "record" of a musical performance, a film "records" the interactive, practical actions of its artists for later "play." In this way, movies join the rest of a culture's cognitive network to shape the neuronal connections of its viewing and listening audience, just like other performances.

The delay in fully realizing filmic agency prompts an interesting question: How far can initial agency and eventual performance be separated from each other and still retain a significant connection in our mediated age? This question is directly relevant to matters of autonomy and embodiment in Enaction theory. In 1961, Nat "King" Cole recorded "Unforgettable" in a New York Studio, and Capitol Records released it as a part of a three-record, long-playing set, *The Nat "King" Cole Story*. Thirty years later, in 1991, engineers in an updated sound studio wired musicians and Natalie Cole, Nat's daughter, with headsets so that Natalie could effectively "sing in unison" with her dead father. The technology involved exhuming the original tape recording from 1961 and matching a slightly reworked version of Nelson's Riddle's music and Natalie's voice on a microphone with her father's singing. Natalie did several takes and the studio engineers mixed three of them into a composite track that became the basis for the final product. In an interview, Natalie recalled a remark made by her producer, David Foster, near the end of production: "At one point David thought, 'Wouldn't it be incredible if not only she answers her father but he answers her, as though he was right over her shoulder?'" (Stanyek and Piekut 2010: 31). Foster and Al Schmitt, a master sound engineer, found that they could lay in Nat's voice slightly behind Natalie's to provide that echo effect. The sound of the final mix for "Unforgettable" in 1991 suggested that the ghost of Nat "King" Cole was hovering behind his daughter as they sang their duet together.

Cole's ghost was not the first and certainly would not be the last of past media stars to haunt the present. In 2010, through the wizardry of mixing old film clips with present digitized media, the "unforgettable" ghosts of Humphrey Bogart and Audrey Hepburn were doing television commercials for contemporary products. Who has agency in these digitized productions? Natalie Cole, together with her producers and engineers, could certainly claim collective agency for the 1991 rerecording of "Unforgettable." But what about Dad? Could we say that Nat "King" Cole continued to exercise agency in 1991, long after his death in 1965? In a 2010 *TDR* article, scholars

Jason Stanyek and Benjamin Piekut disconnect long-term from short-term, immediate agency. For Stanyek and Piekut, the possible effects of agency may be more historically significant than the agent's initial actions. According to Stanyek and Piekut:

> Agency is always distributed and never coterminous with a single body; it is not something that a person collects and, in a moment of purposeful clarity, unleashes... Standard reckonings of agency... often constrict causality to a 'here and now' operation... The topology of causality cannot be reduced to a one-to-one relationship between action and result, for effectivity is enhanced by intra-active and over-lapping agencies in a manner that exceeds commonplace notions of intentionality. Effects are unpredictably durative, and can be indirect, delayed, unintended, and even unmarked. (Stanyek and Piekut 2010: 18)

If we think of agency in terms of its many effects instead of tying it to the intentions that initially motivated it, as Stanyek and Piekut recommend, it is clear that the deceased Nat "King" Cole played an agential role in the 1991 production of "Unforgettable." Nor is this situation unique; film actors Mary Pickford and Charles Chaplin, dead long before Cole, still exert some agency in the present whenever their films are shown. Performances must begin in embodied actions involving brains, bodies, and their immediate surrounds in the present, but the ramifications of their biocultural agency may extend far into the future.

Considered from this point of view, computer games also involve extensions of agency. By manipulating an avatar with a joy stick or through other means, the gamer in a typical video game claims and extends her agency within the world of the video. Although her opponents usually appear to be other figures in the fictional world of the game, these antagonists actually extend the collective agency of the team that created and programmed the video. This agonistic relationship creates special challenges for video creators, who must program for a range of possible skill levels to keep the game interesting for many players. Both gamers and game creators are extending their agency through computerized technologies.

"Unforgettable" extensions of agency through time and technology are the fundamental constituents of culture and communication. By extending agency in this way, human beings take advantage of our capacity to engage in "shared intentionality," Tomasello's term for our ability to share intentions and actions with others that I discussed in Chapter 1. Judged within the framework of evolutionary time, humans have quickly moved from speech, to writing, to print, to electronic media, all the while elaborating and expanding the boundaries of shared intentionality into wider (and eventually global) networks while maintaining some modes of "unforgettable" intentionality that began centuries ago. Even as some genres of performance also expanded their networks – World Cup football, Hollywood and Bollywood films, and broadcasts of Catholic religious rituals – others continued as live and local. Nonetheless, the foundation of all performance in shared human intentions and extended actions continues to inform them all.

Of course the chief example of extended agency in human communications history is the invention of writing and the gradual extension of literacy. Because the ancient Greeks took the time to write down the performance events that constituted *The Iliad* and *The Odyssey*, the collective narrator we call "Homer" can still "speak" to us. But as the Greeks were all too aware, writing and reading are not the same as performing. Unlike performers, writers do not directly communicate through their bodies, with the consequence that reading is a different cognitive operation than spectating. Readers are usually encouraged to imagine the human actions described and narrated in texts – actions often grounded in marvelous subjunctive realities – but projecting animate desires, intentions, and emotions onto material, embodied role-players (or onto their avatars, as in computer games and puppetry) is not a part of reading. Further, writers and readers cannot pick up what they need to know through normal socialization processes. Instead, in most societies, they must attend a school set apart from their families and villages, where learning to read and write requires several years of practice to attain minimum proficiency – and a college education these days to engage in literate behavior with knowledge and sophistication. Little wonder that the skills involved in literacy took centuries to gain normative acceptance in most cultures on the earth, and that illiteracy remains widespread. In contrast, performing and enjoying the performances of others is built upon the kinds of genetic proclivities and cultural sociality that *Homo sapiens* had acquired and was practicing 50,000 years ago, thousands of years before a tiny fraction of the human population learned to read and write. While literacy can help to improve our performative abilities, it is not a necessary prerequisite for it.

How, then, might we understand the shift from biocultures primarily dependent upon live performances to those more modern cultures reliant mostly upon literacy and print? Johnson's logic of continuity provides perhaps the best framework. As in human development and evolution, more advanced processes are usually built upon more basic biocultural capabilities and learning. As we have seen, babies learn shared intentionality before they can play mimetic games as toddlers and later graduate to more imaginative scenarios as four-year olds. Similarly, many mammals became adept at playing before one mammal in particular was able to incorporate mammalian play into human performance. Biocultural development over historical time follows a broadly similar path. The main difference, though – and it is an important one – is that the evolution of performance required new genetic capabilities, while the much shorter development of literacy could build upon biological abilities that were already present in the High Paleolitic era. Following Johnson, then, literacy may be said to have emerged from performance and we can expect that it shares some continuities with it. Literacy often involves the packaging of framed events, and it facilitates the sharing of these subjunctive realities; the importance of narrative for performative and print modes of communication is the obvious link here. Literacy, however, does a better job of preserving those realities (before film and video, anyway) than performance can. Just as animal play is not the same as performance, so performance differs from the activities of literacy. Lacking embodied or extended role-players and spectators, writing and reading are not performances. And just as it would be foolish for us to expect that animal play can be analyzed with the same tools by which we understand human performances, so is it important to distinguish among many modes of analysis that may be fine for literature but are inadequate for performance.

Biocultural enablements and obstacles

This next section begins with the work of an aerial artist, a kind of performance that has been practiced for centuries and (like many circus acts) does not require literacy for the basics of its craft and appeal. Although I have been emphasizing action and its extensions in time and space as the basis of performance, it is evident that the simple human ability to take action within a durative event is not usually enough to constitute a performance that will grab and hold audience attention. Spectators want to follow flows of coordinated action, but they also enjoy watching performers contend with internal and external constraints and overcome the obstacles that they encounter along the way. Further, such conflicts typically work at both biological and cultural levels. Consider the 1974 performance of aerial artist Philippe Petit in New York City.

On August 7, 1974, Petit, with the help of his assistants, strung a tightrope wire between the two towers of the World Trade Center and secured it with guy wires and winches during the night. Shortly after 7:00 am the next morning, Petit stepped to the edge of the South Tower, a quarter of a mile above lower Manhattan, to draw the attention of those below. Many New Yorkers on their way to work stopped to gaze at the small figure in black against the morning sky. Most thought he was a repairman, a window washer, or possibly a jumper, poised at the edge of the building for a suicide fall; few saw the cable stretched between the towers. Spectators on street corners, in Wall Street buildings, and on the Staten Island Ferry craned upward; some exchanged comments with each other; a few shouted at the lone man to jump; all waited to see what he would do. The New York police had seen what was happening and some were already scrambling through the lobbies and up the elevators of the South Tower to stop this public disturbance. Petit had secured no public permit to allow him to attempt what he was about to perform. Finally, the aerialist doubled over from the waist to stretch his body, hoisted a nearby balancing pole and adjusted it in his hands, made a final test of the cable with his thin-soled slippers, and then nimbly stepped onto the wire and walked a few feet forward.

The crowd below was aghast. A few screamed, some turned away, many felt queasy, but most glued their eyes to the tightrope walker and gawked in silent, spellbound amazement. Petit built his act carefully. He had been performing high-wire tricks for several years and knew how to pull in the crowd. He took his time with the first crossing to the North Tower, a 140 feet away, checking the wire for stray ends that might puncture his slippers, adjusting his body and the pole to the occasional gusts of wind at that altitude, and working with the increasing sway of the cable as he neared the center of his walk. Petit was focused but at ease; he would later comment on the freedom, confidence, and even arrogance he felt while losing himself in the flow of his performance. During the forty-five minutes of his act, Petit danced on the wire, hopped up and down, and at one point even lay down on his back, pretending to take a nap, with the balancing pole across his stomach. Many spectators who watched him for a while relaxed from gaping astonishment into admiration, amusement, and joy.

Finally, after eight crossings and the threat of a downpour from lowering clouds, Petit saluted his audience below and ran quickly across the cable and into the outstretched arms of an irate cop. The police hauled him off the top of the building, the City charged him with disturbing the peace, and a local judge slapped him with a small fine and the community service of performing a safer aerial act for city kids. The media had a field day with the event; one newspaper dubbed Petit's escapade "The Artistic Crime of the Twentieth Century." When asked why he did it, Petit said, "When I see three oranges, I juggle, when I see two towers, I walk" ("Philippe Petit," *Wikipedia*, accessed July 26, 2014).

It will be helpful to consider Petit's "walk" from the perspective of Mark Johnson's understanding of image schemas. As noted in the last chapter, the image schema of SOURCE-PATH-GOAL, or simply PATH, underlies our comprehension of all agential movement from one place to another. When Petit crossed between the twin towers, he began at the edge of one tower, his SOURCE, moved across the PATH of his wire, and arrived at his GOAL, the observatory roof of the other tower. Petit and his spectators also unconsciously used the image schema of PART-WHOLE to understand his entire performance as an event. Infants first understand PART-WHOLE relations in terms of their bodies – e.g., "my fingers are a part of my hand, my hand is part of my arm, my arm is a part of my body . . . " Petit and his spectators could not know how many PARTS there might be to his WHOLE performance, but Petit understood that he needed to add some variety to his crossings to hold the crowd's attention. According to Johnson, "(1) Schemata are structures *of an activity* by which we organize our experience in ways that we can comprehend. They are primary means by which we *construct* or *constitute* order and are not mere passive receptacles into which experience is poured. (2) Unlike templates, schemata are flexible in that they can take on any number of instantiations in varying contexts" (Johnson 1987: 29–30). Petit's spectators unconsciously applied the PATH and PART-WHOLE schemas (or schemata) to this activity of aerial artistry and used them to construct their understanding of the event. Both image schemas primarily helped the humans involved to comprehend Petit's agency.

Johnson understands image schemas as primitive cognitive universals based in genetic traits deriving from our evolution. Infants, for example, explore their world through image schemas soon after birth and may begin to experience some of these schemas in the womb. Later in life, people experience and express image schemas in thousands of ways in all varieties of human culture. Johnson's first major exploration of this phenomenon occurred in 1987 with *The Body in the Mind: The Bodily Basis of Meaning, Imagination, and Reason*, where he enumerated twenty-seven foundational image schemas (Johnson 1987: 126). Others besides PATH and PART-WHOLE directly involve agency (ITERATION, MERGING, and SPLITTING), some have to do with physical orientation (UP-DOWN, CENTER-PERIPHERY, and CONTAINMENT), while several center on activities that often oppose human agency (BLOCKAGE, COUNTERFORCE, and COMPULSION). He broadened his investigation of image schemas in *The Meaning of the Body* (2007), linking image schemas to prescient insights from John Dewey. Johnson notes that Dewey "recognized the underlying continuity that connects our physical interactions in the world with our activities of imagining and thinking" (2007: 139–40). For Dewey, the source of this continuity combined the physical and the mental; he termed it the "body-mind." Johnson specifies that experiencing, imagining, and deploying image schemas is a significant and mostly unconscious operation of the body-mind. While image schemas do much more than constitute performances – they structure all human activity – all sports contests, musical events, dramatic performances, and religious rituals have several of these distinctive schemas at their core. Following Johnson's practice, I shall capitalize the names of all image schemas in the ensuing discussion.

In addition to PATH and PART-WHOLE, the artist and his spectators would have unconsciously used several image schemas to comprehend the biocultural enablements and constraints of Petit's daring stunt. The first and most significant of these was the imminent threat to Petit's life if he lost his BALANCE. As we know from our bodies and from the gravitational "pull" of the earth, our UP-DOWN orientation when we walk can be disturbed if the sense of balance located in our inner ears goes askew. Of course Petit was not simply walking on a piece of wire or rope a foot off the ground; he was several thousand feet up in the air, rendering the biological and physical problems of BALANCE and gravity both life-threatening for him and more engaging for spectators. The challenges to Petit's life derived from culture as well as biology: to construct two skyscrapers and stretch an aerialist's wire between them required a level of invention and material culture that was clearly unavailable to our Paleolithic ancestors. (In contrast, slack-rope dancing – an aerialist's ability to maintain BALANCE and move across a low, swaying rope, often tied between two trees – has probably been performed for thousands of years.) Another vital image schema for Petit's performance was CONTACT, the necessary CONTACT between his slippered feet, or occasionally his prone body, and the wire. In Petit's case, CONTACT related directly to BALANCE, but our body-minds can and do experience these two schemas separately. Again, the material, cultural enablements of manufactured slippers, wire, and even the balance pole figured in Petit's ability to maintain his biological CONTACT with the wire. Finally, COUNTERFORCE, the occasional winds at the height of Petit's walk, exerted a force against his body that sometimes threatened his BALANCE and the efficacy of his CONTACT. The spectators below would not have been directly aware of this obstacle (although some probably imagined it), but Petit reported that increasing gusts of wind was one reason that he decided to end his walk when he did.

As a result of experiencing these image schemas together, Petit and his spectators became "coupled" to the same situation. As Johnson relates, ecological psychologist D.N. Lee has worked out how humans and other animals experience an appropriate relationship to their surroundings, which Lee terms "body–environment coupling" (Lee 1993: 43). Because the environment may include other people, coupling often links people to people, a linking that may involve performers and spectators. According to Lee, humans act so that they can experience optic, acoustic, and haptic patterns of flow in order to maintain their orientation within a surround:

> Like all animals, we exist by virtue of coupling our bodies to the environment through action. Inadequate coupling, whether it be on the perceptual side, as when driving in a fog, or on the movement side, as caused by muscular dysfunction, can be a prescription for disaster ... Action in the environment is the root of the ecological self. (1993: 43)

Petit used his eyes, ears, and muscles so as to preserve his BALANCE and CONTACT, and the spectators below him craned their necks to watch in the chance that he might lose both of these orientating patterns of flow and tumble to his death.

Body–environment coupling is a necessary part of individual survival and an important component of social relations, where people couple (ecologically) with each other as well as with the objects that are a part of their surroundings. Following other Enaction scientists, Johnson notes that all social phenomena, in the biological sense of interactions among the same species, arise "out of recurrent structural couplings that require the coordinated participation of multiple organisms" (Johnson 2007: 148). Petit's performance for the assembled spectators coupled all of them together. All performances, in fact, involve such "recurrent structural couplings" for the duration of the event. As we will see in Chapter 4, coupling is a necessary prerequisite for spectators engaged in processing and making meanings out of performances.

All sports events featuring competition among athletes rest upon recurrent couplings among the players, couplings among the spectators, and structured couplings that bring players and spectators together. To begin with, sports events involve several of the same evolutionary and cognitive fundamentals as dramatic performances. "What if we structured a competition between these kinds of players, under these conditions, and with these rules?" is the implicit subjunctive question behind racquetball, football games, and bowling competitions. Sports events are neither narratives like dramas nor exhibitions of skill like circus acts, but they do center on actional events, their beginnings and endings constrained, in this case, by the rules of the game, which includes the game's location, its field of play. The "what-if" reality of a sports event involves athletes in the same kinds of blends that occur in acting. The ice hockey player who performs the role of a Forward, for example, blends certain attributes of himself or herself (that he or she has a well-muscled body and can play aggressively) with the role (Forward on the team) and becomes a self/Forward while on the ice. Like actors, hockey players try to block from consciousness aspects of themselves and their personal situation that would inhibit them from playing their best in the moment-to-moment give-and-take of the game – that the odds-makers favor the other team to win by 5 to 1, for example. In the athlete/position blend, the athlete probably blends in more of himself or herself than does the actor to create an integrated self/role. But the cognitive fundamentals of conceptual integration and subjunctive event are the same.

Sports philosopher R. Scott Kretchmar points to some attributes of games that partly distinguish them from other play activities even as their foundational actions nod to their evolutionary roots. When we invent and play games, he says, "we stipulate relationships between means and ends in order to know 'what counts'" (Kretchmar 2007: 7). As an example, Kretchmar notes that it is not enough to get the ball in the hole to have it "count" in golf; players cannot carry the ball to the hole and drop it in but must hit it into the hole with a golf club. What Kretchmar calls the "logic of gratuity" also applies to games. "This involves the capacity to negotiate a pair of apparent contradictions," he states, "specifically that harder is better and certain experiences of uncertainty trump those of security and certainty" (2007: 7). Basketball is structured so that a three-point shot is harder and less certain than a free-throw, with the justifiable consequence that it counts three times as much. As with performing narrative drama, other animals are incapable of inventing and negotiating the rule-following and risk-inducing behavior that all games require. Kretchmar notes that, while general play came first in evolution, the cognitive demands of playing games mean that this specific form of play has probably been around for only the last 50,000 years.

Kretchmar's "logic of gratuity" may be best defined in the biocultural terms of Johnson's image schemas. To continue with an example from golf, hitting the ball from the tee to the hole may involve the COUNTERFORCE of wind, the BLOCKAGE of trees or ponds, and the many problems that can occur when the ball hits the SURFACE – from the rough to the sand trap to the green. Although modern cultures are adept at manufacturing golf balls and clubs, there are clear biological limits on the distance that any player can drive a ball, even for strong and expert golfers like Tiger Woods in his prime. Similarly, American football provides a good example of "harder is better" and "uncertainty" trumps "certainty"; all of the image schemas of force in golf noted above come into play on the football field. Despite the best padding, helmets, and gear that an advanced culture can buy, it is now apparent that professional football tests the biological limits of its players, too, especially regarding the debilitating effects of recurrent brain concussions.

The image schemas at the core of these and other sports events often spring significant metaphors with long lives in popular culture. This is not surprising. Lakoff and Johnson understand that most metaphors derive from the embodied nature of image schemas: "She's traveling quickly on the PATH to success" and "CONTAIN your anger!" for example. Regarding metaphors from sports and games, young adults entering the job market might see themselves as weight lifters, archers trying to hit a bull's-eye, or as players in an online game of "Monopoly." Later in life, the game metaphors in our body-minds may shift to those of team sports, as we work with other members of our team to "score points" so that we might succeed as a group. It is probably the case that all cultures take their sports metaphorically, seizing on the agonistic dynamics of competition to celebrate the victory of an individual or team as the triumph of their city or, in the Olympics or World Cup of Soccer, the victory of their nation. As historian Roger Kittleson points out in *The Country of Football: Soccer and the Making of Modern Brazil,* soccer has forcefully shaped Brazilian nationalism since the 1950s. Newspaper reporter S. WuDunn, writing about a scandal in Sumo wrestling in Japan, stated, "Sumo wrestling . . . which is the national sport of Japan, is regarded as more than a sport; it is seen as an epitome of Japanese honor and the national ethos" (cited by Sutton-Smith 1997: 77). Football and Sumo wrestling are richly metaphorical for Brazilian and Japanese culture.

Along with blends resulting from conceptual integration, metaphors give meaning to much of our social lives. As Lakoff and Johnson have been repeating in one form or another since 1980 with the publication of *Metaphors We Live By,* "The essence of metaphor is understanding and experiencing one kind of thing in terms of another" (Lakoff and Johnson 1980: 5). No longer seen as a characteristic of language alone, metaphors permeate our lives:

> Metaphors have entailments through which they highlight and make coherent certain aspects of our experience... Metaphors may create realities for us, especially social realities. A metaphor may thus be a guide for future action. Such actions will, of course, fit the metaphor. This will, in turn, reinforce the power of the metaphor to make the experience coherent. In this sense, metaphors can be self-fulfilling prophesies. (1980: 156)

If you understand yourself as a "chain smoker" who is unable to stop, for example, the metaphor of smoking as bondage may actually help to kill you. To return to sports, one person engaged in a contract negotiation may use the tennis metaphor, "The ball is in your court," to indicate to the other person that it is time for her to make a counteroffer. But the metaphor indicates more than "It's your turn." It implicitly defines the negotiations themselves as similar to a tennis volley, with both partners engaged in a kind of game that entails clear and fair rules and results in a win for one person and a loss for the other. Significantly, this metaphor, like most, derives from an image schema, the schema of CONTAINMENT. If a tennis ball is within the boundaries of the court on one side of the net, the court CONTAINS that ball.

The schema of CONTAINMENT recurs in many sports: a squash court, a ping-pong table, and a boxing ring are CONTAINED locations. The space of an urban marathon race may extend for twenty-six miles on city roads, but, still, the runners may not leave that long, narrow CONTAINED track to take a short cut. Other kinds of competitive games are usually centered in a CONTAINED space as well: a card table, the designated board on which "Clue" is played, and the contained space of a computer screen for video games. The schema of BALANCE, primarily in its metaphorical extensions, is also common in many sports and contests. In brief, contest rules must be fair, evenhanded, and equally balanced, as in the allegorical image of Blind Justice holding a set of scales. This is true for all competitions, from traditional Chinese Go, to a Javanese cock fight, to an American spelling bee. The outrage that greeted the TV quiz show scandals of the 1950s in the US, when some contestants were given the answers and other were not, demonstrates what can occur when BALANCE is perceived to have been violated. BALANCE is also important, though not crucial, for fan enjoyment at sports events. We generally enjoy close contests much more than "blowouts," when one team or player dominates and (metaphorically) crushes the other.

Musical events are also performances, in terms of the definition we are developing. Made up of WHOLEs and telescoped PARTs of action (the symphony, the song, the riff, the chord, etc.), concerts of every kind commence when the musicians and auditors are coupled to play and to listen, and end when the program is finished (or, in a late-night jam session, when most are too exhausted to continue). Although rock musicians and their fans often seek to collapse the everyday person and the musical role into a single, "authentic" self, all musicians lead blended lives while performing. Musical metaphors and blends, with or without accompanying words, can conjure a multitude of subtle emotions, images, and experiences that remind listeners of or tease them into imagining an ascent to Heaven, a peasant folk dance, or the loss of a loved one. Music can surge, linger, explode, or fade away, reminding us of similar moments in our own lives. Psychologist Daniel Stern calls such patterns of flow and change "vitality affects" and traces them to the kind of interactions that mothers and infants often share together. Vitality affects often shape the kinds of image schemas that constitute musical expression. Musical BLOCKAGE can hit the listener with explosive force, for example, the ITERATION of the same musical notes can bounce us along, and a surge in volume can help to sustain the schema of COMPULSION.

As these examples suggest, the image schematic rhythms of music pervade our lives. Composer Roger Sessions emphasizes that the experience of music is thoroughly embodied:

> Time becomes real to us primarily through movement, which I have called its expressive essence; and it is easy to trace our primary musical responses to the most primitive movement of our being – to those movements which are indeed at the very basis of animate existence. The feeling for tempo, so often derived from the dance, has in reality a much more primitive basis in the involuntary movements of the nervous system and the body in the beating of the heart, and more consciously in breathing, later in walking. Accelerated movement is, from these very obvious causes, inevitably associated with excitement, retarded movement with a lessening of dynamic tension. The experience of meter has the most obvious and essential of its origins in the movements of breathing, with its alternation of upward and downward movements. The sense of effort, preparation, suspense, which is the psychological equivalent of the up-beat, finds its prototype in the act of inhalation, and the sense of weight, release and finality produced by the downbeat corresponds most intimately to the act of exhalation. (cited in Johnson 2007: 237)

For Sessions, natural movements in time – heartbeats, breathing, and the sounds and moves that bind infants and parents – are the sources of dance as well as musical aesthetics.

Sessions' insights above track easily onto Johnson's image schemas. Repeating rhythms, melodies, and harmonies through ITERATION – with enough variation to make them appealing – is a necessary part of a hip-hop song or a traditional gamelan performance. The extension of musical repetition into movement, from a marching band to a classical ballet, invariably amplifies the cultural resonance of its musical base. Sessions refers to breathing as a combination of FULL-EMPTY and UP-DOWN. Knowing when to inhale and exhale, when to fill the lungs and when to empty them, is crucial to singing and blowing – on a tuba or clarinet, for instance. Inside of our body-minds, inhaling and exhaling also produces an UP and DOWN motion, as the diaphragm moves in concert with the expansion and shrinkage of the lungs. In addition to up-beats and down-beats, à la Sessions, the verticality of UP and DOWN also relates directly to pitch, the vibration frequency that produces musical sounds; "high" notes vibrate the air more rapidly than "low" ones.

Other schemas occur frequently, though not inevitably, in many musics. Composers often deploy the MERGING and/or SPLITTING of rhythms and/or melodies; these are as frequent in an Irving Berlin tune as in a Bach cantata. Finally, PATH is a frequent organizer of musical flow. The PATH of a musical score need not be organized as a series of causal events, as in much dramatic narrative, but the moment-to-moment relations among the parts must be linked in such a way as to suggest an evolving coherence. Perceiving this linkage is usually as much cultural as biological. At the first performance of Stravinsky's "Rite of Spring" that featured Diaghilev's Ballet Russes in 1913, for instance, many Parisian auditors could perceive no coherence among the parts of the dance concert and a near-riot resulted. Nowadays, following the innovations of John Coltrane's "free jazz" movement and John Cage's "Silence," many auditors have no problem finding aesthetic coherence in the avant-garde music of that earlier era. Most westerners, however, still have trouble perceiving the emerging flow of traditional Chinese music.

Musicologist Lawrence Zbikowski, author of the award-winning book *Conceptualizing Music: Cognitive Structure, Theory, and Analysis* (2002), demonstrates that people can understand and respond to musical sounds through the cognitive tools of categorization and cross-domain mapping, which he derives from the insights of Lakoff and Johnson. Zbikowski's work epitomizes the kind of "bottom-up" analysis favored by Johnson and others eager to advance Enaction as the central paradigm for explaining cognition. I will take the beginning of John Lennon's song "Hey, Jude" as an example to demonstrate this approach: "Hey, Jude/Don't make it bad/Play a sad song/And make it be-e-et-ter." If you remember the tune, you do not need to know musical notation to understand that the first, second, and fourth phrase of its opening measures end with what Zbikowski would term a "falling gesture" (Zbikowski 2006: 117). The third, "Play a sad song," in pleasant contrast, ends with a rising gesture. Always seeking to categorize incoming stimuli, our brains, says Zbikowski, will "chunk" the notes of each musical phrase together and look for similarities and differences among the chunks. Chunks need not be identical to each other for the brain to put them, tentatively, into the same category. In *The Meaning of the Body*, Johnson elaborates on Zbikowski's conclusions to point out that cross-domain mapping from the body to our experience of music – from rising gestures to high notes, for example – happens all the time. "It should be expected, then," he states, "that all of the image schemas of force dynamics (e.g., COMPULSION, BLOCKAGE, ATTRACTION, ENABLEMENT, etc.) and all of the structural elements of paths (e.g., starting points, paths, steps along the path, destination, progress toward destination, etc.) will play a role in our experience and understanding of music. And so they do" (Johnson 2007: 257–58).

Johnson's conclusion that our experience of music draws on our bodily memory of force dynamics opens the discussion to an insight about all performances. It is no secret that competitive performances, from chess games to soccer, engage us in the actions of BLOCKING, COMPELLING, and other exertions of physical force; these schemas are an important part of their appeal for players and spectators. And we know from our experience of dramatic action on stage and at the movies (as well as from several theories of drama) that conflict, sometimes directly physical, is often an important source of dramatic interest. With the addition of Johnson's insight about music and force dynamics, it seems evident that nearly all performances have conflicting forces as a significant part of their embodied core. This is as true for Petit's "walk" as for Beethoven's Ninth.

What about role-playing computer games? In his *Caught in Play*, cited earlier, anthropologist Peter Stromberg filmed several gamers in 1996 and 2000 engaged in playing *Mekton*, a science fiction game, and an advanced version of *Dungeons and Dragons* in 1996 and 2000, respectively. As do actors playing dramatic roles, the group of gamers adopted the perspective of their characters within the frame of the game and easily accepted the constraints of time and space imposed by its fictional circumstances. Approaching the full vocal and physical embodiment of dramatic actors, the gamers even gestured and occasionally moved as though they were their avatars, acting within the game's subjunctive reality. Both games, of course, were full of dramatic conflict – PATH, BLOCKAGE, ENABLEMENT, and COMPULSION occur frequently in many computer games – and the gamers typically registered the tensions and emotions of their avatars. Each of the gamers could drop in and out of role and the other players had no difficulty distinguishing between these differences on the basis of their embodied engagement. Such alternation is a necessary part of MMORPGs, the massively multiplayer online role-playing games, in which many players either compete or cooperate to achieve goals. As in many sports events, most gamers alternate between playing and spectating, with no difficulty.

Some online role-playing games are more like dramatic improvisations than sports contests. Networked games such as *Second Life* allow for much more variety, individual agency, and group collaboration among the players than popular games like *World of Warcraft* and *Grand Theft Auto*. Although much of the activity in *Second Life* encourages players to fantasize social interactions for themselves, the game also facilitates the setting up of specific areas in which gamers may pretend to be other people (or monsters or zombies, etc.) with wide freedom to establish their own situations and dramatic conflicts. Other games reward improvised group cooperation. In *Waking Mars*, for example, players become exploring scientists living in the year 2097 who must discover and cultivate new forms of life on the planet Mars because the Earth has become too polluted to sustain humanity. Players help each other to create and sustain ecosystems, which, given the game's programming, necessarily involves learning and patience. As game ethicists Mary Flanagan and Helen Nissenbaum note, "Instead of rewarding players for winning or conquering, the game rewards players for considering cause and effect and, over a longer period than typically is designed into a causal game, it also credits players' attention to sustainability" (Flanagan and Nissenbaum 2014: 43).

Cultural-cognitive ecosystems

Although crafting virtual interactions through avatars and allowing participants to move in and out of role-playing in improvised situations may appear to be recent phenomena, the basic idea behind both activities is an old one. Many religious rituals encourage identification with spiritual avatars and also involve participants in alternating between the activities of immersion in role-playing and the witnessing of spectators. Congregants in most Protestant church services in Europe and the US, for example, move easily from praying and singing together to listening to music or to a minister's sermon. The wide variety of rituals from among the world's religions, past and present, draw on many types of performances and may center on contests, music, or drama – or even all three. As we have seen, *ras lila* relies primarily on dramatic narrative to structure its journey through time. While music also plays an important part in worshipping Lord Krishna in Vrindavan, dramatic conflicts involving ENABLEMENT, ATTRACTION, and RESTRAINT REMOVAL appear to be central.

Other ritual events have also mixed many of the major goals that performances can entail – telling a story, competing for a victory, and enchanting spectators with musical delights. For the Athenians of the fifth-century B.C.E., the City Dionysia, the major theater festival of the year, was also a religious ritual dedicated to worshiping the god Dionysus. Combining public ceremony with their religious services, the ancient Athenians told stories in public speeches to their citizens and imperial vassals that justified their empire. Perhaps because the Greeks enjoyed sports, they injected competition into the five-day event; a panel of judges awarded prizes to the best tragic and comic playwrights. Finally, lyrical expressions of music and dancing played an important role in the rituals; all citizens could participate in a music-filled parade and the audience at the plays enjoyed choric speech, dancing, and singing. Like many rituals, the City Dionysia drew extensively on visual, aural, and kinesthetic interactions, the three primary senses and their corresponding modes of communication that *Homo sapiens* have likely used for performances since the dawning of human time. (The senses of taste, touch, and smell would also have also been important for our ancestors, but these are no longer as crucial to the success of most performances.) Just as clearly, the festival of Dionysus featured COMPULSION, ATTRACTION, ENABLEMENT, and other of the physical forces in all of each of these sensorial modes.

If we can say that performance functioned evolutionarily, at least in part, as a means of exploring the problems and possibilities of social cohesion, its focus on agonistic action is not surprising. The notion that social conflict generates rituals and other kinds of agonistic performances is an old one in anthropology and performance studies, dating from Arnold van Gennep's early twentieth-century work on rites of passage, Victor Turner's incorporation of van Gennep's idea into his theory of social drama, and Schechner's use of social drama as a contrast (and continuation) of western aesthetic theater in the 1970s. In each of these models, performance is a means of addressing the problems caused by social conflict. We will examine the ethical implications of this focus on agonistic action in Chapter 5.

For now, though, it is important to note the probable reason for this link between the simulated or actual conflict embodied in nearly all performances and the dynamics of hunter-gatherer life experienced by our ancestors. In *Hierarchy in the Forest: The Evolution of Egalitarian Behavior* (1999), anthropologist Christopher Boehm found evidence that *Homo sapiens* developed the ability to enforce group-oriented norms that promoted egalitarian behavior. Early humans relied on the social cohesion of their bands for fire, food, shelter, and other basics for survival, he notes, but they did not solve the problem of "dominators" and "cheaters" until around 100,000 B.C.E. Although our species was likely predisposed by that time to behavior within their bands that was generally altruistic (as is evidenced in the few remaining tribes of hunter-gatherers), how to deal with those individuals who would try to hoard resources and dominate others and or who would avoid their fair share of the work remained a problem.

Boehm and others argue that because humans will tend to act on their desires both to dominate or cheat and to avoid being dominated by and/or cheated on by others, early bands of *Homo sapiens* adopted an ethics and politics of rough egalitarianism as a compromise to deal with the problem. That is, altruistic social norms and/or the rules of the band worked to enforce cooperation from both dominators and cheaters, as well as from others in the group. It is important to be clear about this: Boehm is not saying that our hunter-gatherer ancestors agreed to put aside their desire to cheat, their lust for revenge, and other actions motivated by self-interest simply to embrace altruism. On the whole, early *Homo sapiens* probably remained just as self-centered, nasty, and brutish as we are. Rather, the demands of group survival led these early bands to enforce cooperative social norms, which, in turn, opened up a biocultural space in which altruistic practices and emotions might occasionally flourish. I will elaborate this insight in the next chapter.

As noted, humans in these same bands were already performing contests and music at that time, performances that could also reinforce altruistic and egalitarian practices and norms. Consequently, pitting pro-social forces against anti-social ones in agonistic situations was a logical and potentially persuasive way of structuring many hunter-gatherer performances. With the development of common languages, they could also tell stories and sing narrative songs to further embellish the agonistic structures that advanced their social and political values. Because *Homo sapiens* are the most social animals on the earth, it should not be surprising that most of the performances of our species continue to provide models of social antagonism leading to happy reconciliations or unhappy endings.

While the insights from van Gennep, Turner, Schechner, and Boehm are helpful in understanding the cultural side of our penchant for exploring pro- and anti-social forces through performances, we need a more encompassing framework to underline the complete biocultural dynamics of performance events. Philosopher Andy Clark called for just "such a new kind of cognitive scientific collaboration involving neuroscience, physiology, and social, cultural, and technical studies in about equal measure" about fifteen years ago in *Mindware* (Clark 2001: 154). Cognitive scientist Edwin Hutchins, who had already explored the implications of culture as "a complex cognitive ecosystem" (Hutchins 1995: xiv), has been working toward a framework that answers Clark's challenge. Recognizing that most understandings of culture and cognition still anchor cultural knowledge and practice in individual minds and actions, Hutchins recently proposed to expand "distributed cognition" theory to arrive at such a cultural and cognitive framework. His theory begins with the assumption that all human cognition is "distributed" among various networks. Hutchins primarily extends the diversity and scale of these networks; he limits some to neural networks in the brain, notes that others join together the brain, body, and immediate surround of an individual, recognizes that some networks link several people together through kinship and other close ties, and proposes that quite a few connect people of the same culture. At the cultural level, Hutchins cites "the emergence of a shared language" as an appropriate example. Noting that this task cannot be accomplished by a single individual or small group, he states, "The emergence of a language is a cognitive process that takes place in an evolving cognitive ecosystem that includes a shared world of objects and events [i.e., cultural practices] as well as adaptive resources internal to each member of the community [i.e., evolutionary-biological abilities]" (Hutchins 2014: 37). The term that Hutchins finally arrives at to name this process is "the cultural-cognitive ecosystem" (2014: 45), a term that nicely recognizes the necessary and complementary contributions of both culture and biology.

Adapting Hutchins to my purposes, we could say that all performance events are parts of one or several cultural-cognitive ecosystems. In this regard, performances fulfill several of the conjectural stipulations that Hutchins discusses for all events within his system. "Like any ecosystem," he says, "the cultural-cognitive ecosystem can be seen as a constraint-satisfaction system that settles into a subset of possible configurations of elements. It is a dynamical system in which certain configurations of elements (what we know as stable practices) emerge (self-assemble) preferentially" (2014: 45–46). Hutchins adds, "Some of these [mechanisms of constraint-satisfaction] are neural mechanisms; others are implemented in material tools; and still others are emergent in social processes of collective intelligence – the development of conventions, for example" (2014: 46).

Take, for instance, the emergence of musical comedy in London and New York before 1930 as a major genre of mainstream western entertainment. By 1930, the "satisfactions" of attending a musical – both biological and cultural – were evident to many theatergoers in both cities: beautiful girls, catchy tunes, and a hopeful narrative, among the most prominent. Some of the significant cultural-historical "constraints," though less visible at the time, are now clear in retrospect: the necessary link joining musicals to a developing culture of consumerism within industrial capitalism in the West, the mandate that Broadway and West End shows make money for their investors, a fashionable theater (one of Hutchins's "material tools") in which to produce and present the show, and generic conventions limiting the length of performances, the types of songs, the racial casting of the leads, and other restrictions. Within these (and other) constraints and satisfactions, musical comedy emerged out of operettas, revues, and other entertainments to capture a significant market share of middle-class urban entertainment by the mid 1920s. Using Hutchins's theory as a guide, we could trace the "stable practices" constituting the productions and enjoyments of musical comedies that did indeed emerge dynamically and "preferentially" – that is, as a result of the push and pull of its major constraints and satisfactions – during that era.

I have been describing what Hutchins calls "conjectures" about the "global features" (2014: 45) of cultural-cognitive ecosystems. He also lists "conjectures" about a few "local features" (2014: 46) that are relevant to the history of any genre of performance. These include his recognition that "which [cultural-cognitive] practices assemble at any moment depends on the local structure of the ecosystem" (2014: 46). Because the local ecosystem for producing and enjoying musicals differed somewhat between New York and London in the 1920s, for instance, there were some differences in the kinds of musicals popular in each city. Another "local feature," notes Hutchins, is that "learning in the [local] ecosystem includes changes that are outside of the individual person – in artifacts, for example" (2014: 46). Because fashionable dress for female actor/characters (a significant "artifact" in all musicals) differed in some ways between New York and London in the 1920s, women attending musical comedies in one city learned somewhat different practices from their counterparts in the other. Nonetheless, both groups of women easily perceived "family resemblances" (2014: 46) in fashionable attire across the pond and this facilitated borrowing and mixing among Anglo-American fashion-conscious females. This last example accords with Hutchins's insight that the "interpersonal coordination of practices, including communicative practices, is facilitated by the fact that families of practices exist" (2014: 47).

Hutchins acknowledges that his theory of cultural-cognitive ecosystems is primarily geared to illuminate the "web of cultural regularities in which we are all immersed" (2014: 47). His theory, he implies, may not work very well to account for some of the historical changes that have emerged in performance history. Nonetheless, his is one of the first theories that rests upon an understanding of networks as systems of cultural and cognitive learning, continuity, and exchange. Among his tentative conclusions are that the repetition of biocultural practices increases "the predictability of experience" for individuals (2014: 46) and decreases their entropy – that is, the running down of historical cultural-cognitive practices and their systems. He also asserts that the "possibilities for individual learning depend upon the structure of the ecosystem" (2014: 46), primarily because all local ecosystems limit what is available to be learned. Finally, states Hutchins, "the generalization of action across contexts is facilitated by family resemblances among practices" (2014: 46). These observations apply equally well to the cultural-cognitive difficulties and possibilities in which underprivileged poor children in nearby Indian towns are immersed today as to the opportunities for predictability, learning, and action among upper middle-class theatergoers in London and New York in the 1920s.

While Hutchins looks forward to the time when his conjectures may be "rephrased as proper testable hypotheses" (2014: 47), it is evident that his theory has already revealed several avenues of approach and investigation for performance historians and critics. In addition to its other advantages, Hutchins's focus on networks of practice and communication potentially allows historians and critics to bypass notions of culture as necessary CONTAINERS of performance networks – the conventional approach, whether for "cultural" or "multicultural" analyses, in socially constructed histories today. Specific performance networks might flourish within relatively narrow cultural or national networks, of course, but popular genres of performance can easily cross cultural and national lines if transcultural and/or transnational networks exist to facilitate such transfers. This movement has been happening with sports events for decades – witness the global popularity of football – and it has recently occurred as well in the world of popular musical comedies.

In a 2014 *Theatre Survey* article, David Savran presented strong evidence that the so-called Broadway musical is now a transnational brand, thriving in Seoul, Hamburg, and other global cities. "The traffic in the most popular form of theatre in the world can no longer be linked to one metropolis or one national tradition," he notes (Savran 2014: 318). Not only are transnationally networked audiences enjoying "Broadway style" shows (a trend since the 1980s), but similar networks of impresarios, directors, investors, writers, and actor/singer/dancers in Korea and Germany are helping to produce, perform, and market them in the US. Savran's focus on networks as nodes of production and enjoyment is crucial here. Some networks may be coterminous with the general allegiances of cultures and/or nations, but many are more various in size, less traditional in orientation, and easier to join or drop. Understanding genres of performance as the result of biocultural networks bounded by constraints and satisfactions can de-emphasize the loaded issues of authenticity and belonging that have bolstered claims of groupishness; the approach enables scholars to open up a wide range of possibilities for investigation.

Hutchins's theory of cultural-cognitive ecosystems, together with Savran's exploration of transnational "Broadway brand" musicals, also suggests that this nexus of ideas may be deepened and extended through the sociology of Pierre Bourdieu. Bourdieu's "fields" of cultural production and his notion of "symbolic capital" depend crucially upon networks of communication and practice. Further, his notion of "habitus" as a system that regulates embodied dispositions through biocultural constraints and satisfactions is close indeed to Hutchins's sense of the operation of cultural-cognitive ecosystems. Like Hutchins and other Enactivists, Bourdieu understood that the human practices that constitute a social order are both enacted by human agents and help to constrain the actions that those socialized humans might practice.

Networks of cultural-cognitive ecosystems can also be extended historically to understand major shifts in communication and performance history. In his *A History of Communications: Media and Society from the Evolution of Speech to the Internet* (2011), historian Marshall T. Poe draws on the work of Harold Innis, McLuhan, Marx, Ong, and other theorists and historians to chart major eras of communication as biocultural systems of constraint and satisfaction. In particular, he looks at eight attributes of historical media networks that have recurred across time and traces how these attributes tended to translate into social practices and values. Regarding the general attributes of accessibility, velocity, and searchability during the speech era of the hunter-gatherers, for example, Poe notes that when speech was the only means of human communication, it tended to result in social practices that were equalized, democratized, and amateurized – findings largely in accord with Chris Boehm's conclusions about egalitarianism in Paleolitic culture. These practices resulted in specific institutions and norms within each language-bound band or tribe that produced both constraints and satisfactions. Poe recognizes that many cultures in the world today are undergoing a major shift from the top-down, one-way media of most of the twentieth century (radio, film, and television) to the Internet, which features very different network attributes and tends to advance more open and participatory social practices. "Tends" is a necessary modifier for Poe's understanding of these dynamic historical media networks; his history is not based in technological determinism. Although the relative accessibility of the print medium might tend to promote equalized social relations among the literate, for instance, that social effect during the era of print was far more evident in Western Europe than in China, for a variety of historical reasons that Poe's general approach nicely accommodates. In short, Hutchins's theory of biocultural ecosystems opens the orientation of Enaction to several sociological and historical interpretative possibilities.

CHAPTER 3

Sociality, emotions, and empathy

Human affects and emotions play a significant role in shaping both the constraints and the satisfactions of all performances. While the emotions of musicians, athletes, actors, and priests in rehearsing and enacting their performance activities are important and necessary for their success, I will primarily be discussing spectator engagement and response. Because this book is about performances in networks and biocultures, we need to understand how spectatorial experience draws upon and plays out in cultural-cognitive ways. In performance history, spectators have usually outnumbered performers by factors of ten or even a thousand times; their experiences at performance events always shape subsequent performances and are typically more historically significant for the constitution of performance networks than those of the performers themselves. Luckily for our ancestors, their cognitive and emotional experiences guided their response to their performances, and this biocultural mix of influences continues to shape all performance events and networks. Given the importance of affects and emotions for spectatorship, plus the lack of rigor with which our culture tosses around emotional terms, I will put the words that my sources define as emotions in **bold letters** throughout this chapter.

Emotional engagement and sociality

While neuroscientists, psychologists, and sociologists have little doubt that affective involvement plays an important part in the activity of spectating, the nature of that role has not been closely examined. This is partly because most scientists have focused their experiments on emotional interactions in everyday social situations, not on performances. As we will see, some generalizations about social interactions can be applied to the more specialized realm of performer-spectator relations, but others cannot. Social situations generally involve face-to-face relations among people who address each other in personal terms. Such familiarity is unusual among

Emotional engagement and sociality

players and audiences, however, who rarely engage in any direct back-and-forth at all. Imagine a jazz trumpeter breaking off her solo to talk to a stranger in the first row or a fan with a bullhorn who tries to initiate a conversation with an outfielder during a baseball game. While people do alternate between the roles of spectator and player in rituals and computer games, most performances do not allow for this alternation. Rather, many performances are structured so that audiences do not physically interrupt the performers. Instead of face-to-face interaction, many performances involve observation-at-a-distance, as when a group of people at one end of a room watch a specialized type of interaction among a smaller group at the other end.

Nonetheless, spectators are always invited to respond to events that have been framed to evoke their emotions. Spectators go to entertainments knowing and desiring strong emotional engagement. As noted in the last chapter, the agonistic structure of sports, music, and other performances heightens the emotions of spectators within that cultural-cognitive network. Audiences engage performances through voluntary, intentional action, and their attention to and occasional immersion in its image schemas and consequent emotions is a part of their activity. In addition to emotional involvement, spectator actions include making decisions that put them in front of a performance event (either live or mediated), paying attention to the event by moving their bodies (which includes focusing their eyes and attuning their ears), integrating the players they watch into discrete person/role blends, and blending all of those actions together (plus the actions of other spectators) into a performance event. To return to Boyd's key insight, when they engage with players in a performance, spectators seek to attend to patterns of action and respond to what they perceive. Consequently, any adequate definition of performance must involve spectator emotions. To cite the old philosophical saw for the ontological validity of phenomenological experience over some notion of objective reality: If a tree falls in the forest (if actors perform on a stage) and no one is there to hear it (and no audience gets caught up in its emotions), did it make a sound (did a performance really occur)? The Enaction answer: No, for both situations.

Perhaps the most common mode of involvement for spectators is taking sides in the performative conflict. A spectatorial decision to root (noisily or silently) for one side or another occurs in many sports contests and plays, but it also happens in rituals and music – Baptist congregants sing for God's ENABLEMENT over the ATTRACTIONs of Satan, and concert-goers are often relieved when the violinist completes the necessary complex variations of the concerto to return to the PATH of the familiar melody. When the heroes and villains of the performance can be personified, the action of picking a desired winner usually leads to two other major emotional investments – condemning the undesirables and celebrating your own players. Again, this is most apparent in sports events, but it also occurs when spectators respond with **anger**, **fear**, and/or derisive laughter to the negative characters in dramas and dances. The **antipathy** that results from this cognitive-affective process (and the **sympathy** inspired by positive actor/role-players) is a mode of psychological projection. That is, spectators project their own emotions, values, and desires onto blended players in a performance. We want our dramatic hero, our Marine Corps Marching Band, or our rugby team – the All Blacks of New Zealand, making warrior faces and chanting the Hakka – to succeed! Likewise, although we do not always admit it, we desire the failure of those forces that oppose us. Again, the psychological mandates of groupishness lead us easily into agonistic rooting.

Spectating as taking-sides may seem a radical simplification, but it builds upon primordial biocultural needs that continue to inform audience response and action in significant ways. Aligning ourselves with "us" over "them" is the downside of human altruism. As evolutionary biologist Mark Pagel notes, the "ultra-sociality" of our species has predisposed us to form altruistic bonds not only with our family but also with those in our social groups upon whom we depend (Pagel 2012: 73). Humans are the only species that will occasionally sacrifice their lives for non-relatives; soldiers in combat who willingly die for their buddies – an action that occurs in all cultures throughout the world – is perhaps the most obvious example. At the same time, says Pagel, "the nature of our altruism can also help us to understand some jarring facts about our social behavior. It is a melancholy feature of our species that there are two situations in our everyday lives in which humans can act with such explosive violence toward others as to make us question if it is ever safe to trust another of our kind, and both of these are linked to protecting our societies" (2012: 88).

Although Pagel's names for these two situations are relatively neutral, his examples of "parochialism" and "moralistic aggression" make it clear that the first can escalate to genocide, while the second animates the persecution of suspected treason from within. Pagel points both to the fossil record and to recent history to suggest that both impulses have been a part of human sociality for a long time. There is evidence that *Homo sapiens* were competing with each other and with their near relatives, the Neanderthals and other species of the *Homo* genus, when they moved out of Africa and into Eurasia beginning around 100,000 years ago. Our ancestors had lived in small groups for several million years before then and had already perfected tools that allowed them to exterminate many species of game animals; by then, other groups of *Homo*s had become their primary competitors for hunting and gathering. As a result of the ties that bind us to our own culture, says Pagel, "it would seem that humans are capable of throwing a switch in their minds that allows them, even with little or no provocation, to treat members of other societies … as something considerably less than human in moral terms" (2012: 89). Pagel cites the Hutu massacre of 800,000 Tutsi tribesmen in 1994 as a modern instance of parochialism leading to genocide. And he quotes the Roman politician Cicero on the need for moralistic aggression against traitors: "[The traitor] rots the soul of a nation – he works secretly and unknown in the night to undermine the pillars of a city – he infects the body politic so that it can no longer resist. A murderer is less to be feared … " (2012: 91). Although it has worked for centuries to open our hearts to others of our own race, religion, and nation, human groupishness can lead to slaughter as well as altruism.

Some performance studies scholars, preferring Brechtian *verfremdungseffekt* to raw emotional appeal, have assumed that spectators can and should distance themselves from their emotions while witnessing a performance, in part to prevent the eruption of parochialism noted by Pagel. In rejecting the emotional extremes of German Expressionism for Marxist rationalism in the 1920s, Bertolt Brecht accepted the conventional distinction that divides reason from emotion. As is well known, he was concerned that spectators caught up in the irrational emotions of a dramatic illusion would have no interest in or energy for starting a communist revolution. Philosopher Martha Nussbaum, however, points out that "if emotions are suffused with intelligence and discernment, and if they contain in themselves an awareness of value and importance, they cannot … easily be sidelined in accounts of ethical judgment … " (Nussbaum 2001: 1). Nussbaum's *Upheavals of Thought* demonstrates this proposition through copious examples from the cognitive sciences, Greek philosophy, and personal experience. Significantly, from an Enactive perspective, Nussbaum shows that emotions proceed from "value judgments, which ascribe to things and persons outside the person's own control great importance for that person's own flourishing" (2001: 4). Rather than welling up from our "animal instincts," emotions are linked to our goals and intentions. People respond emotionally, in part, because they value what others are praising or attacking. As I have demonstrated in previous work, Brecht-the-playwright and theatrical radical actually understood this very well, even as Brecht-the-theorist argued in the late 1920s for what he and many others took to be the rationality of Marx (McConachie 2006: 9). Cognitive critic R. Darren Gobert has also shown that Brecht's understanding of spectatorial emotions evolved over the course of his career (Gobert 2012: *passim*).

The psychological projection that animates **sympathy** and **antipathy** is foundational to spectating in other ways as well. We have already considered the importance of projection in rituals and films; by projecting intentionality onto inanimate objects, we can endow the statue of a deity or a series of photographs on celluloid with the human ability to act. Later in the chapter, we will see that projection is also central to empathy. Following such projections and attributions, however, the emotions and intentions of blended figures in a performance are usually apparent to audiences through direct observation and interaction. Most of what spectators see and hear does not require complex mental operations to interpret and understand. This is partly because the rules of the game, the demands of the music, or the staging of the drama usually work toward transparency; witnesses can see why that hockey player BLOCKED an opponent into the boards, why that musical ITERATION at the rock concert evoked a smile from the soloist, and why that actor/character in a drama wept at the COMPULSIVE behavior of his spouse. As a result of our shared biology and similar experiences with caregivers as infants and children, humans are primed to perceive a great deal about the emotional and mental lives of each other. Regarding our direct grasp of facial emotions, for example, Ludwig Wittgenstein remarked, "'We *see* emotion.' – As opposed to what? – We do not see facial contortions and make the inference that he is feeling joy, grief, boredom. We describe a face immediately as sad, radiant, bored, even when we are unable to give any other description of the features" (Wittgenstein 1980: 570). Wittgenstein's insight is borne out by the extensive experiments on facial emotions done by Paul Ekman and his colleagues; people from a wide sampling of international cultures have identified the same faces as **happy**, **sad**, **angry**, etc.

Our generally direct access to the emotions of others has led some scholars to question the assumptions of Theory of Mind (ToM), an approach that has dominated many discussions of self and other relations in cognitive studies. In their introductory chapter to *The Shared Mind: Perspectives on Intersubjectivity* (2008), the editors propose an Enactive perspective on the commonalities of human subjectivity that opposes the assumptions of ToM. ToM starts with the proposition that there is a foundational separation between the minds of selves and others that must be bridged through some folk theory or imaginative simulation that will enable one person to "read" the mind of another. In contrast, the Enactive scientists in *The Shared Mind* present compelling evidence that human evolution and psychology already interconnect our species through many shared cognitive and affective processes that make such complex bridging unnecessary. This is because our culture and evolution as a species during the hunter-gatherer era of our history selected for groups and individuals who could "read" each other's minds easily and instantly to facilitate group cooperation. Primarily through visual cues, embodied interactions, and straightforward projections, our species can usually understand – or believe that it understands – what conspecifics in homogeneous social groups are intending, doing, and feeling. Likewise, we do not need the mental gymnastics of theories and simulations to understand most of what is going on in a hip-hop piece of music, a baseball game, or even a production of *Waiting for Godot*. (Identifying possible meanings in these performances, however, is a different matter, as we will see in more detail in the next chapter.) I will be using insights from *The Shared Mind* in the forthcoming discussion.

While Ekman's Facial Action Coding System underlines the straightforward communicative nature of several emotional states, it also points up a general problem in the scholarship of emotion. On the basis of his surveys and our commonly shared facial muscles, psychologist Ekman identifies six emotions as "primary": **Happiness, sadness, fear, anger, surprise**, and **disgust**. Working from his experiments on the neurobiology of emotion systems in mice and similar higher mammals, Jaak Panksepp picks out seven rather different primary emotions in our species, as we will see below. This kind of scientific disagreement is only the tip of the iceberg when it comes to scholarly differences for dealing with affect and emotion. An additional complication for performance studies scholars, as for investigators in other areas in the arts and humanities, is that several post-structuralists have bypassed the scientific work on human emotions and jumped to definitions that ignore the need for empirical confirmation. One of the most popular of these is an approach based in the theories of Gilles Deleuze and Felix Guattari. Their work is cited prominently in *The Affect Theory Reader*, a 2010 anthology of selections that promises to introduce students to eight different orientations about affect and emotion, none of which draw substantially on empirical science. As a result of this confusion, if researchers google "affect," "feeling," or "emotion," they will encounter a sea of approaches, several of which generate much scholarly heat these days but little light. There is no point in trying to sort through the potpourri of orientations to arrive at a possible synthesis of these options; too many are unscientific to begin with and even those that can claim some good evidence and a measure of validity often rest on incommensurable assumptions. Among the best reasons for proceeding from within a paradigm such as Enaction is the current scholarly cacophony surrounding affect and emotion.

Amidst this noise, Giovanna Colombetti's essay "Enaction, Sense-Making, and Emotion" provides a reliable place to begin. She asks how our affects and emotions help us to regenerate the conditions of our own survival, adapt to our environments, and make sense of our situations in ways that assist us in pursuing our goals. As we will explore in the next chapter, intentional goals related to survival impinge directly on the perception–action systems of all spectators. Colombetti recognizes that "living systems necessarily establish a *point of view* [about their internal and external environments] and moreover a *concerned* point of view that *generates meaning*" (Colombetti 2010: 148). A definition of emotion compatible with the Enaction paradigm must link emotions to meanings; individuals encounter and perceive the world as meaningful, not simply as a neutral place awaiting attribution. In contrast, some approaches to emotion assume that our cognitive appraisals of the environment within and around us occur separately, distinct from the embodied experiences of affect and emotion. Colombetti lays out the evidence to argue that such a separation "implies a disembodied view of appraisal that is both phenomenologically and structurally implausible" (2010: 157). Instead, she endorses Jaak Panksepp's and Antonio Damasio's approaches to the science of emotion because both relate emotion to "meaning-generating and adaptive mechanisms" (2010: 150).

Panksepp's *Affective Neuroscience* (1998), updated in 2012 (and co-authored with Lucy Biven) as *The Archaeology of the Mind*, provides copious evidence for seven distinct neurobiological emotion systems. These systems are: **seek, fear, rage, panic/grief, lust, care,** and **play**. All have lower-level emotional states as well, such as "anxiety" in the **fear** system and "loneliness," a less extreme form of **panic/grief**. For neuroscientist Panksepp, these and other primary emotions proceed from the activation of discrete emotion systems. In his experiments on the emotions of mice, which are very close to those of our own, Panksepp distinguished among different emotions on the basis of "whether a coherent emotional response can be activated by localized electrical and chemical stimulation along specific brain circuits, and whether such arousal has affective consequences as measured by approach and avoidance responses" (Panksepp 1998: 14).

Emotions for Panksepp, in other words, link brain chemistry, neuronal circuits, hormones, and muscular responses to animate and guide human action. Like many scientists working on mammalian emotions, Panksepp also distinguishes between emotions, which are entirely unconscious, and feelings, which can occur when the chemical and behavioral results of our emotional systems rise to consciousness. As he notes, emotional arousals in humans are usually "accompanied by subjectively experienced feeling states that may provide efficient ways to guide and sustain behavior patterns, as well as to mediate certain types of learning" (1998: 15).

In addition to Panksepp's seven primary emotions, I will also refer to secondary, or social, emotions in the upcoming discussion. To understand those dynamics, I turn to the ideas of neuropsychologist Antonio Damasio, who based much of his experimentation on insights gained initially through his therapeutic work with patients suffering various kinds of brain damage. Damasio recognizes that the biocultures that shaped our ancestors also altered our emotional dynamics by layering social emotions on top of our primary ones. While our primal emotions date from the evolution of the limbic system in the brains of early mammals many millions of years ago, our social emotions emerged more recently, probably as a part of the coevolution of culture and genetics. Damasio's list of social emotion systems includes **humiliation, guilt, antipathy, sympathy, pride, shame, contempt**, and **embarrassment**. Although not as basic to our survival as primary emotions, these and other secondary emotions help us to regulate and modify our social relationships. Much like primary emotions, social emotions may be sparked by internal or external stimuli, which lead to the activation of dedicated neuronal networks in the brain, which then play out in the body through hormonal response, increased blood flow to specific body parts, and changes in muscle tone, etc. that prepare the body for action.

Although some mammals also have social emotions, they are more highly developed in *Homo sapiens* than in any other species. As already noted, social **sympathy** and **antipathy** helped our ancestors and continue to aid groups of our species in separating "us" from "them." At the same time, our ancient kin were learning to cooperate with others in their bands to forge successfully for food and to manufacture tools, clothes, and shelter. To accomplish such tasks, they needed to establish group norms to assure workable divisions of labor and to pass on their acquired knowledge. Our emerging social emotions generally reinforced these norms. Although social norms vary widely among human cultures, "there does seem reason to suspect that normative thought is a universal feature of human society and of normal agency," states philosopher and anthropologist Kim Sterelny (Sterelny 2012: 160). As he points out, moral norms typically regulate human action in family structures, economic relations, religious commitments, political hierarchies, and in most other significant social institutions in all biocultures. Further, young children pick up the norms of their caregivers and neighborhood adults with surprising rapidity, both by direct observation and through instruction. Notes Sterelny, "The narrative life of a community – the stock of stories, songs, myths, and tales to which children are exposed – is full of information as to what actions are to be admired and which are to be deplored" (2012: 163). While he agrees that human evolution prepares youngsters for such moral education, Sterelny makes a good case for the importance of "the organization of our developmental environment, [that works on children] through specific perceptual sensitivity and by our prosocial and commitment emotions" (2012: 165). In other words, children inherit a proclivity for normative behavior and learn social norms by watching others and experiencing primary and secondary emotions in the course of their social interactions.

As Sterelny recognizes, his position on moral cognition marks him as an advocate of the Humean revival; he is an ally of the eighteenth-century moral philosopher David Hume, who taught that emotions are an important source of moral action. Other Enactivists, including Martha Nussbaum and Evan Thompson, have also endorsed modified versions of Hume's perspective. In support of his position, Sterelny cites the experiments of Tomasello and those of his co-workers, which show that most human children, in contrast to young chimps, naturally behave prosocially and cooperatively with their peers by the time they reach four years of age. According to Sterelny:

> We are perceptually tuned to the emotions and emotional responses of others, and our own emotional responses to those others. We are typically aware of, and emotionally responsive to, others' distress. We do not just respond emotionally; we notice our own emotions by some internal analogue of perception... Our suite of emotional reactions – especially those concerned with reciprocation, sympathy, empathy, disgust, and esteem – shapes and constrains, though certainly does not determine moral cognition. According to this view, moral cognition develops from an interaction between emotions, exemplar-guided intuitions, and explicit principles. (2012: 166–67)

And the development of moral cognition in the young, of course, helps to shape the ethical norms of adult life in all biocultures. As we will discover in more detail in Chapters 4 and 5, the emotions experienced by spectators in performances play a crucial role in meaning-making and ethical perception.

Emotions and meanings

In his *Moving Viewers: American Film and the Spectator's Experience* (2009), cognitive film critic Carl Plantinga adapts several of Panksepp's and Damasio's insights, along with those of philosopher Robert C. Roberts, to forge an approach to film viewing that generally works within the principles of Enaction. As we will see, the insights in *Moving Viewers* can be extended to account for the role of affect and emotion in all kinds of performances, filmic or otherwise. Plantinga's experiential approach includes attention to curiosity and suspense (both varieties of Panksepp's **seeking**) and similar matters that have usually been understood as parts of viewer cognition by other film theorists. For Plantinga, emotions are "concern-based construals" (Plantinga 2009: 56); they "result from someone's perception or construal of an event or situation in relation to her or his concerns" (2009: 29). This general definition accords with Colombetti's stipulation that emotions establish "a *concerned* point of view that *generates meaning*."

Incorporating the work of several scientists, Plantinga discusses emotion as a kind of affect, but also distinguishes between the two. "Affect is any [bodily] state or feeling," he says (2009: 29), which may range from feeling hot or cold, to a general mood of happiness or gloom, to experiencing a headache. Emotions are also affects, affirms Plantinga, but they are tied to a person's values and concerns. Unlike other affects, emotions are always about something; "they are directed at something or someone, whether real or imagined," he states (2009: 57). Following other evolutionary psychologists, Plantinga also separates emotions from other kinds of affects through evolution. Most affects have an ancient pedigree; they date from the time that our reptilian ancestors could only experience pains, moods, instincts, and reflexes. Emotions are more highly evolved; all mammals, as previously noted, are hard-wired for **play, fear, lust**, and the other primal emotions. While he differentiates moods and other affects from emotions, Plantinga also recognizes that they are mutually influential; a general mood of sadness produced by several days of cold, wet weather will tend to heighten the emotion of **panic/grief**, and vice-versa. Finally, Plantinga is clear that affect and attributed meaning are indivisible, in films as in life: "Affective experience [in general] and meaning are neither parallel nor separable, but firmly intertwined." The viewer's affects guide the emergence of meaning, and "a lack of attention to, or inability to understand, affective experience could well lead one to misunderstand the thematic workings of a film..." (2009: 3–4). The same could be said for the ties linking emotions and other affects to meanings in sports, rituals, and musical events.

Plantinga recognizes the importance of a spectator's **sympathetic** or **antipathetic** responses to performers in blended roles. This is not to say that audiences will "feel the same" as a sympathetic protagonist in a drama – after all, a character may experience extreme pain – but it does mean that spectators will take the well-being and goals of specific performer/roles as their focus and respond to their actions and situations accordingly. Such concern-based construals are fundamental to the competitive nature of all performances; an audience desires to take sides and usually does so. Nonetheless, because a spectator's emotional response to a blended figure in a performance is often complicated and changeable, the term "identification," used by some psychologists, is too inexact to serve the purpose. "Willy Loman really is a terrible father," we might come to believe near the end of *Death of a Salesman*, reversing our previous feeling of **sympathy** for actor/Willy to **antipathy**. In addition to these two responses, other social emotions may enter into a spectator's feelings about a musical or sports figure, depending on the circumstances.

Plantinga's typology of the different ways emotions play out over time is especially useful for understanding the dynamics of affects and emotions in performances. "Local emotions" are the briefest. Spectator **panic** when Lon Cheney turns around to reveal his ghoulish face in the *Phantom of the Opera* or **rage** when the other team intercepts a forward pass in an American football game is usually quick and intense. Local emotions typically cause an immediate spike in hormones and heart rate, but quickly subside. Plantinga's "direct emotions" are the next longest in duration. These are caused by an incident in the forward action of a performance event, but last longer than local emotions. For example, Judy Garland as Dorothy in *The Wizard of Oz* establishes her wish to travel to a land "where troubles melt like lemon drops/away above the chimney tops" when she sings "Over the Rainbow" early in the film. Because most of the audience already **cares** for Garland/Dorothy and knows that the narrative of the film is a fantasy, they will **seek** to discover how her wish may come true. This combination of **seeking** and **caring** reaches its climax in the tornado scene and ends temporarily when Dorothy's house lands on the Wicked Witch of the East in Munchkin Land. "Global emotions" endure the longest. Like the other two, the overall forward action of the game, drama, or song causes a global response, which will usually last, in varying degrees of intensity, throughout the time of the performance. These include the **lust** that pervades an erotic film or the combination of **pride** and **care** that sustains Woodie Guthrie's "This Land Is Your Land."

In addition to local, direct, global, and sympathetic or antipathetic emotions, Plantinga notes that spectators sometimes respond to the technique of a performance. All of the emotional responses discussed so far occur while spectators are experiencing the flow of the fiction or game, while they are "living in the blend," to use Fauconnier and Turner's terminology. As we have seen, however, audience members often step back from their involvement in a performance; they unblend their player/role integrations and perhaps the blend of the performance itself to criticize or celebrate the ritual or game in other ways. They use their higher-order consciousness to directly recognize the constructed, subjunctive realities of the performance before them. Plantinga calls these "artifact emotions," implicitly referring to the celluloid artifact that constitutes the material reality of a film. Examples of artifact emotions in film viewing include the admiration (a variety of **pride**) a spectator may feel for the cameraman after watching a long and involved tracking shot or perhaps a response of **embarrassment** in the realization that a normally good actor turned in a mediocre performance. While appropriate for film spectating, the term "artifact emotion" does not translate well for most other types of performance. A better designation might simply be "production emotion," which implicitly distinguishes between the productive work that must happen "backstage" before a performance can occur – the work of architects, writers, managers, directors, designers, broadcast technicians, etc. – and the performance level of the show, which always involves the doubleness of blending. Because spectators generally want to concentrate on the game, the story, or the ritual, most production emotions do not last for very long.

Although this section has necessarily focused on the general emotional dynamics of spectating during performances, I want to close its discussion by emphasizing that Plantinga's Enactive approach also opens up questions of aesthetic complexity and the emergence of meaning. In his chapter on "Negative Emotions and Sympathetic Narratives," Plantinga asks how viewer pleasure can accommodate painful emotions caused by film narratives that end in death; he focuses on the ending of James Cameron's melodrama *Titanic* (1997) as his chief example. Plantinga recognizes that this question has broad ramifications for theories of emotion in dramatic tragedy as well as melodrama. Despite the drowning of many **sympathetic** characters in the story, particularly the death of Jack (Leonardo DiCaprio) from freezing as he and Rose (Kate Winslet) await rescue in the water,

Plantinga claims that Cameron uses "various techniques... to control the pain and transform it into pleasure" (2009: 169). While acknowledging that this romantic melodrama is not *King Lear* or *The Trojan Women*, Plantinga rightly points out that spectators must work through immense sadness and loss in these and similar narratives before they can arrive at some resolution and meaning for themselves. He rejects several of the usual explanations for this process, including the psychoanalytic position that audiences are inherently masochistic and the Aristotelian one that they undergo a purging, a catharsis, of pity and fear.

Instead, Plantinga adopts a modified version of Hume's claim that spectators at a dramatic tragedy convert their negative responses into positive emotions and feelings through the pleasure they take in the artfulness of the presentation. Although Plantinga does not make the connection, Hume's claim that spectators can use their perception of beauty to gain some distance from their immediate immersion in the emotions of the moment aligns with Grodal's insight that spectators may deploy their higher-order consciousness to temporarily focus on the constructed qualities of the film as an artifact. With regard to *Titanic*, as Plantinga points out, the opportunity for spectators to **admire** the artfulness of the film is evident in Cameron's handling of DiCaprio/Jack's death and his ghostly farewell wave to Winslet/Rose. Soon after Winslet/Rose awakens from her watery stupor, prompted by calls from a nearby rescue row boat, she discovers that her lover has died. For many spectators, this moment was probably the high point of **panic** and **grief** in the film. Then a curious thing happens. Even as Winslet/Rose releases DiCaprio/Jack's hand from her own to let him sink, she says, "I'll never let go, Jack." Instead of keeping audience focus on Winslet/Rose's **grief**, however, Cameron, says Plantinga, shifted to "a high-angle point-of-view shot [that showed DiCaprio's] body descending silently into the blue, gradually disappearing into the deep as his face points upward and his arm stretches out above him, as though he salutes Rose or waves his final good-bye" (2009: 180). Cameron leaves spectators with two questions: What did Rose mean by saying she would "never let go" and how was Jack's final gesture an apparent "response" to Rose's odd affirmation? Both questions, of course, move the narrative along even as they soften the **grief** of the moment. Although Plantinga recognizes that this shift may have mollified spectator response, he also knows it was unlikely to erase it. Some spectators, though, may have temporarily moved out of the immediate flow of the film – they may have suspended their belief in its actual reality – by adopting what I am calling a production emotion for a second or so during that moment. That is, the camera shot, lighting, and music may have shifted them temporarily into **admiration** for the film's beauty and away from the characters' situation.

Plantinga emphasizes, however, that Hume's insight into tragedy is only partly correct for *Titanic*. DiCaprio/Jack's wave good-bye does emerge as a possible meaning at the moment of his disappearance into the deep, but the full potential of that meaning, plus the resolution of Winslet/Rose's statement, must be answered by later scenes in the film. Soon after Winslet/Rose is saved, Cameron shifts from the circumstances of the Titanic disaster in 1912 back to the frame story in the present, in which an aged Rose (now played by Gloria Stewart) must come to terms with her memories of that fateful night. The diving crew that has discovered the remains of the Titanic on the ocean floor has not emerged with the priceless blue diamond, "Heart of the Ocean," that once belonged to Rose and has come to symbolize the **care** and **lust** she felt for Jack. In the last episode of the film, we discover that Rose still has the diamond and Cameron invites us to speculate what she will do with it, now that she has climbed onto the deck rail at the back of the modern ship, much as she did with Jack on the Titanic eighty-five years ago. Stewart/Rose decides to return the Heart of the Ocean to the sea and the audience watches it sink out of sight, just as they watched Jack gradually descend a few minutes before. Stewart/Rose has answered Jack's wave good-bye and honored the memory of their love; now at the end of her own life, she is finally ready to "let go" of Jack's metaphorical hand by letting go of the diamond. *Titanic* invites spectators to feel **admiration** for her gesture of self-sacrifice, an action that echoes Jack's many gestures of **care** for her.

As Plantinga points out, Cameron's ending offers spectators a funeral-like ritual of celebration designed to restore moral order through the idealization of romantic love. The film, he says, expresses "a belief in the transcendence of love, a hope that love can survive death, loss, and separation. [It] offers . . . a connection with loved ones who have died" (2009: 186). More of a melodrama than a tragedy, *Titanic* crafts a narrative that seeks to move spectators beyond lingering negative emotions to deliver a positive "fantasy of assurance and control" (2009: 188). As a theater historian, it is interesting to me that Cameron's script rests on that reliable chestnut of nineteenth-century drama, the symbolically charged prop, to wrap up his well-made melodrama. On the whole, of course, this conventional device probably made *Titanic* more emotionally appealing to spectators than it might have been otherwise. What is undeniable in all of this is Cameron's Oscar-winning ability to marry the revelation of possible meaning to the elevation of spectator emotions.

Varieties of emotional response

For her performance piece "America, The Beautiful," Nao Bustamante created an on-stage ecology for her art with several costume pieces, a table with an old record player, and two ladders. The video of "America, The Beautiful" on her official website, shot at a live performance in 2002, shows her taking off all of her clothes, wrapping tape around her stomach and legs, smearing make-up on her face and plastering a sex-kitten wig on her head with too much hair spray, then climbing onto the top of a short ladder, where she perches to "dress" herself in two pumps and two long, white gloves. All the while, Bustamante creates her own sound effects by playing old recordings of "Love is a Many Splendored Thing," "Someday My Prince Will Come," and a bouncing, circus-like tune as she stands and bends awkwardly on top of the ladder to get her shoes on. Given the music and her apparel, Bustamante seems to be preparing herself to perform a grotesque beauty pageant presentation. She occasionally pushes a frightened smile at the audience when, as the character she is performing, Bustamante/pageant contestant has completed a part of her act. Her initial dressing on the short ladder is only a necessary preface for her much longer climb to the top of a twelve-foot ladder, where she pretends to hold sophisticated conversations with others and performs shadow animals in front of a spotlight against a curtain backdrop with the fingers of both hands. The apparent effect of her narrative performance on the off-camera audience was frequent laughter, some gasps of concern for her safety, and occasional stretches of tedium, especially during the several minutes it took her to put on her pumps.

What was going on emotionally in Bustamante's audience to spark the laughter and the gasps? One critic for a San Francisco paper summarized what he took to be the meaning of the performance by stating that she plays a grotesque beauty queen who "climbs the metaphorical ladder of success" (Nao Bustamante website, accessed July 27, 2014). While this is true on one level, it is also obvious and significantly incomplete. Yes, Bustamante is satirizing the trappings of female beauty in the US, especially when those norms are applied to large Latina bodies. Her character tries to hide her excess flesh under wrapping tape, doll up her face and hair, and put on the appropriate shoes and gloves – all to enable her to climb to success. In terms of one primary image schema for this sequence, it is clear that Bustamante was drawing on CONTAINMENT; she sought to CONTAIN her flesh under tape and her Latina ancestry under the conventions of Anglo beauty. No doubt some of the laughter in the audience erupted from their **embarrassment** for her character – a direct emotion in Plantinga's terms – as spectators watched her trying to cover up that which could not be CONTAINED. Through performance, Bustamante was partly stating that the ideal of American beauty cannot be made to fit larger-sized bodies; her attempt to squeeze her body into that ideal led to grotesque physical images that provoked laughter.

But this observation does not take account of Bustamante's precarious BALANCING acts as she performs these many feats. Most of the fifty-minute video tape shows her struggling to keep from falling off the two ladders, a struggle made more difficult by the fact that her costuming, wig, and shoes get in the way of the tasks her character is driven to complete, apparently to win the beauty pageant. At one point, Bustamante/pageant queen slides her hefty body between two rungs of the left side of the two-sided tall ladder to reach her leg out to the other side, passes herself through two rungs on the right, and, finally, emerges with her entire body on the right side of the ladder. And she does this without losing wig, shoes, or gloves. In image schematic terms, this action couples CONTAINMENT with BALANCE. Although this ladder feat and others like it appear to imitate circus acrobatics, Bustamante's genuine precariousness have the opposite effect of a smooth, rhythmic, everything-is-under-control circus performance. If Bustamante only wished to critique successful American beauties, she could have accomplished this far more easily, quickly, and gracefully. The gasps from the audience suggest that her awkward, precarious BALANCING act evokes **anxiety** and sometimes outright **fear** in her witnesses. More pervasive overall in her performance piece than **embarrassment**, **fear**, and its less extreme cousin **anxiety** were the dominant global emotions of "America, the Beautiful." Spectators experiencing this emotional range in Bustamante's performance might come to understand that the attempt to conform to Anglo norms of beauty can cause Latinas actual physical and psychological harm.

Martha Nussbaum's interpretation of the first of five *Kindertotenleider* by Gustav Mahler also explores the many links between audience emotion and meaning-making. Mahler set to music five poems about the death of children penned by a grieving German poet, Friedrich Rükert. Rükert did in fact lose two of his children to scarlet fever in 1833 and wrote the poems soon afterwards. Nussbaum understands that music cannot work emotionally in the same ways as a language-based narrative; Mahler is a good example for her because he claimed that his symphonic writing began at the point where the power of words ended. Instead of involving spectators through their emotional responses in the actions of characters, music for Mahler, says Nussbaum, crystalized "general forms of emotion" with the power to evoke "dream-like" states of mind (Nussbaum 2001: 266). For Nussbaum, all orchestral music, not just Mahler's, "is especially well-suited to express parts of the personality that lie beneath its conscious self-understanding... Lacking the narrative and objectual structures to which we are accustomed in language, it frequently has an affinity with the amorphous, archaic, and extremely powerful emotional materials of childhood" (2001: 269). Induced to enter a kind of dream state, auditors of symphonic music may experience musical forces directly through their bodies in ways that call forth half-conscious pressures, flows, and visions. Although Nussbaum recognizes that any translation of musical emotion into words can only be partial and impressionistic, her general knowledge of music, scholarly research into this *leider*, love of Mahler, and eagerness to share his music with her readers drives and guides her comments.

For Nussbaum, Mahler's *Kindentotenleider* calls forth images of **grief** – Panksepp names the emotion **panic/grief** to emphasize the sense of abandonment coupled with loss that the death of a loved one can bring – that go beyond the texts of the poems upon which they are based. Nussbaum acknowledges that the poems orient the general dynamics of the music but insists that "the music has its own independent contribution to make to the work's emotional trajectory" (2001: 280). Because the songs take the perspective of a grieving mother or father, most listeners will feel immersed in the parent's pain, unable to move to a third-person, **sympathetic** point of view.

According to Nussbaum, "[T]he first song expresses the isolation of personal grief and pain within the exuberant and indifferent life of nature, which by contrast seems not at all consoling, but falsely sweet and sinister" (2001: 283). Mahler achieves this contrast primarily through his choice of instruments, his spare use of a female singer's voice, and by his musical dynamics. He begins with a plaintive, mourning oboe, soon accompanied by descending notes played on a horn, then joined by the searing quality of the female voice pitched above the instruments. The effect, says Nussbaum, is "that of a mind tormenting itself, biting into itself in silent isolation, after a night of utter sleeplessness" (2001: 284). In sharp contrast, the strings and harp swell into this picture of desolation to suggest the rising of the sun, denoted by the sung words of the poem. While the strings suggest that the cycles of nature simply continue, regardless of human **grief**, the otherworldly sweetness of the harp signals Mahler's point of view, says Nussbaum. "The sun is rising and light begins to flood the world – for everyone but the one who has lost a child in the night" (2001: 285). The mundane arrival of sunlight is an unwelcome intrusion into the parent's **panic/grief**. Next enters a glockenspiel and chimes six times, reminding the parent/listener that the child's funeral must soon occur. The toy-like, high-pitched ringing of the glockenspiel conjures images of a child at **play**, notes Nussbaum, ironically grinding in the fact that the parent's past **joy** of playing with the child has ended.

Mahler works variations on these musical dynamics in the second and third strophes of the song. In the second part, the oboe again carries the forlorn melody of mourning, but more strings are added to the bland swelling of the sunrise. Suddenly, says Nussbaum, "the oboe cuts in as if in a protest against the onward march of the light..." (2001: 286). The glockenspiel sounds again, but with fewer notes, as if it were a wind-up toy running down. In the third strophe, the woman's voice inverts the mourning melody heard throughout by the oboe but the oboe enters to accompany the voice with its original tune. According to Nussbaum, "The inversion of the grief melody represents the voice's attempt to conquer its own grief...; but the oboe, persisting with the melody's original form, insists that this effort is in vain" (2001: 286). The song ends with soaring strings and arpeggios from the harp, which seem to "snatch the child out of the parent's arms into the world of natural process and decay," says Nussbaum (2001: 286). "It is impossible not to feel that the usual polarities of light and darkness are being reversed here," she states. As the music swells to a climax, the little bell of the glockenspiel returns, but seems to stammer, as if the memory of the child's **joy** is being extinguished. The bell continues, sounding on the offbeat, but diminishes, as even the oboe joins the strings and harp to welcome the light. Then silence. Nussbaum ends her interpretation with this comment: "The little bell sounds once more, alone, its painful memory of joy sounding in the void, with a high and inexorable stroke" (2001: 287).

Like Johnson's descriptions of musical effects on listeners, Nussbaum's comments rely throughout on Daniel Stern's "vitality affects" to imagine musical movement. Mahler's *Kindertotenleider*, says Nussbaum, surge, fade, explode, fall, and swell, implicitly imitating the movements of a newborn child as it emerges into life. Nussbaum's invocation of these musical effects reinforces her attempt both to depict the dream-like feelings that an auditor's immersion in music can effect and the emotional tensions it probably evokes in many listeners. As both Johnson and Nussbaum acknowledge, however, language can never fully capture what music does to us. Further, because each listener bodies forth and inhabits somewhat unique worlds, one person's emotional response will likely differ from another's.

Nonetheless, Nussbaum is probably right that music often taps into the "emotional materials of childhood" for most people. It is difficult to imagine that most sensitive listeners would not respond with **panic/grief** or at least with **sadness**, the primary emotion's minor register, to Mahler's *Kindertotenleider*.

Watching two choreographed versions of the character of Eliza derived from *Uncle Tom's Cabin* at a dance concert, many spectators likely experienced **fear** and **anger**. The occasion was a 1990 performance of *The Last Supper at Uncle Tom's Cabin/The Promised Land*, produced by the Bill T. Jones/Arnie Zane Dance Company and choreographed by Jones. Like Mahler's *Kindertotenleider*, the dance evoked memories – in this case bioculturally shaped memories based in the experience of slavery by black bodies and minds in the American South of the nineteenth century.

I will focus on two sections of the second scene of this dance, entitled "Eliza on the Ice," loosely based on the chapter in H.B. Stowe's 1851 novel in which the runaway slave Eliza, with her child in her arms, flees her pursuers by leaping on ice floes to cross the Ohio River to freedom. Typically a gripping part of stage adaptations of the novel in the late nineteenth and early twentieth centuries, the melodramatic scene often featured wind and snow effects, moving cakes of ice across the stage, slave catchers with barking dogs on one side of the river, and Eliza's rescuer on the other. In the theater, as in Stowe's novel, Eliza's heroism was meant to demonstrate the fearless determination typical of a light-skinned, quadroon mother – nearly all Elizas were played by white actors – to rescue her child from the degradations of slavery and join her runaway husband, who had already made it to Ohio. A hundred years ago, most U.S. theatergoers had seen several productions of *Uncle Tom's Cabin* and many had also watched a film version of the piece; its racialist ideas and images were thoroughly embedded in the culture of the nation. And, arguably, still are.

The Jones/Zane version of "Eliza on the Ice" both demolished such sentimental expectations and refashioned selected elements of the Eliza scene to explore contemporary African American womanhood for its spectators in the 1990s. Four actor-dancers portrayed different versions of Eliza in near-solo succession and the scene further undercut Stowe's elevation of individual heroics by celebrating the collective action of all of them at the start and finish of the twenty-minute scene. Given the distinctive skin pigmentation of each dancer/Eliza, the piece also ignored Stowe's belief that only a Negro who was partly white, and hence closer to ideal femininity and motherhood for antebellum white culture, could have attempted such dangerous leaps to protect her child. Crucially, in the Jones/Zane scene, none of the five Elizas carries a baby; motherhood is no longer the emotional center of the danced action. Rather, each of them develops different movements that embody various historical experiences of African American women. For some people living today, these experiences may still live in the memories of their families, passed down through actual physical embodiments from generation to generation. For most in the audience, Jones's and the dancers' choreography and performances will open a window on the historical past that continues to provide a warning for African American women today. In discussing two of these four dances, I will rely primarily on Ariel Nereson's description and interpretation of the dance in her dissertation, "Feeling History: Emotion, Performance, and Meaning-Making in Bill T. Jones/Arnie Zanes' Dance Company" (2014), and a videotape of the dance provided to me by Nereson.

"Eliza on the Ice" begins with buffo military maneuvers performed by the males of the company dressed as attack dogs, a parody of the mastiffs that appeared in melodramatic stage productions of the novel. Jones costumed and choreographed them to appear both ludicrous and alarming; dressed in black tank tops, jockstraps, combat boots, and muzzles, they drill and exercise under two large cutouts of vicious dogs, held aloft on poles like military crests by two dancers. During the dances of the first two Elizas, these embodiments of the terrifying and foolish aspects of slavery hover near the periphery of the stage, occasionally making quick entrances and exits without interrupting the Elizas's solos.

The dogs return in force, however, with the entrance of Betsy McCracken as Eliza 3. Like McCracken/Eliza 3, the dogs wield what look like long wooden paddles, held vertically and occasionally turned in the hands like batons. For some spectators, the paddles, in conjunction with a painted scenic backdrop of a southern river scene (definitely not the ice-filled Ohio), may suggest that the dogs and McCracken/Eliza 3 are engaged in crossing a river in a long canoe, but the evident tensions between her/Eliza and the dogs suggest a standoff in which little progress is possible. This Eliza can never get to the other side of the river and, even if she could, she would still be trapped in slavery. Motivated primarily by **fear**, McCracken/Eliza moves with speed to protect herself from the dogs. Alternating between bodily jerks and quick, linear strides, she deploys the same military-like movements as her opponents, twisting paddle and body to keep the dogs at bay. States Nereson, "The effect of these extremes of linearity and tension is that emotionally this character [McCracken/Eliza 3] is in control of her situation, but that this control comes at a high price – the total erasure of pleasure and comfort" (Nereson 2014: 64). By copying the moves of the dogs, McCracken/Eliza 3 is able to maintain a watchful COUNTER-FORCE against them, but at the price of reproducing the conditions of her enslavement. As a spectator watching the video of the performance, I was worn down by McCracken's guarded **fear** and began to feel as exhausted as the character she portrayed.

Working for extreme contrast, Jones shifts primary agency for most of the next section of the dance from his Eliza figure to the male dogs. Jones consciously uses Maya Saffrin's biracial identity to suggest the fate of the "tragic octoroon," often depicted as sexually desirable in nineteenth-century U.S. white culture. Like the other Elizas, Saffrin wears a white dress, but in her case it is in the style of "a coquette from a turn-of-the-century French postcard," according to Jones (cited in Nereson 2014: 66). As Nereson relates, "The choreography of Eliza 4 is a sequence of throws... One man sets her up in a precarious balance or lift, for the purpose of watching her fall, prey to another dog/man... Saffrin's Eliza cannot control her own self, let alone the dogs, and is frequently manipulated into positions of risk" (2014: 67–68). As the dogs toss her around like a sexual plaything, Saffrin registers the emotional effect of her character's physical availability through her rag-doll body and blank expression. The dogs turn her into a dehumanized object for manipulation, finally leaving her in a heap on the ground. In response to the dogs' enjoyment of their grotesque **play**, most of the spectators likely experienced **anger** and probably some **sadness** for Saffrin/Eliza 4. That was certainly my experience as I watched the scene.

Following the dogs' exit, the first dancer of Eliza 1 returns to the stage and attempts to help Saffrin/Eliza 4 by teaching her a simple social dance based in the black vernacular tradition, a dance that had been performed earlier. But the dogs return and haul Eliza 4 off stage. Two previous Eliza dancers join the dancer of Eliza 1, creating a trio of social dancers. Next, the dancer playing H.B. Stowe brings Saffrin back onto the stage and attempts to comfort her, but Saffrin/Eliza 4 shakes her off, expressing her own **anger** for the first time and aligning her body with those of the other dancers. According to Nereson, "the presence of the other Elizas has literally given Eliza 4 strength, as her body has increased its tension, amplitude, and linearity through embodying their [vernacular] choreographies" (2014: 71).

"Eliza on the Ice" concludes with the four women exiting in rhythmic unison; below the waist, they are performing the same rolling-walk step all have practiced before, but above the hips, each woman is executing gestures unique to her singular Eliza. Nereson states that "this choreography illustrates Jones's overarching concept of each woman as a facet of the same figure, giving them the same choreography on the lower body but allowing for individual expression of the upper body" (2014: 71). For me, the final movements of the Eliza dancers evoked **sadness** but also some **pride** and **sympathy,** as the dancers moved together both individually and in unison. Following their exit, the dancer playing Stowe crawls painfully off stage and the scene ends. Evidently, the four Elizas have made a choice that carries contemporary moral force: Better to maintain traditional practices and risk brutal encounters with men than to accept the reduction of the self to a sentimental cliché. By reaching back to include the movement histories of slave women through metaphors of dance, Jones and his dancers sought to extend the cultural-cognitive ecosystem of his contemporary audience into the historical past. In effect, the five dancer/Elizas in "Eliza on the Ice" connected the 1990 spectators to a network that included both the experience of slavery for women over 150 years ago and one sentimental refraction of that experience in Stowe's *Uncle Tom's Cabin*.

Empathy and the emotions

From the perspective of current cognitive science, empathy is generally defined as the ability to experience and understand the intentions, emotions, and beliefs of another. Though not an emotion itself, empathy often leads to negative or positive emotional engagements with others; it is ubiquitous and commonplace. When we try to understand what a cellphone caller really meant by a particular vocal inflection or imagine the facial response of a loved one to a possible gift, empathy is involved. Without our evolved ability to engage in empathy, role players could not coordinate their performances, and spectators would have little incentive to watch them, much less attempt to figure out what they were doing. As these examples suggest, the cognitive processes of empathy are mostly unconscious, although humans can (and do) educate themselves to improve their empathetic perceptions. Nussbaum's discussion of Mahler's understanding of a parent's grief makes it clear that the composer's empathetic skills were finely tuned, indeed. In retrospect, it is evident that I empathized with each of the dancer/characters as I watched the taped performance of "Eliza on the Ice."

The contemporary scientific understanding of empathy differs significantly from the nineteenth-century meanings of the term. German romantics used the word *Einfühlung* – which was later translated into English as "empathy" – to mean the ability of individuals to project themselves into the situation of another person or into nature. The romantics believed that *Einfuhlung* could help them to solve imaginative problems such as how a poet might temporarily merge his identity with a famous Renaissance figure or how a romantic painter could come to feel what it is like to be a gnarled tree on a hilltop. From their point of view, this aesthetic notion of identification and mystical merging involved conscious projection and the temporary loss of the self in another object or person. This was the conception of empathy that Bertolt Brecht opposed in several of his theatrical essays. Brecht's primary problem with *Einfuhlung* was the loss of agency for spectators that the romantic conception of the term entailed. Drawing on the German romantic understanding of *Einfuhlung*, Brecht believed that empathy began as a conscious aesthetic choice and that spectators could turn away from empathetic engagement if induced to enjoy performances in other ways.

No current scientific definition of empathy assumes that spectators (or anybody else) can control empathetic engagement in this way. Nor do current definitions suggest that empathy involves a loss of agency and the mystical merging of the self with some other. This is not to say that cognitive scientists agree on a definition of empathy, however. In a 2009 survey of contemporary uses of the term, C. Daniel Batson singles out eight related but distinct understandings of empathy. Finding that researchers generally use empathy to provide an answer to two very different questions, Batson separates these definitions into two groups. Two of the eight link empathy to **sympathy**, says Batson, and attempt to determine "what leads one person to respond with sensitivity and care to the suffering of another?" (Batson 2009: 3). Most definitions, however, are responses to how one person can "know what another person is thinking and feeling" (2009: 3). Within this predominant range of definitions, observers have noted two major approaches, which tend to emphasize different, though related aspects of the cognitive process. Neuropsychologist Simone G. Shamay-Tsoory calls these "cognitive" and "affective" empathy and discusses the different research traditions and agendas that have informed them (Shamay-Tsoory 2009: 215–16).

Shamay-Tsoory notes that "cognitive empathy" is generally understood as perspective-taking. That is, the person engaged in empathy attempts to adopt the thoughts and feelings of another person in order to predict his or her future behavior. Researchers interested in perspective-taking have often explored this form of empathy through Theory of Mind psychology, discussed earlier. In contrast, affective empathy, as the name suggests, links the empathizer to the other through physical and emotional expressiveness and response. Many experiments since the 1970s have validated and underlined the importance of affective empathy for social interaction. Researchers following this approach, also known as empathetic simulation, emphasize the embodied rather than the mental side of empathy. Simulation involves a kind of mimesis; the empathizer perceives and unconsciously embodies the emotional behavior of the target person. Perceiving the facial expression, muscle tension, and physical posture of **rage** in another, for example, the empathizer will begin to feel **rage** in herself. Alternatively, a spectator watching a happy actor/character in performance will experience a degree of that happiness himself.

The recent discovery of mirror neurons has given hope to those who are pushing for a unified theory of empathy. As noted in Chapter 1, networks of neurons in our brains effectively "mirror" intentional motor activity produced by another person and perceived by the empathizer. If a spectator watches an aerialist take a step on a high wire or sees a hockey player flick the puck toward the stick of a teammate, for example, the same group of neurons in the empathizer's brain is activated as in the player's brain; neurologically, it is almost as if the observer had taken the step or flicked the puck himself. By working through our perceptions, bodies, and minds, our networks of mirror neurons unconsciously attune us to each other. Vittorio Gallese, one of the first scientists to investigate mirror neurons in monkeys, terms the mirror neuron system in primates "the basis of social cognition" (Gallese et al. 2004: 5).

Evan Thompson, whose many books and essays take a phenomenological and Enactive perspective on neurobiology, agrees with Gallese about the foundational importance of mirror neurons but believes that other parts of the brain and body are involved in the later stages of empathy. In his *Mind in Life: Biology, Phenomenology, and the Sciences of Mind* (2007), Thompson understands empathy as a four-stage process, each one more reliant on higher-order consciousness than the stage that precedes it. His types, which follow normal human development, begin with "sensorimotor coupling," which centers on the work of mirror neurons, and culminate, three stages later, in the possibility of "moral perception." As we mature, we gain the abilities to resonate with other's feelings and intentions, to take the perspective of another person, to turn that perspective toward ourselves in order to gain self-awareness, and finally to see the other as a person who deserves concern and respect. Thompson is quick to add that empathy does not exhaust moral understanding, but it does provide a significant entry point into it. I will adopt Thompson's point of view on empathy, both because it accords with Enaction and because it joins empathy to ethics, a connection I will develop further in Chapter 5.

From Thompson's Enactive point of view, the "sensorimotor coupling" of mirroring puts humans in tune with each other and results in many of the low-level unconscious affective links that are usually explored as a part of affective empathy. This mutual mirroring may lead to a second, more complex form of empathy, which he terms "imaginary transposition" (Thompson 2007: 395). As the name suggests, imaginary transposition allows the empathizer to attempt to place herself or himself into the mind of another; it is identical in most ways to what other psychologists mean by perspective-taking. To link sensorimotor coupling to imaginary transposition, Thompson draws on recent evidence about child development. Soon after they are born, most infants are driven to mirror the intentional facial expressions of their caregivers and this mutual mirroring continues between infants and caregivers throughout early childhood (and much longer, in most cases). By about nine months, the normal child can use other cognitive skills, plus the knowledge and memory that he or she has gained from mirroring, to engage in imaginary transposition. This begins with the child's recognition that other humans are intentional agents "like me" and leads the developing baby to project herself/himself into the mind of a nearby adult. Later the child may even imagine what an adult may be thinking, feeling, and intending when that person is absent.

Soon after children can accomplish the basics of imaginary transposition, they gain the ability to play with "reiterated empathy." Thompson borrows this term from phenomenologist Edith Stein to denote the ability to conceptualize oneself from the point of view of another person. As he explains, "Empathy thus becomes reiterated, so that I can empathetically imagine your empathetic experience of me and you empathetically imagine my empathetic experience of you" (2007: 398). For toddlers, this ability often signals the onset of **shyness** and/or **confidence**, because the child can now begin to perceive how others feel about him or her. In adults, reiterated empathy may register as **embarrassment**, indifference, or even **guilt**, depending on how successfully a person believes others have interpreted his or her intentions and emotions.

Thompson notes that the fourth level of empathy, "moral perception," is "not the same as any particular feeling of concern for another, such as sympathy, love, or compassion. Rather, it is the underlying capacity to have such other-directed and other-regarding feelings of concern" (2007: 401). Reiterated empathy rises to moral perception in children when they begin to understand others and themselves as agents who can take action in the world. Despite its later complexities, moral perception is rooted in the experience and imagination of the self as a five-to-seven-year old while perceiving the feelings, plans, hopes, and goals of others.

Applying Thompson's four stages of empathy to a speech given by Nelson Mandela suggests some of the ethical possibilities of empathy for political performers. Mandela spoke to the newly constituted South African Parliament on May 24, 1994, soon after his election to the Presidency. Not only did the oration demonstrate Mandela's politically graceful and ethically savvy use of empathy. Because the speech occurred at the birth of the new post-apartheid nation, it also underlined the constitutive possibilities of all performances – a possibility especially true for political rhetoric. Significantly, Mandela's first parliamentary address deployed empathy both as a means of constituting the new nation and as a step toward reconciliation among the peoples of South Africa.

According to rhetorician Philippe-Joseph Salazar, Mandela faced a difficult challenge on that day in 1994. Recognizing that his speech would begin the process of governing the newly (re)constituted nation-state, he also knew that he could not claim to be the only legitimate voice to speak for the people of the nation; he understood that the elected Members of Parliament (MPs), to whom he addressed his talk, must also share in the responsibilities (and the potential failures) of governance. Salazar believes that this reality led Mandela to set the opening sentence of his oration at an indefinite moment in the future: "The time will come when our nation will honor the memory of all the sons, the daughters, the mothers, the fathers, the youth, and the children who, by their thoughts and deeds, gave us the right to assert with pride that we are South Africans, that we are Africans, and that we are citizens of the world" (Mandela 2003: 148). By evoking a future moment of national concord that looks back on what remained a very discordant and potentially dangerous present, Mandela was able to establish his goal of a peaceful and honorable transition without downplaying the possibilities of civil war and the difficult political work that lay ahead for all of the MPs. The opening sentence also announced that the new nation, in achieving that goal, would be able to claim an honorable place among the other peoples of the world, a status that South Africa had lost during the boycotts and sanctions in the last years of the apartheid regime.

In terms of Thompson's levels of empathy, Mandela's opening certainly grabbed the attention of the MPs, visitors, and representatives of the press in the parliamentary hall and ensured that most of them experienced "sensorimotor coupling" with him. Coupling an attentive body with the body of any orator entails the neuronal mirroring of the muscular exertions of the speaker, which would include the flexing of the vocal chords as well as his or her gestures and whole-body movements. Whether they approved of his politics or not, the crowd in the parliamentary chamber was unconsciously attuned to the sounds and movements emanating from the new President's body. To pay attention effectively couples your body with another.

Next, Mandela singled out an Afrikaans woman poet who, he said, "transcended a particular experience and became a South African, an African, and a citizen of the world. Her name is Ingrid Jonker" (2003: 148). Mandela acknowledges that Jonker took her own life, but not before she wrote poetry that realized her "commitment to the poor, the oppressed, the wretched, and the despised" (2003: 148). In fact, as many in Mandela's audience knew, Jonker had publically committed suicide to protest the apartheid regime and to **shame** her father, one of the legal architects of apartheid. As Salazar remarks, Jonker's "[s]elf removal from the false nation of the apartheid regime allowed her to enter the proleptic or projected nation-to-be-born, the one Mandela is now summoning into being" in his speech. (Salazar 2002: 24) Mandela then quotes most of the poem that Jonker wrote in response to the anti-pass demonstrations in Sharpeville in 1960. Noting that a child who had been killed in the massacre "is not dead," Jonker's poem concludes with these verses:

> The child is present at all assemblies and law-giving
> the child peers
> through the windows of houses
> and into the hearts of mothers
> this child
> who only wanted to play in the sun at Nyanga
> is everywhere.
>
> The child grown to a man treks on through
> all Africa
> the child grown to a
> giant journeys
> over the whole world
> without a pass!   (Mandela 2003: 149)

As well as honoring a fallen hero in the fight against apartheid, the poem echoes Mandela's earlier invocation of citizens claiming their rightful place in South Africa, Africa, and the world.

None of the listeners would have missed the "imaginary transposition," in Thompson's terminology, at the heart of Mandela's decision to speak the emotional words of Jonker's poem. By putting yourself in the poet's place and experiencing the Sharpeville massacre through her eyes, the new President implicitly promised, you can experience the "thoughts and deeds" of one of our new nation's martyrs. Politically and ethically, Mandela's invocation invited all South Africans – the formerly named "blacks," "coloreds," "Afrikaners," and "English" – to envision themselves as heroes in the struggle for freedom and democracy. Of course this empathetic mode of identification would have challenged nearly all of his listeners (and later, the readers of his speech) to adopt an identity and play a political role that was very different than the one they or their parents and kin had inhabited and played during the last eighty years. The vast majority of South Africans had rarely, if ever, imagined themselves crossing the enforced norms of color and ethnicity to play a suicidal role in ending apartheid. And for many Afrikaners in 1994, Jonker remained a traitor. In short, the new President had resurrected a dead poet who had written about a painful episode in the past, and who, until that moment, had been an outsider to nearly all of the major groups of South Africans. For most citizens of the new nation, the call to step into the shoes of Jonker and imagine playing her suicidal role would have been surprising or even shocking. But also, and partly for these reasons, potentially transforming.

As Salazar relates, Mandela's decision to set his speech in an imagined, subjunctive future allowed him to move forthrightly into the rhetorical realm of *ethos*, the invocation of moral values to support a (sometimes) questionable argument. Mandela could not be sure, however, that all of his listeners would accept Jonker as an ethical model. States Salazar:

> It is clear that under other circumstances his *ethos* would not have been so readily accepted, nor allowed him enough credibility to quote, in English, an Afrikaans poet on the sufferings of African children. In other circumstances, he might have alienated everyone at once. However, on this occasion, he offered a vision that was also a fiction. And such a move, if we consider it, was even bolder. (Salazar 2002: 25)

Salazar also notes the immense *pathos* of Mandela's speech, his recourse to emotional appeal. Indeed, the *pathos* involved in speaking of Jonker's suicide and the *pathos* of the poem itself, which centers on a dead child's eventual triumph, is the primary rhetorical lure for listeners to accept and engage in Mandela's proffered imaginary transposition. By first projecting themselves into Mandela's vision, they experienced **sympathy** with the speaker. Then, by empathizing with Jonker and expanding their range of transposition to the child himself, witnesses could experience various iterations of **pride**, through the child's journey from hope, to struggle, to eventual victory. In crafting his speech, Mandela apparently understood that he was inviting a huge leap of faith from many of his listeners and that, consequently, he needed to provide them with emotional rewards for the empathetic risks they had taken.

While imaginary transposition was the primary empathetic tool of Mandela's speech, he also left room for Thompson's third level of engagement, "reiterated empathy." Reiterated empathy centers on ethical self-reflection; having stepped into another's shoes, people turn the imagined gaze of the other toward themselves to discern how well they might measure up to the other's expectations. After concluding his reading of Jonker's poem, Mandela summarized its primary meanings for the assembled listeners: "And in this glorious vision, she instructs that our endeavors must be about the liberation of the woman, the emancipation of the man and the liberty of the child." He then proceeded, more prosaically, to outline his political goals for "creating a people-centered society" (Mandela 2003: 149). For his audience in the Parliament, the details of Mandela's "Reconstruction and Development Programme" (2003: 150), understood in the context of Jonker's poem, prompted the potentially **shame**-laden question: "Dare I disappoint Jonker's expectant gaze in the coming months?" Wielding the ethical leverage he had gained though his bold vision, Mandela asked the assembled MPs, and implicitly all of the citizens of the new nation, to pass laws and embrace international treaties that would move South Africa toward his program.

Unlike reiterated empathy, "moral perception" does not involve the spur of conscience in which an imagined person of superior morality is looking over your shoulder and judging your actions. Toward the end of his speech, Mandela proclaimed that "[t]omorrow, on Africa Day, the dream of Ingrid Jonker will come to fruition" (2003: 150). In elaborating what he meant, it soon became clear that the President was not proclaiming the imminent arrival of a national utopia. Rather, he was anticipating the movement of the new South Africa into history, with the unfurling of a new flag, the lifting of the last remaining sanctions against the old regime by the United Nations, and other imminent actions on the international stage. This was indeed part of Jonker's vision, if not the whole of it. Nonetheless, by proclaiming the fruition of Jonker's dream, Mandela softened her ethical mandate into an ambiguous affirmation celebrating immediate political change as well as encouraging eventual reconciliation. This would echo through the rest of Mandela's address. For example, the combination of celebration and challenge in a paragraph near the end of the speech caught both sides of his intended ambiguity: "We have learnt the lesson that our blemishes speak of what all humanity should not do. We understand this fully that our glories point to the heights of what human genius can achieve" (2003: 151). Regarding Thompson's levels of empathy, Mandela was evoking the hope of unencumbered moral perception, in which all South Africans might experience true ethical concern for each other, but also locating moral perception near the "heights of what human genius can achieve." A practical politician as well as a visionary, Mandela rested most of his immediate hopes for South Africa on the empathetic rhetoric of imaginary transposition and reiterated empathy, not on the occasional "genius" of moral perception.

Significantly, though, Mandela's gesture toward moral perception kept open one route to achieving "truth and reconciliation," an initiative already begun in the transition that would continue in the work of the Truth and Reconciliation Commission, beginning in 1996. Given the occasion of his May 24 speech, however, Mandela surely understood that this address was not the appropriate time to take more concerted action on that difficult front. But he had already deployed the first three stages of empathy to help to constitute the nation as a place where people could expect that others would try to see the world through their eyes and would work to improve their ethical actions in the eyes of others. Whether Mandela created expectations for empathetic and **sympathetic** exchanges that no governmental commission concerned with reconciliation could ever fulfill is a question that remains unanswered; this part of his legacy for South Africa is both a hope and a burden for the future.

In his oration to the Parliament, Mandela apparently sensed that creating the culture of any new nation is fundamentally about translating subjunctive imaginings into new practices, norms, and institutions. Of course the results of such speech acts have not always been beneficial. Cognitive anthropologist Henry Plotkin remarks in *The Imagined World Made Real* that evolution has usually favored groups rather than individuals of the same species, and that groups can be coercive. He states, "If culture is imagination made real, one of the forces that compels each of us to believe in and adhere to extraordinary imaginings is [the] sheer weight of numbers of others believing in them. This does not mean we are all enslaved to the majority all of the time. It merely means that most of us are so predisposed some of the time" (Plotkin 2003: 285). Plotkin's pessimism reminds us that the networks of distributed cognition that have constituted most of the world's cultures for most of recorded history have often foregrounded the **fear** of group survival and, consequently, led our species into tyranny, superstition, genocide, and oppression. I will argue in Chapter 5, however, that humans have made some ethical progress over time and that progress remains possible; the abolition of apartheid in South Africa can surely stand as one such example.

Performativity and its discontents

When subjunctive action has practical effects, as it certainly did in the case of Mandela's address to the new South African Parliament, theorists in performance studies generally term such actions "performative." Scholars have pushed and pulled definitions of performative and performativity in several ways during the last fifty years. Philosopher J.L. Austin coined the adjective "performative" in 1955 to apply it narrowly to a particular kind of utterance in everyday speech that performs a real action. He distinguished between an utterance that is "*doing* something rather than merely *saying* something" (ital. in original) (Austin 1961: 222). Such utterances, as when a minister says, "I now pronounce you husband and wife," are performative because they make something new happen and do not simply describe an existing reality. Noting that an actor playing a minister on stage could not actually marry anyone, Austin distinguished performative language from speech used in theatrical fictions. Austin's initial definitions and discussion led some later thinkers to distinguish sharply between the reality of performative utterances in everyday life and the fictitious nature of stage performance. In contrast, others found that staged (and filmic and televised) fictions were just as real (though for different reasons) as actual life. Theorists continue to modify and debate possible meanings of performative and performativity.

Ten years ago, two performance artists entered into this debate in a way that directly challenges Austin's example of marriage. In 2004, when the Mayor of San Francisco began allowing gays and lesbians to marry, Annie Sprinkle and Elizabeth Stephens attempted to tie the knot at City Hall, only to have the Superior Court of California reinstate the ban on gay marriage on the day before their scheduled ceremony. Soon after that, the women staged two participatory marriages to challenge the ban and to celebrate the many possibilities of a married relationship. As performance studies scholar Peter Dickinson pointed out in 2010, Sprinkle and Stephens used their two weddings to inaugurate "a new subjunctive

temporality. The particular anti-structure of their ... nuptial celebrations – where the performative witnessing of Sprinkle and Stephens's exchange of vows is always secondary to the witnessed performances of their friends and collaborators ... – sets the stage (quite literally) for the multiple 'as if' scenarios of their life together that they will document throughout the coming year in still more performance modalities" (Dickinson 2010: 118). Dickinson adds, "Part of what is being 'undone' in their wedding project is the idea that marriage is the institutional ... precondition of the normative, nuclear family structure as it has been celebrated, defended, lamented, and mourned by religious fundamentalists, political pundits, and talk show hosts across North America" (2010: 120–21).

Finally, in 2007, Sprinkle and Stephens held their wedding ceremony in Calgary, Alberta, where same-sex marriage was legal under Canadian law. In 2007, what was an acceptable and actual reality in one country remained an unacceptable and subjunctive reality in another. Modifying Dickinson's claim slightly, however, it is clear in hindsight that Sprinkle and Stephens were not simply countering a conventional social norm; they were establishing a new one. Within their network of friends, gay marriage was already becoming the new normal, a situation in their minority bioculture that Sprinkle and Stephens helped to legitimate and hurry toward wider acceptance. As we have seen in this chapter, performances may not change the law right away, but they often nudge social norms in one direction or another. The increasingly widespread legality of same-sex marriage in several states and the constitutional logic of equal protection under the law finally led the Supreme Court to legalize same-sex marriage across the nation.

Austin's 1955 attempt to distinguish between performative utterances that are consequential and fictitious statements that have no real-world results was misleading. Following Enaction theory, we may call something real when it can cause something to happen. As already noted, all modes of speech, "performative" in Austin's terms or not, cause real actions and all actions – whether on stage, in a wedding ceremony, or behind a presidential podium – have consequences. They may not have the same kinds of consequences, of course, but performances do shape distributed networks, from neuronal connections to cultural-cognitive ecologies, and, like Mandela's speech-making, can alter contingent realities. As noted in Chapter 1, languaging is primarily another way of taking action; it is not simply a representational matter of symbols and signs. From an Enactive perspective, all performance is performative, even in the narrow sense of the term meant by Austin.

Fearing the possible constitutive role played by performance, some rulers, churchmen, and philosophers have sought to restrict the role of performance in their cultures, especially in the theater. Theater scholar Jonas Barish reports that antitheatrical prejudice may be traced in western culture to the philosophy of Plato. In *The Republic*, he banned the theater from his notion of a utopia because he believed that most citizens should not use their imaginations to think beyond the roles assigned to them by the state. As Barish illustrates, many western rulers and churchmen restricted the kinds of roles that actors could perform, persecuted their profession, and even prohibited actors from burial on sacred ground. Antitheatrical prejudice in the West flourished among Puritans and strict Catholics from 1550 to 1900 and even surfaced during revolutionary times. Jean-Jacques Rousseau argued against the theater on the grounds that role-playing simply masked and confused a person's true identity, which should be transparent to all in a virtuous republic. Many ardent republicans took up Rousseau's prejudices during the French Revolution. During the American Revolutionary War, the Continental Congress banned all theatrical performances because it feared the theater would sap the single-minded energy needed for the fight. It is probably safe to say that no patriotic American at that time (even George Washington, who loved the theater) ever imagined that an actor, Ronald Reagan, might one day become the President of the United States.

There is probably a cognitive basis for antitheatrical prejudice. A good case can be made that many of those who attack the theater suffer from anxiety about the inherent flexibility of the embodied self and the cognitive operations of metaphor and blending that allow our species to play subjunctive games with identity and reality. Barish suggests that the very nature of the theater evokes "ontological queasiness" in some people because of their fear of "impurity, of contamination, of 'mixture,' of the blurring of strict boundaries" (Barish 1981: 3, 87). The blurring of concepts, of course, is what metaphors and blends are all about; role-players involved in sports and music as well as in the theater primarily "live in the blend" during their performances. For this reason, although the theater may evoke more "ontological queasiness" than other genres of performance, it makes sense to rename the problem the "antiperformative prejudice."

CHAPTER 4

The dynamics of making meanings

While affects guide meaning-making, they do so within the broader context of a dynamic system that brings together embodied interactions among our brains, bodies, and surrounds. Many scientists working within the Enaction approach turn to dynamic systems theory (DST) for guidance in proposing and testing their hypotheses. The basic idea that people and/or other animate beings are parts of systems (i.e., involved with others through recurring patterns of mental, bodily, and ecological interactions) and that these systems are dynamic (i.e., capable of self-generating change over time) has been an accepted part of cognitive and social scientific explanations for a long time. I have already used parts of DST to explain Edwin Hutchins's notion of the cultural-cognitive ecosystem as an approach for understanding the history and emergence of performance genres.

Chapter 4 synthesizes insights from previous chapters to provide a sketch of the major components of DST for spectators at all performances. A part of our general perception–action system, the "spectating system," to coin a term, entails interactions and emerging dynamics among goal setting, sensual perceiving, experiencing image schemas, remembering, and learning – all within affects and emotions that guide the system. While the precise relations among these processes cannot yet be mathematically specified, these elements do appear to be important in maintaining spectatorship and generating change in the system over time. Most of these processes occur in a matter of milliseconds and remain below the level of consciousness, but occasional moments of feeling and learning may surface. Following my overview of DST for spectators, the rest of the chapter examines some of the consequences of this spectating system for performance theory, criticism, and history.

Starting performance events

Before audiences can engage their spectating systems, they must be ready to experience what they will see, hear, and do during a performance.

As discussed in Chapter 1, nearly all performance events require some preparation before they can get going. For spectators, this process may range from preparations that include (1) season ticket purchasing, arranging for a babysitter, travel and parking, dinner, walking to an opera house, finding reserved seats, chatting and reading the program, and applauding the conductor as s/he makes an entrance and the houselights begin to dim; to (2) sitting down on a couch in a living room, finding the remote, turning on the television, and pushing a few buttons to get to the right station; or even to (3) clicking a computer mouse a few times to open up the right website. Each of these processes assumes that the production, whether an opera, a TV sitcom, or a pornographic video, is spectator-ready and takes the viewer from the beginning to the end of the start-up process.

Aside from these kinds of actions, spectator preparation for any performance also involves expectation, which is necessarily keyed to memory and the local cultural-cognitive ecosystem. Within this ecosystem, genre-specific networks include a working knowledge of conventional practices for most spectators. One way of approaching the tricky problem of a spectator's expectations is through James J. Gibson's notion of "affordances." Gibson wrote about ecological psychology in the 1960s and 1970s. From his perspective, organism-surround interactions involve reciprocal relationships; all organisms have certain potentials for interactions within an environment, given the capabilities of the organism and the possibilities and constraints of the environment. Gibson termed such allowances "affordances," moving the verb form of "to afford" into a noun. One affordance of a chair, for instance, is sitting, allowing for a reciprocal relationship between human sitting and the environmental possibility of a chair. Although Gibson used his notion of affordances primarily to chart organism-spatial interactions, the term can also be used metaphorically to look at the potential fit between genres of performance and audience enjoyment.

All performances afford certain kinds of experiences (and not others) for spectators. Audience members at a live opera may enjoy the mix of music, acting, and spectacle from a fixed point in the auditorium, for example, but they cannot shift their visual perspective on the action to another point in the theater because the affordances of a live performance (unlike a film) do not allow it. Watching a popular law enforcement melodrama on television can provide a viewer with some assurance that her life in the city will be safe, but (unlike some church rituals) it will not afford her the security of knowing that ultimate justice rules in the universe. Finally, the masturbator watching pornography cannot direct the naked couples on the video to proceed at the speed of his own arousal; unlike his lived experiences with the performance of a prostitute, for example, he will know that his affordances when watching porn cannot include the possibility of control over the pace of the video sex. Just as the affordances of all performances rule out some expectations, they also heighten others. Operagoers desire to be reduced to tears by certain arias, viewers of law and order melodramas often want their sense of social morality confirmed, and masturbators seek to watch the right kinds of kinky moves among the right kinds of couples for their pleasure. The affordances of all past performances will invariably shape viewer expectations about the performance to come.

While spectators at some performances may hope to re-live exactly what that performance delivered for them in the past – some spectators return many times to the same musical comedy, stand-up performer, or even the same sports event hoping to replicate their experience – most spectators use the start-up period (however short it may be) to separate themselves from their normal lives and to begin the transition to play. Because performance derives evolutionarily from mammalian play, it is not surprising that some of the relaxation, happiness, and focused attention that accompany animal play should begin to animate many spectators preparing to enjoy a performance. Significantly, Panksepp and Biven understand **play** as both a type of activity and the emotion produced by that activity. They borrow a recent definition of childhood play from Gordon Burghardt, who notes several criteria of play that recur in all young mammals, three of which are particularly relevant for adults enjoying performances: "(1) play is a spontaneous activity, done for its own sake because it is fun (pleasurable); (2) play exhibits many repetitive activities, done with abundant variations, unlike serious behaviors that are not as flexible; and (3) animals must be well fed, comfortable, and healthy for play to occur, and all stressors reduce play" (quoted in Panksepp and Biven 2012: 352). Like children, adults choose to **play**, they enjoy repeating play activities, with many variations, and too much stress, from any source, cuts into the positive emotion of **play**.

Panksepp and Biven emphasize that rough-and-tumble play – i.e., pretend fighting – tends to be the most pleasurable form of play for all young mammals. In such contests, the young tacitly agree not to hurt the other as they test and refine their physical abilities through play fighting. Scientists have found that only the nervous systems of "winning" rats deliver dopamine rewards in real fighting – losing rats in a real fight get no chemical payoffs – whereas all young rats receive dopamine gratification in rough-and-tumble **play**. "How do we know **play** 'fighting' is affectively positive?" they ask. "Both 'winners' and 'losers' of play 'fights' rapidly learn instrumental tasks, such as making fast and appropriate choices in a T-maze, *in order to gain the opportunity to play* [again]," they state (2012: 363). In other words, all players can become dopamine "winners" when they engage in pretend fighting. The importance of rough-and-tumble play for all mammals suggests two other conclusions, as well. First, we should not be surprised that activities of performance for adults can encompass negative as well as positive emotions. Sports teams lose, actor/characters in dramatic tragedies die, and sometimes flesh-and-blood people must be sacrificed in religious rituals. Sometimes the "bad" things that occur to individuals in all play activities may work toward "good" social ends, but sometimes not. In any case, mammalian play cannot be reduced to anodyne "fun," as some theorists of performance have tried to do. There is much more going on in play fighting than amusement and escape. Second, although Panksepp and Biven do not say so, it may be that nearly all adult play and performance take the form of social conflict because such agonistic "us vs. them" relationships are reminiscent of childhood rough-and-tumble **play** for adult spectators.

For most, active spectating probably begins soon after they couple their attention to the performers and to their surround near the end of the start-up period. I noted in Chapter 2 that coupling is a normal, even necessary part of animal life to ensure that living things are in touch and in tune with the relevant cultural-cognitive elements in their ecological surrounds. Human survival depended upon such unconscious coupling in the past, and we continue to rely on visual, auditory, kinesthetic, and sometimes haptic coupling today. Spectators attend all performances with the bodily knowledge that they have coupled their awareness with performance situations in the past and they usually expect, without even knowing that they do so, to continue such coupling in the future. Unless a spectator is ill, mentally impaired, or very distracted, coupling will happen automatically. Coupling, then, is not the same as spectator immersion in a performance narrative or contest, although it may lead to such rapt attention later in the event; it is simply an awareness of the general affordances of the performance situation, allowing for the engagement of mirror neurons should animate, intentional action occur. A spectator's eyes, ears, and memory tell him or her, in effect, "Here I am in a large space with many others attending to actor-singers performing on stage," or "Here I am clicking my mouse and waiting for some hot action." Coupling is only the first step in engaging with a performance, but without it there can be no future emotional rewards.

Because all stressors impair playful engagement, the places for performances are usually free of distractions that might get in the way of spectatorial expectations. This aspect of spectating depends upon a safe and secure ecological surround, a surround that often includes other people. While optimal viewing conditions in the West typically vary among sports events and classical musical concerts, both sports stadiums and concert halls provide a mix of social stimulation and opportunities for focused attention that are appropriate to the expectations of sports fans and music lovers. Unfortunately, mediated performances on television or computer screens at home are often interrupted – by live distractions, commercials, or through a spectator's search for more immediate stimulation – with the result that many viewers today probably have lower attention spans for performances than previous generations of audiences. Although having to decouple and recouple attention from performances on home entertainment systems can be frustrating, most spectators are now accustomed to such interruptions.

Unless viewer coupling with a performance faces too many initial obstacles, most spectators will usually **seek** to entrain their bodily rhythms with the rhythms of the performance during the start of the show. As A.C. Bluedorn defines it, "Entrainment is the process in which the rhythms displayed by two or more phenomena become synchronized, with one of the rhythms often being more powerful or dominant and capturing the rhythm of the other. This does not mean, however, that the rhythmic patterns will coincide or overlap exactly; instead it means the patterns will maintain a *consistent relationship* with each other" (cited by Clayton, Sager, and Will 2004: 10). Such consistent rhythmic relationships are common throughout nature – in the synchronized flashing of fireflies at night, the shared speech rhythms of a human conversation, and the repetitious pattern of menstrual cycles among women who live together over several months, for example. Chronobiologists who study such matters have found that most of the body's major systems – breathing, heart rate, digestion, emotional response – are loosely entrained together. Like coupling, entrainment occurs unconsciously.

Regarding performances, performers generally take the lead in entraining audiences. That is, they will establish recurrent patterns in the rhythms of their own moving, breathing, vocalizing, musicing, etc. that will gradually lead most spectators to adopt a consistent relationship with the rhythms of the performance. In the film *Titanic*, for example, Cameron took his spectators underwater for several of the opening sequences, inducing a slow-motion (and dream-like) rhythm appropriate for the start of his memory-infused drama. Because of their reliance on musical rhythms, concerts, together with operas and dance events, can usually establish a fairly tight bond of entrainment with their audience. Entrainment tends to be looser in sports events and other contests, primarily because the moment-to-moment rhythms and energy levels of most games vary widely. (Spectators at sports competitions sometimes make up for this fact through rhythmic cheers involving physical moves, such as body "waves," to induce more entrainment than the game itself can usually sustain.) Nonetheless, spectators generally seek to entrain themselves to the rhythms of a performance; it is more enjoyable that way. One music researcher found that even listeners to sounds with widely varying beats would "entrain to what s/he perceives as the 'centered' or medium period length" of the rhythm (Clayton, Sager, and Will 2004: 15). Because performers in musical and dramatic events usually begin as the dominant forces in setting the rhythms for their shows, they will pay a penalty in spectator discomfort if they abruptly break from their established patterns and shift to widely varied rhythms.

Spectators, by contrast, can and do drop in and out of the entrained rhythms of a performance. As we have discussed, the conceptual integration that spectators unconsciously use to merge players and their roles in a performance can be consciously unblended to examine player or role separately. Questions such as "Why did that singer covering Bob Dylan's 'Tambourine Man' decide to perform it very differently from him" become possible when the new singer's performance is de-blended into its component parts. It seems that imagining different possibilities for the singer or the song can momentarily knock an auditor out of her or his entrainment with the general flow of the piece, which partly depends on engagement in the subjunctive reality of the blend. The auditor will usually remain coupled to the performance situation during this time, though, because the material circumstances of the performance, whether live or mediated, will not have changed. Because entrainment heightens enjoyment, however, most auditors most of the time will prefer to remain in the comfort zone of the patterned flow. A few drop-outs from an entrained audience will have little effect on most live performers, but the widespread scrambling of entrained audience rhythms – often signaled in musical concerts by an eruption of coughing among many auditors – can unnerve performers. While these general relationships among coupling, entrainment, and blending probably occur as I have discussed them, I am aware of no empirical experiments that have validated these conclusions.

Toward a spectating system for performances

Following the usual establishment of coupling and entrainment by the "end of start," most spectators will **seek** to become fully engaged in the performance. As noted, spectators may break from their entrainment at any time – to look at the program, channel surf, run to the kitchen for a slice of pizza, or to unblend the experience to consider where else they may have seen that performer – but they will usually **seek** to reconnect with the performance upon their mental and physical return. This is simply because, for most of us most of the time, immersion in **play** is more rewarding than other ways of passing the time. Our immersion engages what may be called a "spectating system" for performances. This dynamic system, a part of our general perception–action system, usually works intermittently until the performance is over. One of the primary takeaways from this section will be the importance of dynamic processing for the generation and emergence of spectatorial meaning.

Scientists have applied dynamic systems theory (DST) to kinds of systems that vary widely in scope and duration – from single cells within a human heart to individual humans in a given city population and from the millisecond activation of visual attention to the weeks-long process that infants go through when they learn how to extend an arm and hand to be able to grasp an object. As these examples suggest, experiments based in the assumptions of DST have been helpful to scientists interested in testing for specific kinds of autonomy, sense-making, and experience within the Enaction paradigm. Very little of the evidence gained from DST experiments so far, however, is directly relevant to the concerns of performance studies scholars. A few scholars have applied the generalities of DST to performance situations, including John Lutterbie and Evelyn Tribble, but even this descriptive work is still in its infancy. My interest here is in outlining the likely major components of spectating as a dynamic system and in suggesting how they probably interact to produce self generating changes over time. I hope that this book will encourage scientists oriented to Enaction and DST to begin probing our field for testable hypotheses and experiments that provide confirmable results.

In their *Mind as Motion: Explorations in the Dynamics of Cognition*, editors Robert F. Port and Timothy van Gelder use an example from a tennis game to illustrate the kind of situation that DST is designed to account for, describe, and eventually measure. This example has particular relevance for common and recurrent situations in performance studies:

> The ball is approaching; you are perceiving its approach, are aware of the other player's movements, are considering the best strategy for the return, and are shifting into position to play the stroke. *All this is happening at the same time.* As you move into place, your perspective on the approaching ball is changing, and hence so is activity on your retina and in your visual system. It is your evolving sense of how to play the point that is affecting your movement. The path of the approaching ball affects which strategy would be best and hence how you move. *Everything is simultaneously affecting everything else.* (ital. in original) (Port and Gelder 1995: 23)

Port and Gelder describe this example as a relatively closed system with its own neuronal, corporal, and ecological parameters (the nervous system and brain of the player, the player's moving body, an approaching ball and moving opponent within the bounds of a tennis court, etc.). Their perspective is first-person, centered on one player's brain, body, and immediate surround. Following the rigors of DST description, Port and Gelder also specify that the system evolves in real time (perhaps the three seconds or so it takes a ball to travel from one side of the court before it is hit by the player on the opposite side). Assuming the second player successfully returns the tennis ball, a new system at this level of play could be discerned and investigated to describe the next exchange from the first player's perspective.

Next, notice the similarity between the moment-to-moment points of a tennis game as a DST system and this example from Richard Kemp, which occurs near the beginning of his *Embodied Acting: What Neuroscience Tells Us About Performance*:

> It all happens at once. It has to. The impulse, the breath, the speech, the gesture, the walk, the awareness of the guy in the fifth row who's nodding off, so I punch up the end of the line that bit harder. And because I punched harder, my partner is surprised and jolted into her response with that extra calorie of spontaneity, which crackles the air, and the audience almost imperceptibly sits up, drawn in, more alert. It all happens at once. (Kemp 2012: 1)

Again, the author describes a system – here an instance of two actors sparking a heightened audience response – that also occurs over time, in this case perhaps three seconds during a theatrical performance. One difference between this system and the tennis example is that it is centered on interactions among three people (and eventually more, because the whole audience is pulled into it by the end). Kemp also emphasizes a minor adjustment made by him that ends up shaping the course of the interaction in a major way. As we know, tennis games tend to work in the same ways; the intentions and relative autonomy of the agents matter in the ongoing interactions of the dynamic system as a whole.

Notice that the brain-, bodily, and ecologically based interactions in the tennis game and theatrical performance are coupled; these three components of the system are continuously interacting in time. If we could freeze the evolution of a dynamic system to examine an fMRI snapshot of one of its brain-based components in operation, we could get a sense of that neural component for a particular millisecond, but it could not be the whole picture. Enactive systems do not "begin" in the head and radiate outward into the body and environment. In a real sense, they do not "begin" at all; even in sleep, our brains, bodies, and surroundings are in continual interaction. Our mental and corporal coupling with the world only ceases when we die. Until that time, "everything is simultaneously affecting everything else," as Port and Gelder affirm. This is an exciting insight that holds significant potential for performance studies, but as yet it is more suggestive than scientifically predictive.

While Port and Gelder note several mathematical models that have successfully captured the dynamics of various human systems, they also recommend other alternatives for systems in which time-series data are unavailable and probably impossible to isolate and track. One of these is "dynamical description;" Port and Gelder give as an example the work of Esther Thelen, who has described the process by which motor skills emerge and change in infants as they attempt to reach and grasp for nearby objects. According to the editors, "Thelen pays close attention to the exact shape of individual gestures at particular intervals in the developmental process, and focuses on the specific changes that occur in each individual subject, rather than the gross changes that are inferred by averaging over many subjects. It is only in the fine details of an individual subject's movements and their change over time that the real shape of the dynamics of development is revealed" (1995: 17). Thelen's "dynamical description," her focus on changes in particularities over short intervals of time, offers a possible future model of investigation for joint projects between performance studies scholars and cognitive psychologists.

Lacking such fine-grained studies, however, we must approach DST for spectating at a more general level. Walter J. Freeman, in his engagingly titled book, *How Brains Make Up Their Minds* (2000), provides an appropriate way forward for an approach to the perception–action system that animates spectators:

> Our actions [which for Freeman would include the actions of spectators] emerge through a continuous loop that we can divide into three stages. The first stage is the emergence and elaboration within our brains of goals concerning future states. The goals are in nested layers, ranging from what we do in the next few seconds to our ultimate survival and enjoyment of life. The second stage of the loop involves acting and receiving the sensory consequences of actions and constructing their meanings. In the third stage, we modify our brains by learning, which guides each successive emergent pattern. These three stages are accompanied by dynamic processes in the brain and body that prepare the body for forthcoming actions and enable it to carry them out. My view is that we observe and experience these preparations as emotions... (Freeman 2000: 91–92)

For Freeman, the spectator dynamic system may be said (arbitrarily) to begin with human intentions and goals, move to actions and receptions, and conclude with learning, before cycling forward again.

We can look for some validation of Freeman's educated hunch about the importance of the emotions in this process from the synthesis of neuroscientific, psychological, and behavioral evidence concerning emotion and sense-making offered by Giovanna Colombetti, cited in the previous chapter. Objecting to current conceptions of emotion that rely on "abstract cognitive-evaluative processes," Colombetti insists that "emotion should be conceptualized as a faculty of the whole embodied and situated organism" (Colombetti 2010: 146). She draws on Varela's understanding of autopoiesis to note that emotions are the primary means by which human organisms arrive at goals to "continuously regenerate the conditions of their own survival" (2010: 147). In her recent book, *The Feeling Body: Affective Science Meets the Enactive Mind* (2013), Colombetti notes her agreement with Freeman's general approach to DST. She summarizes the evidence that all affects, including emotions, continually exert regulating and energizing influences on our actions, including conscious cognition. As she explains, affective episodes do not constitute a distinct step in the perception–action sequence. Rather, emotional durations are "an inescapable, pervasive dimension of brain activity on which sensory information impinges and from which action progresses" (Colombetti 2013: 64). Contrary to the common understanding of cognition channeling emotional energy to perform tasks, our emotions energize neurocognitive resources to guide intentional actions, which, in turn, set the stage for meaning-making, which is also suffused with emotion. How all of this fits together within the dynamic system of spectating is still beyond scientific confirmation, but Colombetti's insights, which draw on the work of Panksepp and Damasio, at least provide a clearer understanding of the probable links among affect, goal-setting, and learning.

Freeman emphasizes the importance of learning in his perception–action system. Recall from Chapter 1 that learning requires prior action and builds upon the attribution of meaning, plus the temporary storage of that meaning in memory. The example I gave in that chapter involved learning the differences between a growling guard dog and a whimpering puppy and creating simulations in our brains for both types. Following Freeman, our learning leads to memories of past interactions with dogs and we can use that learning to help us elaborate future intentional goals (both immediate and long range) regarding possible relations with "man's best friend." Learning often occurs more quickly than that, however. Even within a second – as when a smile aimed at another person produces a glance away, which then leads the smiling person to change his face to a serious expression – we can see that Freeman's third stage of learning will often produce new action. Freeman notes that his three stages work together to create recurring loops of interactivity that continuously generate actions. Most Enaction theorists would agree that this notion of ever-changing loops spiraling forward to shape our lives through time is a good metaphor to describe an agent's dynamical sense-making, goal-setting, learning, and survival. The main question for this section, then, is how the goals, actions, and learning of spectators generate, modify, and perpetuate these dynamic, intentional loops.

Over the duration of a performance event, spectators set various goals for themselves, some of which are realized very quickly while others may take the entire performance to accomplish. In general, these goals probably function within the durations of Plantinga's local, direct, and global responses, though this had not been confirmed empirically for all kinds of performances. **Seeking** to discover if the basketball team will score in the next round of play and gradually learning who will win the game are related, nested goals of different magnitudes, as Freeman suggests. And both goals are a part of an individual's, and sometimes a society's, sense of well-being and potential for survival. "Winning" teams, characters, and even musical rhythms help biocultures to feel good about their heroes, their values, and their actions, and individuals often adopt goals that will facilitate such social affirmation by the end of the performance. By transforming negative emotions into positive ones, *Titanic* served that purpose as well as others.

In his *Dynamic Patterns: The Self-Organization of Brain and Behavior* (1995), J.A. Scott Kelso recognizes the importance of coupling and entrainment among animate beings as the basis for their dynamic interactions. Kelso's ideas are generally in line with Freeman's and Colombetti's thoughts about DST. Like Varela, Thompson, and Rosch, Kelso also separates living systems from inanimate ones on the basis of autopoiesis. In *Dynamic Patterns*, Kelso distinguishes DST from other approaches that have dominated past thinking about brains, bodies, and behavior – behaviorism, ethology, and a computational understanding of cognition. I will rely on Kelso's *Dynamic Patterns* to describe the primary elements of dynamic systems and the general process that causes the patterns of the spectating system among spectators to emerge and change through time.

Enjoying Richard Pryor's heart attack

Many of the systems that Kelso describes in animal brains and bodies are barely within the reach of intentional goal-setting – cell mitosis, the development of locomotion in lamprey eels, and the emergence of color and line patterning on the wings of butterflies, for example. Midway through his book, Kelso turns to intentional activities among humans and asks, "How does mind get into muscle? How can intentionality... be understood in terms of a physically inspired theory of biological and behavioral self-organization?" (Kelso 1995: 137). He finds that the general dynamic processes are the same, though more complex, for systems in which higher-order thinking also matters, as it certainly does for watching a game of squash or participating as a congregant at an evangelical Christian ritual. Kelso specifies four major elements involved in taking the brain, body, and the ecological surround through Freeman's three-step DST process: boundary conditions, attractors, perturbations, and phase shifts. Kelso's articulation of these interacting elements has been widely influential. As we will see, these four elements constitute the constraint-satisfaction system of dynamic processing noted by Hutchins.

I will use the stand-up routine and recorded audience response to part of a classic comic monologue performed by Richard Pryor to illustrate Kelso's four dynamic elements. In *Richard Pryor: Live in Concert*, initially recorded at a theater in Long Beach, California in 1978 and released the next year, Pryor tells many funny stories to the racially mixed audience, most with himself as the butt of the joke. About a third of the way into his concert, the comedian recounts his experience of a recent heart attack, widely reported in the media, which nearly killed him. As Pryor demonstrates, he was walking along in his front yard when the attack grabbed him – which he personifies as a huge wrench tightening around his heart. The attack forces the comedian onto one knee, then down on the ground, where Pryor writhes on his back. Still hanging on to his microphone, he makes an emergency call to God, only to be put on hold by a bored female angel in Heaven. Pryor passes out and later wakes up in an ambulance surrounded by white people. Thinking he has died and gone to the wrong heaven, he says, "Now I got to listen to Lawrence Welk for the rest of my days." Following this comic climax, Pryor pulled his audience out of the situation with sincere compliments to the doctors, nurses, and interns who saved his life. The audience in 1978 loved this two-and a-half minute turn and I still laugh out loud every time I watch it, now in digitized format for computer viewing. Perfectly attuned to white guilt and U.S. racism in the 1970s, Pryor was a master at ramping up black–white anxieties for comic and progressive effects. (Although Pryor's treatment of women in this self-authored concert now comes across as woefully sexist, that part of his act had little effect on audible audience response in 1978.)

In order to formulate a possible goal with regard to a specific stimulus – in this instance, how to respond to Pryor's simulated heart attack in the midst of his concert – intending spectators in 1978 worked within what Kelso calls the appropriate "boundary conditions" of the situation, also known as "control parameters." Let us assume that these boundary constraints will include the fact that the spectator is sitting in the Terrace Theatre in Long Beach in 1978 and has been enjoying Pryor's concert. While s/he knows that several cameras are recording the show, that knowledge has receded in memory as more immediate comic stimuli have commanded his/her attention. As a part of the set-up to his story, Pryor mentions his heart attack, which will lead the viewer to expect some comic riffs from him on this personal experience. The spectator may be wondering how Pryor could get any fun out of his recent brush with death, but is probably ready to find out; the comic has already insulted foolish white people, parodied fussy black women, and personified sympathetic talking dogs – so why not? Boundary conditions for spectatorship, then, involve the physical surround of the spectator, relevant biocultural learning concerning the situation (including, in this case, some knowledge of U.S. racial relations, an awareness of Pryor's politically radical and foul-mouthed reputation, and a general knowledge of the usual conventions of stand-up comedy), plus recent memories generated by the images and sounds of the performance so far. All of these factors can help our spectator to predict and make sense of what is coming next. They are the "parameters," the constraints within which the auditor expects to gain the general satisfaction of laughter while enjoying Pryor's retelling of his heart attack story. Of course the spectator will also bring her or his own sense of racial oppression, entitlement, emotional baggage, and any other personal memories experienced as relevant into this mix as well. Nonetheless, by setting up expectations, boundary conditions help both to constrain and to guide our spectator's future responses and intentional actions.

In the case of listening to Pryor's heart attack story, the spectator may be initially torn between two possible actions: to join in **sympathy** with Pryor and empathize with him about this experience or, secondly, to shut out any stories about heart attacks – perhaps the spectator is just recovering from his own heart problems – by disengaging from Pryor's storytelling. The first alternative would allow him to remain within the fictional flow of the comic narrative, while the second would temporarily end the story's claim on his attention and emotions. Both possibilities are what Kelso would term "attractors"; either might be a desirable response to the immediate stimulus within the present boundary conditions of the spectating system. In general, attractors are satisfying because they evoke emotions that will promote long- and short-term survival and flourishing. Following Freeman, we can say that the immediate and long-term goals of the spectator shape the construction of both attractors. In effect, our recent heart attack victim needs to decide, "Can I stand more **fear**, which might get my heart racing, or should I just try to relax and enjoy myself?" Both options have some likely near-term survival value. This is rarely a completely conscious decision, of course; the body-mind of the spectator will sense the better possibility and prepare accordingly.

Let us assume that the spectator has enjoyed himself so far and that his body seeks further relief from tension through the laughter that a good comic can provide. He unconsciously sets a goal of seeking more of the same emotional release and continues to empathize and **sympathize** with Pryor. All of this has happened in the fifteen seconds or so that it takes Pryor to set up his heart attack story. By the end of this introduction, he is walking casually on stage, just as (presumably) he was walking easily in his front yard, when suddenly he stops and commands himself in the voice of Mr. Heart Attack, "Don't breathe!" Finely attuned to the differences between the norms of white and black U.S. speech, Pryor barks the line like a tough white boss commanding the new black man on the job. The image schema at play here is COMPULSION, which has gripped Pryor around his heart and is twisting him into obedience. Already frozen in mid-stride, Pryor, surprised by a sudden jolt of pain, starts to crumple physically and gasps, "I'm not breathing" several times under his breath.

In Kelso's terms, this is a "phase shift." Actually, the spectator will experience two phase shifts here, one quickly following another. The first is Pryor's shift from introductory remarks to the audience as he walks across the stage to his abrupt stop and his voiced command as Mr. Heart Attack. The second shift is Pryor's "I'm not breathing" response to the Man. From a situation involving casual conversation with his spectators about heart attacks, Pryor has suddenly immersed the audience in the viciousness of an actual attack and then shifted again to reexperience that attack through his own body and voice as the Victim. Pryor's experience of COMPULSION generates pain and **fear**. Perversely – and probably only half-consciously for most of the audience – Mr. Heart Attack sounds like a white boss and the Victim of his inflicted pain, of course, is a cringing black man. Pryor must have known that this added racial dynamic would heighten the comic effect; judging from the laughter in 1978, he was right.

Perhaps the most common reason for a phase shift in spectating is new learning. Assuming our spectator was paying attention at the time and not distracted by others in the audience, he saw and heard the two phase shifts and learned from both directly through the attunement of his body to Pryor's. Specifically, he learned through emotional experience what a heart attack feels like. Kelso is clear that learning leads to major shifts in dynamic patterns: "Learning doesn't just strengthen the memory trace or the synaptic connections between inputs and outputs; *it changes the whole system*," which often includes some of the boundary conditions and most of the attractors (1995: 161). In the case of *Richard Pryor: Live in Concert*, the two phase shifts led immediately to two contrasting emotional responses from spectators: **fear** of Mr. Heart Attack and the withdrawal of **sympathy** from the Victim. Audience members will continue to empathize with Pryor, to understand his point of view as he suffers, but most will restrain their **caring**. This is because Pryor objectifies his body at the moment when the heart attack strikes – he turns it into a quivering lump of pain – and spectators welcome this comic objectification because they do not want to feel that pain themselves. The logic of this objectification is the same as what occurs when we laugh at a man who slips on a banana peel and falls down; if we felt his pain, the incident could not be amusing. The old saw about pain never being funny unless it happens to someone else is absolutely true here, and it relates directly to our survival-based need to avoid pain and increase pleasure. Comic performers of their own pain often use phase shifts to constrain spectator **sympathy** and to enable their satisfaction.

Pryor's decision to immerse the audience in the experience of his heart attack changed the initial basis of the skit. Spectators who probably anticipated some first-person, self-deprecating jokes about heart attacks from a **sympathetic** narrator are now confronted with the disappearance of Pryor's comforting narrative voice and presence and the emergence of a third-person orientation to what they are watching, a dramatized attack involving two characters, the Man and his Victim, both played by Pryor. In effect, Pryor has reblended himself; no longer Pryor/Narrator, he is, alternately, Pryor/Heart Attack and Pryor/Victim. This shift alters the initial boundary conditions and leads to the heightened importance of one of the initial attractors. Although the spectators know that Pryor will not die from this attack – he has survived, after all, to tell his tale – they do not know what will finally release him from the wrenching grip of death. This leads very quickly to what Plantinga has called a "direct emotional response" to the narrative because it sets up the **seeking** that will motivate the rest of the two-minute heart attack story. **Seeking**, from the start a part of most spectators' goals, has become much more "attractive." Spectators will want to continue to avoid the wrenching pain that the COMPULSION of the attack is causing Pryor/Victim and a quick resolution to the story is the best way out of this problem.

Following these two phase shifts, Pryor/Heart Attack twists the chest of Pryor/Victim, forcing him down on one knee, then onto his back with a comment about all of the pork his victim has been eating. During this inexorable tightening of pain, all Pryor/Victim can do is plead, "Don't kill me" many times, very fast. The mounting tension as Victim surrenders to Attack is palpable in Pryor/Victim's voice and body, relieved only by his willing and very funny compliance with anything that Attack demands. From a DST perspective, these quick jabs that reduce Pryor to quivering jelly are "perturbations." In physics, scientists use "perturbation" to denote a change in the orbit of a revolving particle of matter or energy, as in the orbit of an electron around a nucleus or a planet in the solar system. Perturbation has much the same meaning in a dynamic system. If the life-sustaining processes of rhythmic systems that carry life forward are imagined as a series of recurring loops, a perturbation is an alteration in the orbit, the loop, of one of those systems. For our spectator watching and listening to Pryor/Victim as he crumples from standing to one knee to doubled-over on his back during this twenty seconds or so, the rhythmic loops involved in triggering chemical changes in the brain, neuronal firings, hormonal releases, and muscular tension that shift the spectator's body rapidly between tension and release are perturbations, wobbles in the loops of the spectator system moving forward. Perturbations may raise memories from the past (other times when Pryor has personified an authoritative white man who causes him pain, for instance) and sometimes they call attention to new stimuli in a system. Although perturbations do not alter the boundary conditions of the system, they may create new attractors to go with the old ones and cause a change in the relative importance of all attractors in play. In this case, the wrenching pain of COMPULSION will likely heighten spectatorial **seeking** for most spectators; finding relief from the tightening agony will become even more important.

As noted, the perturbations above increased the tension in Pryor's body, which also led to heightened tensions and occasional releases through laughter in the bodies of his spectators. The idea that increased tension and its sudden release often lead to laughter is fundamental to Robert Latta's "cognitive shift" theory of humor. A psychologist who has looked closely at numerous examples of funny situations, Latta finds that laughter almost always occurs in the third step of a three-part process. First, the person who will laugh experiences an increase in physical tension. Next, some stimulus event produces a "cognitive shift" and the person realizes that the state of tension she or he has adopted is no longer necessary. Finally, the spectator "relaxes rapidly or fairly rapidly through laughter" (Latta 1999: 44). Folding Latta's theory into my "spectating system," it is evident that each rise in spectator tension that was resolved through laughter while Pryor was rolling on the ground in pretend pain was a new "perturbation," which caused small changes in the "attractors" already in play in the fictitious situation. Put another way, Pryor the comedian took the audience in and out of his (own) victim's pain, sometimes emphasizing it to raise spectator tensions and at other times commenting on it to induce us to see that the comedian was still in control, thereby popping that tension to release laughter. These perturbations, these rapid shifts in tension, were attractive to audience members in 1978 primarily because they came to Pryor's performance expecting to enjoy themselves through laughter and Pryor delivered. Laughing is fun.

Following these perturbations, several more phase shifts occur during the remaining parts of the story. Pryor returns to his narrative voice and talks directly to the audience about his unending string of "Don't kill me"s and, a moment later, explains to his auditors that he started to think about placing an emergency call to God. Then, miming a telephone in his hand, he returns to the dramatic frame of the story to plead, "Can I talk to God right away, please?" This leads to Pryor/Victim's comic confrontation with the female angel-operator in heaven, neatly impersonated by a nasal-voiced Pryor/Angel, an instance of seraphic BLOCKAGE that causes more laughter. Next comes a rebuke from Pryor/Heart Attack, "Was you trying to talk to God behind my back?" and more laughter. By this point in his story, Pryor has somewhat relaxed the grip of pain on his chest, allowing his spectators to relax as well and enjoy his comic inventiveness. Three-quarters of the way into his heart attack narrative, Pryor leaves room for what I have called, following Plantinga, a "production emotion." That is, the audience is given some breathing room to step back from their entrained immersion in the story, allowed to deblend Pryor from his several characterizations, and encouraged to appreciate him as a comic writer. The wonderful silliness about getting put on hold by an angel and trying to talk to God behind Death's back may easily lead to **admiration** for Pryor's comic genius, a critical judgment based in higher-order consciousness. Following that moment, most spectators will reimmerse themselves in the blends of the performance to experience a final phase shift in Pryor/Victim's recognition, upon his waking up in the ambulance, that Heaven is segregated and he's been taken to the wrong one. COMPELLING Pryor to listen to Lawrence Welk for eternity is the ultimate in victimage!

Because I continue to enjoy Richard Pryor's stand-up routines, it has been easy for me to imagine the typical spectator of 1978 as someone like myself, a liberal white guy aware of America's racist past. On the other hand, I know I have become more knowledgeable and sensitive about such matters in the last thirty-five years; I remember that my response to Pryor when I first heard his recordings many years earlier was more ambivalent – mostly **surprise** and **delight**, but also some confusion and **anger**. My point is simply to underline the continuing importance of racially salient social categories for audience response to performers in the United States. As bad as it is (and partly because of that tension-inducing reason), American racism continues to be a significant source of stand-up humor. In a 2006 study on social cognition, Nalini Ambady et al. discovered that a participant's self-identified race was an important factor in that person's ability to successfully develop empathy for another person. Participants were asked to identify the emotions on the faces of three different "racially salient" targets (white, African American, and Asian American). Not only did the participants display a greater ability to successfully match the facial expressions with the emotions of others in their own social group, they also exhibited more **fear** and **anger** when shown faces that were not a part of their in-group. Ambady et al. found an increase in the activity of the amygdala, the site of these negative emotions, when most of the white participants explained their responses to African American and Asian American faces. The study concluded that "these findings suggest that neural regions specifically involved in recognizing fear and anger show differences in signal change depending on the race of the person expressing the emotion" (2006: 213).

While this experiment was not conducted among audiences and performers, the implications for spectatorship are clear: perceived racial differences probably alter the degree of empathetic response. Pryor's heart attack story depends upon spectatorial empathy for its comic success; what Thompson calls "imaginary transposition," the ability to take the perspective of another person, is key here. At some level, Pryor certainly recognized that he needed to play the victim and the fool, at least part of the time, to ease, if not completely allay, the likely fears of his white spectators in order to encourage their empathetic response to him and his roles. Tellingly, he also chose situations in his concert that easily crossed racial lines – sexual desire, human affection for dogs, and heart attacks, for example. Nonetheless, racial dynamics certainly played an important role in the response of every spectator in 1978, likely affecting memory and learning as well as empathy and the emotions.

This sketch of Freeman's three stages of action within the perception–action system of a spectator outlines a DST approach to the major elements of spectating by focusing primarily on only a minute or so of the video. Even within this limited time frame, I have simplified my discussion of the spectator system to be able to present a general overview of the dynamics involved. Among my simplifications was the timing; in the two-and-a-half minutes of Pryor's heart attack story, the coordinated rhythms of any spectator's perception–action system would probably cycle forward about a hundred times. Working within a DST approach, neuroscientists are presently able to measure neuronal firings, instances of memory recall, muscle activation, and the other dynamics of the perception–action system in milliseconds. While this level of experimentation is not yet possible for spectator–performer interactions, it is clear that timing and duration play crucial roles in the actions and perceptions of audiences.

Timing and meaning

Some contemporary scholars have set up experiments that suggest when meaning actually kicks in for spectators experiencing a dance performance. In her "Structure and Aesthetics in Audience Response to Dance," Kim Vincs places such experiments in the context of an ongoing debate between "poststructuralist" dance scholars who hold that spectators primarily construct the meanings of their experience after the dance is complete and "aesthetic" critics who believe that dance primarily induces spectatorial meaning-making through the moment-to-moment play of moving bodies in space and time. On the poststructuralist side of the debate, according to Vincs, Matthew Reason asserts that "culturally mediated processes of interpretation" during post-performance reflection generally override whatever spectators may have experienced while the dance was occurring. In contrast, Vincs cites Laurence Louppe as representing the importance of the spectators' moment-to-moment construction of meaning during the dance itself. From Vincs's perspective, Loupe believes that "the poetics of dance in fact lie within the organization of the body and its movement – an organization that takes place spatially, in the materiality of the relationship between body parts, and temporally, via the trajectories of the body in space/time, rather than through the naming of movement after the fact" (Vincs 2013: 133).

While the experiments cited by Vincs could not fully settle the debate, they do tend to support what she understands as Louppe's aesthetics over Reason's poststructuralism. As one of the principal investigators in several of the experiments she cites, Vincs herself does not pretend to neutrality in this debate. She notes that the post-performance survey and discussion methodology used by many researchers in the past – wherein spectators were questioned about what they saw and heard during the performance – has tended to favor the social constructivist position of the poststructuralist critics. To counter this method, Vincs and her colleagues equipped spectators with palm-pilot devices that allowed them to continuously record their levels of "engagement" during the dance. By engagement, Vincs means "compelled, drawn in, connected to what is happening, interested in what will happen next" (2013: 135). She and her fellow researchers measured the responses of spectating groups of dance students and experts to a range of dances and then tracked these responses against videos of the dances themselves. "The results of these experiments show that audiences do display some agreement in their responses to dance and that choreographic phrasing in the sense of tension and release – increasing expectation and the fulfillment or delay of expectation – has some bearing on these responses," concludes Vincs (2013: 132). Of particular interest to these empirical researchers were what they termed "gem moments," those spikes in spectator engagement triggered primarily by sudden shifts in movement and the arousal of new expectations.

The conclusions of Vincs and her colleagues about spectator response may be partly understood through the lens of dynamic systems theory (DST). Although Vincs does not use Kelso's DST terminology, it appears that the dynamics of boundary conditions, attractors, perturbations, and phase shifts helped to structure the engagements, expectations, and gem moments she reports. The boundary conditions of spectator–dancer interactions during the performances tested in the experiments apparently facilitated spectator coupling and entrainment. Looking in particular at muscle tension and release, Vincs and others found that spectators distinguished between average levels and spikes of muscle tension through their palm-pilot devices. This is not surprising, of course; it indicates that attuning themselves through their bodies to the variations (perturbations in DST terms) among tension levels was an ongoing attractor for the spectators. To continue their engagement and enjoyment, spectators sought to maintain their sensorimotor coupling with the dancers through their mirror neurons, a matter of low-level empathy. The sudden shifts in tension and movement dynamics that led, says Vincs, to different "expectations," were probably what Kelso would describe as phase shifts. The researchers' experiments were not designed to test the conjunction of emotion, memory, and learning that occurred in those milliseconds, but these instances of meaning were clearly distinctive enough to merit the term "gem moments."

"Gem moment" is an apt metaphor for any instance of performative meaning. For Vincs and her colleagues, these were moments of heightened engagement when the body-mind of the spectators they were testing experienced a moment of clarity about what it means for humans to live and move within the spatiotemporal logic of our world. For Vincs, the ability of dance researchers to isolate and describe gem moments supported her contention that the approach of Laurence Louppe and other "aesthetic" critics provided a better way of describing the kinds of non-verbal insights apparent in audience response to dance than did the methods of poststructuralism. Significantly, Vincs does not deny that the social constructivism favored by Reason and others may occasionally prove insightful. Her point is simply that body-mind responses come first and their timing may have significant consequences, as well, for the post-show construction of meanings. Further, Vincs does not oppose critical attempts to put the emergence of bodily experienced meanings into words. Knowing that meaning precedes language, however, she denies the poststructuralist's strong claim that language invariably constrains how and what performances can mean.

Another reason to prefer "gem moment" as a metaphor for the kind of learning that performance can prompt is the hard materiality and formal clarity implied by the term. Unlike the assumption that knowledge gained from performative experience is invariably vague and evanescent, gem insights have a toughness and stability to their contours that suggest the hard-won rigors of performance artistry. Singers can either hit high "C" or they cannot, a baseball catcher either succeeds or fails to throw out a base runner trying to steal second, and actors faced with a Shakespearean soliloquy either manage the necessary breath control to make sense of the speech or they do not. Much of the best of performance is unforgiving in these ways, and spectators who know this have more opportunities for gem moments of pleasure and insight than those who do not.

While Vincs and her collaborators focused primarily on timing and tension, the possible meanings of a performance for its spectators are also dependent upon memories and image schemas. Like most gems, once they are cut and placed in a setting, image schemas do not change over time. As previously discussed, image schemas depend upon pattern recognition, which relies upon the brain's ability to pick out and "chunk" together similar configurations in action. As cognitive psychologist Raymond Gibbs notes, this makes image schemas "emerging points of stability in a [cognitive] system as it engages in real-world interaction" (cited in Paavolainen 2012: 86). Image schemas provide stable bridges between the flows of action among performers and the perceptions of audience members. Although spectators may still make a variety of meanings from what they are seeing and hearing – although meaning-making remains contingent upon many factors – the significant image schemas of any performance will tend to constrain the kinds of interpretations made by spectators. Vincs reports a similar basis for commonality in the actions that link performative to perceived movements and rhythms. To put this insight in Hutchins's terms with regard to the cultural-cognitive ecosystem at play in a performance, image schemas will tend both to constrain possible attributed meanings and to provide satisfactions within those constraints. In Pryor's heart attack story, for example, the more Pryor experienced the constraint of BLOCKAGE, the more his audience tended to find satisfaction in his comedy.

Unlike concepts, image schemas recur as bundles of interacting relationships that involve our brains, bodies, and immediate material environments. To put this in Enaction terms, these relationships center on recurring structural couplings embedded in flows of action that are prototypically perceived and embodied as experiential gestalts; that is, despite their several interacting parts, we perceive image schemas as complete wholes. For BLOCKAGE to occur in Pryor's role-playing and for his audience to feel it, there must be someone or something preventing a second someone or something from moving in an intended direction. Even in its most abstract form, BLOCKAGE always already entails an embodied scene involving necessary relationships among entities, intentions, and forces, which emerges in perception for both performers and spectators as a coherent whole. Second, as previously noted, role-players create and spectators perceive image schemas across sensory modalities. We can hear BLOCKAGE in a popular song as well as see it in a hockey game. Finally, most image schemas require interaction with a material surround – with an actual place on earth – in order to be realized. Before it can happen, BLOCKAGE in a basketball game, on a chess board, or during a stand-up routine needs at least the force of gravity and a surface upon which the blocking action can occur. Players and spectators need no explanation to understand such embodied realities in space and time; we know them from living on earth. Similar constituent elements are also necessary for MERGING, SCALE, LINK, BALANCE, and the other image schemas that recur in all performances.

Back in the 1980s, many theater and performance theorists and critics looked to semiotics as a relatively stable system of signs by which artists and audiences might understand the meanings of the words, objects, and behaviors in a production. Semiotics, however, was based on the assumption that the meanings of performances could be read like a language and that understanding the performances of different cultures required knowledge of different semiotic "languages." Further, semiotic codes were not cross-modal; moving among visual and behavioral signs usually required different codes, and no one ever invented a reliable semiotics for music and other sounds. In contrast, the image schemas that recur in all performances (and indeed in all human activity) are based in foundational, cross-modal, gestalt types of actions and perceptions. While image schemas are universal to all humans, their meanings may vary widely; how people understand performative instances of BALANCE and BLOCKAGE will depend, as we have seen, on memory, emotion, and the other dynamics of the spectating system. For this reason, image schemas do not offer a new and improved semiotics. But the basis of image schemas in human commonality at least takes away one level of otherness separating genders, classes, races, and cultures from each other that the previous commitment to semiotics could not transcend. As *Homo sapiens*, we know when ATTRACTION, ITERATION, COMPULSION, and the other image schemas are in play in performances and in other areas of life, even though our bioculture does not usually prompt us to recognize these universals. While the full meanings of such actions and perceptions may be illusive, they at least provide a common ground of human experience that semiotics could not facilitate.

The biocultural derailment of *Streetcar*

There is no guarantee, however, that the dynamic interactions among performers and spectators will necessarily lead to what might be called the meanings of a performance generally intended by the artists who made it. Given the importance of memory and timing for the dynamic emergence of learning and meaning, early misperceptions by an audience can become the basis for subsequent misinterpretations, which can later mushroom into wholesale misunderstandings over the duration of a performance. Although I have discussed the importance of current memories for meaning-making, I have said little about the broader neurocognitive networks of memory that spectators always bring with them to performances. Because all performances occur within the constraints and satisfactions of their historical biocultures, as Hutchins has helped us to understand, few spectators are ever completely free of the biases and beliefs prevalent in their cultural-cognitive ecosystems.

One way of investigating the effects of spectator memory on the meanings audiences can make of a dramatic performance experience is to find a past production in which it is clear that most spectators badly misunderstood what the artists of the piece hoped they would find in it. In examining such a case, the cognitively attuned performance historian can do some detective work to figure out where and why during the performance the audience probably "went wrong," even though, in another sense, the perceptions of individual spectators responding within the norms of their bioculture are never completely at fault. Knowledge of human emotions, DST processing, the stages of empathy, and local ecological considerations within the place of the performance might all play a role in such an investigation.

The moderate success of *A Streetcar Named Desire* in 1947 on Broadway and its later triumph on the silver screen provides just such a case. Most New York theater critics greeted the premiere of *Streetcar* with mixed reviews; they recognized the excellence of Williams's play, admired Elia

The biocultural derailment of Streetcar

Kazan's directing, and praised Marlon Brando's Stanley, but a majority found Jessica Tandy's Blanche neurotic and unlikeable (Kolin 2000: 1–33). When the film of *Streetcar* based on a shortened and censored version of the play appeared in 1951, the film critics applauded Vivien Leigh's nuanced and sympathetic Blanche as well as complimenting Kazan and Brando, but they continued to discover many of the same meanings in the script and performances that their Broadway colleagues had discerned – meanings that radically departed from Williams's intentions. Despite their perception of very different Blanches, most of the theater and film critics at mid-century badly misunderstood Williams's protagonist and, consequently, what *Streetcar* might "mean."

In 1947, most of the nine theater reviewers identified Blanche as a sexually voracious, decadent southerner, who was out of touch with reality. Eight of the nine used the term "prostitute," "nymphomanic," or a near-synonym of these words to describe her. Howard Barnes, for example, identified Blanche as a "boozy prostitute," while Robert Coleman typed her as a "paranoic-nymphomaniac." Seven of the nine critics also explained Blanche's actions in the play by referring negatively to her Southern heritage. According to Richard Watts, Blanche represented "a long line of decadent Southern aristocrats," while for Ward Morehouse, she was simply "the faded, shattered daughter of the South." Most reviewers also found fault with Blanche for her delusions and neurosis. John Chapman noted that Blanche "shuns the reality of what she is and takes gallant and desperate refuge in a magical life she has invented for herself." Less charitably, Louis Kronenberger flayed Blanche as "the most demonically driven kind of liar – the one who lies to the world because she must lie to herself." In sum, most of the reviewers in 1947 saw Blanche as sexually predatory or a lying tramp, whose southern past had left her deluded and neurotic (Coffin 1948: 249–52).

Not surprisingly, perhaps, the 1947 critics preferred Brando's Stanley to Tandy's Blanche. William Hawkins summed up this general preference in his comment that Stanley is "an honest animal who needs no motivation for anything he does other than he wants to do it at that particular time." Five of the nine reviewers expressed variations on this theme, which effectively eliminated Stanley's agency in the climactic rape scene of the play. While none of the reviewers applauded Stanley's rape of Blanche, most ignored it or used euphemisms to evade its implications; the word "rape" occurred in none of the reviews. Complementing this perception of the story, three reviewers also dismissed Blanche as fated and hopeless. For Richard Watts, for instance, *Streetcar* was the story of "a doomed Southern girl."

Richard Barnes called attention to the universal qualities of Blanche's "tragic destiny," her inevitable "degradation" in the midst of "cruelty, kindness, and sheer animal living" (1948: 249–52). For these critics, Blanche, predestined for destruction, was doomed to end up in an institution even before Stanley laid a hand on her.

The eight national film critics that reviewed *Streetcar* in 1951 spoke more frankly about Stan's violence and several blamed him for Blanche's destruction. Although the critics continued to praise Brando, several of them found his Stanley both more vicious and vulgar than had their theatrical counterparts in 1947, in part due to camera close-ups of the **anger** and **disgust** expressed on his face. Nonetheless, several film reviewers continued to suggest that Leigh/Blanche's situation was hopeless to begin with; Manny Farber in *The Nation* called her "a rotten old Dixie apple fated for squashing," for example (Farber 1951: 173). In addition, despite Hollywood censorship of some of Blanche's more erotic moments, two reviewers retained the adjective "nymphomaniac" to describe her. The film critics of Vivien Leigh's Blanche also understood her as deluded and neurotic, but tended to cite factors beyond her control for this problem. Where most Broadway critics avoided expressing warm **sympathy** for Tandy/Blanche at the end of the play, Leigh's softer Blanche did evoke more pity; three film reviewers used the term "poignant" to describe their general feelings about Blanche's situation. On the whole, however, these critics sympathized with Leigh/Blanche because of her presumed mental illness. The critic for *Newsweek* who found Blanche "very moving" cited "a pathetic mixture of feminine grace and dementia" as the reason for his response (1951: 87).

Only two critics came close to Tennessee Williams's hope for a generally **compassionate** response to his protagonist. For the playwright, Stanley's rape of Blanche was "the ravishment of the tender, the sensitive, the delicate, by the savage and brutal forces in modern society" (cited in Cohan 1997: 318). Brooks Atkinson was the most **sympathetic** Broadway critic regarding Blanche; he concluded his review, "Out of poetic imagination and ordinary compassion, [Williams] has spun a poignant and humane story." (Coffin 1948: 251). Among the film reviewers, *Commonweal* critic Philip T. Hartung believed that Blanche, despite her difficult past, "could still be saved." Williams and Kazan, he said, tell "the story of a woman's loneliness and desperate need for love," which becomes a "study of Blanche's demoralization and the need for charity..." (Hartung 1951: 596). Perhaps the other critics were too immersed in the emotions of outrage sparked by their culture to engage much of their higher-order consciousness in achieving a critical understanding of Williams's imaginative artistry.

Clearly, the northern urban culture of New York City did not prepare most theater and film spectators to experience Atkinson's and Hartung's **compassionate** response to Blanche. While collective, biocultural memories are never monolithic, some may be widely shared, and these usually shape audience expectations and initial meaning-making in all popular dramatic presentations, filmic and theatrical. Soon after they settled into their auditorium seats to enjoy *Streetcar* in 1947 and 1951, most spectators in New York City found themselves experiencing a dramatic presentation that touched on concerns that were linked to several clusters of significance in their memories. I have singled out five of these clusters that, judging from the play, the reviews, and from a general knowledge of post-war U.S. history, appear to have been important in helping New York spectators to generate initial meanings about *Streetcar*: The American South, female sexuality, heterosexual marriage, the moral status of male veterans, and female mental health. Williams introduces all of these clusters in the first scene of *Streetcar*, and New Yorkers were primed by biocultural tradition and recent history to respond to them. While these expectations produced some pleasure for their audiences, they also exerted significant constraints on the meanings spectators would generate about Williams's protagonist and play. In short, these five clusters of memory and emotion pulled New York audiences of *Streetcar* toward several groupish orientations and away from others: northern versus southern values, sexism versus equality in gender relations, patriotic versus unpatriotic affiliations, and normal versus abnormal psychology and sexuality.

From the perspective of post-war New Yorkers, the South of Blanche DuBois was a foreign country. The inheritor of plantation-era southern traditions and sensibilities, Blanche and her kind probably represented the faded gentility, aristocratic pretenses, and emotional extremes that they associated with Hollywood films and romantic novels about characters who attempted to live by the values of the Old South. As Flannery O'Connor noted at the time about such figures, "... [A]nything that comes out of the South is going to be called grotesque by the Northern Reader, unless it is grotesque, in which case it is going to be called realistic" (O'Connor 1961: 40). For northerners, the most popular U.S. guide to such traditional character-types in the 1940s and early 1950s was W.J. Cash's *The Mind of the South* (1941). As historian John Shelton Reed notes, Cash presented the South as culturally distinctive, resistant to change, willfully individualistic, and extravagantly romantic, all qualities that New York audiences could easily attribute to Williams's Blanche (Reed 2003: 15–27).

If they were familiar with Cash's analysis, New Yorkers likely perceived sharp contrasts between their own beliefs and southern traditions. While watching *Streetcar* and judging Blanche's immersion in southern culture, most spectators could define themselves as more cosmopolitan, more accepting of progress, more cooperative, and more rational than Blanche. Indeed, in terms of the acting and directing choices of the 1947 and 1951 productions, audiences could also perceive the two Blanches as more southern that the other major characters. None of the other actors (not even Kim Hunter as sister Stella) attempted a "thick" southern accent, with the consequence that Tandy's and Leigh's Blanches seemed even more isolated from the rest of the characters in the French Quarter of New Orleans and more peculiar to the audience.

Social constraints on expressions of female sexuality, conservative enough in peace time, became more repressive during the war years of 1941–45, a potent source of memory for most U.S. citizens into the early 1950s. Not only were stateside married women expected to remain faithful to their husbands fighting overseas, but it was widely believed that unmarried women should refrain from involving "our boys" in romantic entanglements when they had more serious matters to attend to. Such values were apparent in the restrictions on women who joined the WACS and the WAVES and on those performing in USO troupes. These social norms also played out in Hollywood films during and after the war, which depicted deceptive, immoral women who had betrayed brave hubbies during the fighting (*The Best Years of Our Lives*) and emphasized the combination of heightened sexuality and unreliability in the numerous *femme fatales* of film noir. In the popular imagination, attractive women remained dangerous "bombshells" through the early 1950s (McConachie 2003: 126–33).

Although many women experienced some loosening of such restrictions by becoming temporary Rosie-the-Riveters during the war, post-war society quickly removed most women from such jobs after 1945, in the widespread belief that a woman's "normal" place was in the home. The result of these constraints was what historian Elaine Tyler May has called a domestic version of CONTAINMENT from the mid 1940s into the 1960s: "Within [the home], potentially dangerous social forces of the new age might be tamed, where they could contribute to the secure and fulfilling life to which postwar men and women aspired. Domestic containment was bolstered by a powerful political culture that rewarded its adherents and marginalized its detractors. More than merely a metaphor for the Cold War on the home front, containment aptly describes the way in which public policy, personal behavior, and even political values focused on the home" (May 1988: 14).

The postwar consensus embraced heterosexual marriage and a happy home as the answers to CONTAINING the sexual desires of men and women.

Blanche's presence in the Kowalski household, of course, presents a direct threat to the norms of domestic CONTAINMENT. Her decision to move in with her sister and brother-in-law would have reminded many New Yorkers at mid-century of similarly difficult and potentially combustible situations during the war, when a lack of housing forced distant relatives and even strangers to share temporary living quarters. While New Yorkers might have understood the "end of the line" desperation that drove Blanche to New Orleans, many would have had direct or imagined (through novelistic and filmic depictions) experience of the sexual tensions that could erupt between men and women in such a CONTAINED domestic situation. Consequently, given the widespread desire to return to "normal" gender relations after the war and to begin building a home and family, most would have seen Blanche as a potential home-wrecker and blamed her for the heightened tensions in the Kowalski household. From this perspective, it is partly understandable that the male critics in 1947 could not bring themselves to call Stanley's attack on Blanche a "rape." Her presence in the house, her flirting with Stanley, and her apparent sexual availability, from their point of view, had simply caused the poor boy to explode.

The image of Stanley as a heroic veteran also played a role in spectator response. While there is little in Williams's play that comments directly on Stan's wartime experience, the mere fact of his having served would have elevated him in status in the eyes of most New Yorkers. The popular mythology surrounding "the good war" tended to conflate "our boys" – all veterans were implicitly "boys" regardless of their age – with America itself. The suddenness of the Japanese attack on Pearl Harbor shocked Americans into an image of their enemies and themselves that would stay with them for a generation: treacherous evildoers had violated the trust of innocent, vulnerable Americans. But most also believed that the same good-hearted innocence, coupled with brash toughness and a can-do attitude, became America's best defense in waging a war for democracy and freedom. Hundreds of war films in the 1940s and early 1950s delivered variations on these themes (and none of them showed American soldiers raping local women). In short, if a veteran sexually molested a woman, he must have been driven to it; to think otherwise raised more questions about our boys, the war, and American intentions than most patriots wanted to consider. Consequently, many New York spectators, female and male, would have understood the sexual tensions between Stanley and Blanche and the eventual rape as a case of "she was asking for it" (McConachie 2003: 56–61).

From the point of view of Cold War spectators after WW II, however, women were not altogether accountable for their actions. Freudian psychiatry, never more popular in the US than in the two decades after the war, had long warned that women were more vulnerable to psychological problems than men. Further, postwar psychiatry, especially the Freudian version of "ego psychology" widely practiced in the US, preached that rebellion against normative social roles could lead women to psychological distress and neurosis; social conformity, in other words, was the key to female mental health. Again, Cold War Hollywood provided several films that demonstrated the vulnerability of women to psychological disorders (*The Snake Pit* and *The Three Faces of Eve*) and prescribed normative cures for their problems (McConachie 2003: 61–64, 202–03). It would not have mattered to most spectators that circumstances beyond her control had eliminated Blanche's options for a "normal" life. Her presence, her past, and her demands that she had a right to find a place for herself were an affront to the values of Cold War American life that had emerged by 1947.

When they came to watch stage and film versions of *Streetcar*, New York spectators were constrained by various ideas, images, and prejudices in their memories about the South, female sexuality, marriage, male veterans, and the psychological vulnerability of women. These expectations provided many of the boundary conditions for their perception of the drama, especially in its opening scenes. How individuals in the audience connected the dots among these clusters of themes and applied them to Blanche cannot be known, of course, and may have varied widely. Broadway and Hollywood, after all, had long enchanted many northerners with southern women who shared some of the same traits as Blanche DuBois, and these institutions would continue to enthrall American audiences with similar figures throughout the Cold War. Further, while it is probable that memorial expectations, in general, worked against a positive evaluation of Blanche, biocultural memories alone could not have led most New Yorkers to conclude that she was a tramp or a nymphomaniac. What was it that led most critics (and presumably many other New Yorkers) to conclude that *Streetcar* was "about" a female sexual predator?

To answer this question, we need to shift gears and look more closely at the likely response of spectators to Blanche in specific scenes of the play. What kind of dynamic processing did auditors do to arrive at these conclusions? How did the constraints and satisfactions of the drama play out in Scene One (as designated by Williams in his stage script of *Streetcar*), for example? The first scene shows Blanche under extreme duress; she drinks compulsively to quiet her nerves and later lies about it, careens between extremes of **affection** and **combativeness** in her initial interactions with Stella, and sinks into depressed memories of death when she recalls the recent parade of funerals at Belle Reve. Given what northern spectators already believed about the South, the suspect status of single women, and about female vulnerability to mental disease, it is not surprising that many New Yorkers in 1947 and 1951 might have initially assumed that Blanche was a southern neurotic — another grotesque victim of the Old South and female psychological weakness.

Put another way, many New Yorkers likely projected their negative learned memories of female southerners onto Tandy/Leigh/Blanche when they watched her in the first scene. People tend to project negative stereotypes onto others when they have had few actual encounters with members of their group, when their bioculture educates them to be wary of such people, and when they meet them for the first time. According to social psychologist Daniel R. Ames, if people perceive a social other to be like them, they will tend to project their own positive traits onto that person in a first encounter. In contrast, if they perceive the other to be dissimilar to themselves, they tend to draw initially on negative stereotyped images from their memories (Ames 2005: 164). This generalization about social interaction can be applied to the spectator's "meeting" of an actor/character on stage as well.

According to Ames and others, projecting stereotypes onto strange others tends to fade with time, as biocultural generalizations give way to immediate observations. Unfortunately, for the audience assessment of Blanche, the next scene of the play probably confirmed and extended their initial negative stereotype. Scene Two, the trunk scene, offered theater and film audiences for *Streetcar* some possibilities to begin constructing Blanche as sexually voracious. The scene begins with Stan obtusely insisting on his right to a share of the profits from the "sale" of Belle Reve and then "unpacking" the contents of Blanche's trunk to show his wife how Blanche has squandered their money. Stella, trying to avoid a conflict between her husband and sister, fails to quiet his **anger** and exits. Then Blanche emerges from the bathroom in a slip and red satin robe and immediately begins to flirt with Stanley, presumably because she heard parts of their argument and seeks to win him over. Spectators who had stereotyped Blanche as a potentially neurotic and decadent southerner in Scene One, however, might easily read a different motive into this strategy. Using their empathetic power of "imaginary transposition," they may have understood Blanche's flirtation, together with her red-robed and fresh-from-the-bath, perfumed body, as an attempt to seduce Stanley. Stanley is clearly aroused and accuses her of being a tease, but Blanche is soon dressed and the erotic mood of the scene momentarily dissipates.

Next Blanche makes what some spectators probably thought was another provocative move. She sends Stella off to the drugstore to buy her a coke so that she can speak to Stanley alone. Perhaps believing that she has the upper hand with Stan, Blanche resumes her flirtation, probably as a means of securing her victory and beginning to set up a relationship that will give her long-term control without sexual consequences in the household. Williams is clear later in the play that Blanche has often relied on playful flirtation to manage her relations with men. But in the midst of Scene Two, the audience could not yet have been sure that controlling Stanley was her intention, and some evidently believed that she had gotten rid of her sister in order to have another chance at seducing her brother-in-law. Blanche's stratagem – whether perceived as control or seduction – fails, however, when Stanley rips off the ribbon from the stack of letters from her dead husband and begins to paw through them. Blanche is unnerved, grabs them back, and drops her flirtation. Audience members who had put themselves into Blanche's shoes and assumed that the motive of seduction lay behind her flirtation were probably relieved that Stanley had put a temporary end to her machinations.

The empathetic operation of imaginary transposition can lead spectators to imaginary narrative constructions. That is, once audiences believe they have established a likely intention behind a single action of an actor/character, they desire to understand that intention in terms of a larger narrative pattern. In an article concerning how people make inferences about the social goals and personality traits of others, authors Stephen Read and Lynn Miller draw on several studies to conclude that "we comprehend other people's minds by creating a coherent narrative or story of their actions, organized around their goals" (Read and Miller 2005: 125). Following this process of narrative creation, the perceiver-creator can ascribe specific traits to the other person. For Read and Miller, ascribed traits are 'frame-based [mental] structures that identify the central actions of a sequence of behaviors and the goals of and reasons for that sequence" (2005: 133). "X" can term "Y" "helpful," "selfish," or perhaps "a nymphomaniac," because X has constructed a narrative of Y's past actions that links them together into a causal pattern. In DST terms, creating a narrative to explain the seductive behavior of Blanche in Scene Two would have constituted a definite attractor for many spectators near the end of that scene.

Perhaps the story constructed by audience members to account for Blanche's behavior went something like this: "Older sister loses husband in mysterious circumstances; is unsuccessful in marrying again in her small town and worried about her advancing age, so decides to change her territory and move in with her younger sister, whom she can boss around; older sister is immediately attracted to younger's stud husband and decides to seduce him to wreck their home and steal the husband; husband apparently interested so older sister orders younger sister out of the house to make her move; seduction might have worked, except that older sister is neurotic as well as sexually predatory." This is not Williams's understanding of Blanche's past and her goals, of course, but for many northern spectators at mid-century that had only watched the first scene and a half of the play, such a narrative probably seemed plausible. The story weaves together many of Blanche's significant actions, grounds them in the actual circumstances of what the audience understood so far about her past and present, and tracks her life in terms of an overall goal – to get a husband – that would have been believable to many of the spectators who created the narrative and perceived it to be true. The story also explains why so many spectators in 1947 (and quite a few in 1951) attributed the trait of nymphomania to Blanche's personality. In fact, to turn the question around, it is difficult to explain why so many spectators probably believed her to be a sexual predator if they had not created a narrative much like this one to explain her actions. Given the constraints of their biocultural lives, most New Yorkers who watched *Streetcar* probably took satisfaction in branding Blanche, the outsider, as a nympho.

A few reviewer-empathizers, however, apparently arrived at a more **sympathetic** understanding of Blanche's situation at the end of Scene Two. As we know, imaginary transposition can lead an empathizer to **sympathetic** as well as **antipathetic** assumptions. At the end of the scene, Blanche recovers herself after grabbing back the letters, drops her posing and flirting, and admits her vulnerability to Stanley concerning this failed part of her past. Blanche then tells Stan he can have access to all of the papers concerning Belle Reve, reacts with **joy** to the news of Stella's pregnancy, and jokes with her sister at the end of the scene. Spectators who had continued to engage in imaginary transposition would likely have concluded that this was a very different Blanche than they had witnessed so far. When not exhausted, cross, and defensive from traveling or playing up to a man to win some advantage, Blanche could be humorous and pleasant.

After Stella returns, Blanche laughingly admits that she was flirting with her husband, hardly a comment she would make if her intention really had been to seduce Stanley. Nor would Blanche seem morbid, over-emotional, or self-dramatizing to an empathizing spectator at the very end of Scene Two. In short, this brief look at a nearly normal Blanche might prompt some spectators to question their assumption that Blanche was a neurotic nymphomaniac. For others who had already reached that conclusion, however, Blanche could appear to be "play-acting" at the end of Scene Two; they would dismiss her actions as more evidence of her lying and profligacy.

Those same spectators would also type Blanche as a tramp in Scene Three, the Poker Night, for her flirtation with Mitch. Blanche and Stella interrupt Stanley's poker game with his buddies in the front room of the flat and then retreat to the back bedroom to undress and gossip after their night on the town. Blanche shows off her body through the curtains that divide the rooms, finds some rhumba music on the radio, and lures Mitch back to talk with her while Stella is in the adjoining bathroom. For spectators who already believed that Blanche was man-hungry, the ecology of the bedroom scene with Mitch could suggest to the audience that Blanche, as a predatory *femme fatale*, has arranged the surround of the space to capture Mitch in her spider's web. As in the earlier scene with Stanley, Blanche wears her sexy satin wrapper. She gets Mitch to sit on the bed with her to light her cigarette and bends toward him so that she can read the poetic inscription on his cigarette case. Blanche asks Mitch to cover the naked bulb in the room with a small Chinese lantern after she lies to him about her age, an action which turns him into an obliging southern gentleman even as it hides the wrinkles on her face. Although she plays the role of a prim schoolteacher (a position the audience knows she no longer holds), Blanche works the conversation around to adolescent sexuality to enhance her flirtation. By the end of their short scene together, Blanche has cornered Mitch in a CONTAINED space, plied him with rhumba music, and enticed him into lowering the lights. At this point, those spectators who had put together a narrative about "Blanche the Nymphomaniac and Husband-stealer" were probably adding "Blanche the Tramp" to their list of negative attributions. They could say to themselves, with satisfaction, "Blanche does not care who she sleeps with; she's after anything in pants." Of course for an empathizing spectator who had arrived at a more **sympathetic** estimation of Blanche at the end of Scene Two, her intention of getting Mitch interested enough in her fading charms to propose marriage would have been more understandable.

Scene Four, set in the apartment the next morning, culminates for Blanche in her "Don't hang back with the brutes" tirade to Stella, but the victory goes to Stanley, who wins an embrace from his wife, which is also an explicit snub to her sister, at the very end of the scene. This is preceded by Blanche's fantasies about Shep Huntleigh, her hysterical call to Western Union, and her insults to Stella – all of which probably revived the stereotype of the neurotic southern belle for many northern spectators. Although Blanche announces that her intention is to flee with her pregnant sister to escape the brutish Stanley, most in the audience probably believed that this was yet another of Blanche's strategies to wreck their marriage. For some, it may have led to a revised narrative about the vamp's plans for the future: "Older sister will separate younger sister from husband, then return later to claim her prize." By Scene Four of *Streetcar*, many in the audience had a stake in continuing to believe that their initial suspicions about Blanche were correct.

In DST terms, by Scene Four, many spectators had confirmed a significant "boundary condition" present in their memories at the start of the play – that their initial suspicions about southern women were correct. Following their empathetic engagements, imaginative narrative constructions, and ecological understandings in Scenes Two and Three, spectators actively perceived a Blanche who was a neurotic and dangerous tramp, a sexual predator, and probably both; this perception had hardened into a stable and persuasive attractor. In addition, it is apparent from the reviews that many audience members were both **repulsed** by her and **feared** what she might do to Stella and Stanley's marriage. The nymphomaniac could also be a home-wrecker! Although negative stereotypes often fade when spectators are given more information, this does not always occur. Social psychologist Daniel Ames, cited earlier, notes that "*cues signaling negative social intentions may dominate neutral or positive cues*" when people try to understand others (ital. in original) (Ames 2005: 169). Ames adds that "negative *moral* information is more attention-grabbing [than other kinds] and is weighed more heavily in [immediate] impressions" (2005: 168). This was evidently the case for many spectators with regard to Tandy's and Leigh's Blanche. Despite evidence to the contrary, their initial suspicions about Blanche, derived from northern biocultural memories concerning the war, the South, and female mental instability, stuck, deepened, and warped.

Given audience perception of Blanche's moral threat to Stella's marriage, a threat that involved a vital social institution for many postwar men and women, most spectators probably embraced DST attractors that would isolate and punish her for violating a norm that struck close to the survival of their bioculture. Stella's pregnancy – a fictional counterpart to the postwar baby boom embraced and (literally) propagated by so many Americans – would only confirm the importance to spectators of punishing anyone who tried to threaten the happiness of the next generation. Little wonder, then, that the Broadway reviewers in 1947 were silent about Stanley's violent rape of Blanche; not only did tramps and nymphomaniacs deserve rough treatment, but home-wreckers should be punished and banished (to an asylum or worse) so they could do no more harm to American families. No doubt spectators experienced many "perturbations" along the way to what they perceived to be their righteous, ritual scapegoating of Blanche. And some of these perturbations probably centered on **fears** that the *femme fatale* might actually get away with one or another of her neurotic plots.

But after Scene Four, the first "act break" in the theatrical production and a significant transition point in the film, most spectators probably took solace from Stella's embrace of Stanley and Stan's victorious smile at Blanche. And many in the audience would continue to construct meanings for the production that relied on such prejudicial perceptions for the remainder of the drama. What was *Streetcar* "about" for these spectators? It was about saving Stan and Stella's marriage from the delusions and depredations of a dangerous woman.

While I have emphasized the deleterious effects of biocultural memory on the meanings that the audience perceived about Blanche and *Streetcar*, there were likely other reasons for this response as well. Kazan bears some of the blame for believing that he, through his direction of Tandy and Leigh, could initially emphasize Blanche's negative traits in his stage and film versions of the drama and later convince spectators that Blanche was worthy of their **compassion**. To judge from the reviews, many spectators had already made up their minds about Blanche by the end of Scene Four and simply ignored later evidence that contradicted their assumptions and conclusions. Jessica Tandy and Vivien Leigh might have allowed audiences to feel more sympathy for Blanche early on, despite Kazan's direction. And perhaps Williams misjudged the openness of his northern spectators to southern female misfortunates; he might have found more opportunities to emphasize Blanche's positive traits in his first two scenes. Such "might have beens" are finally beside the point, however. Given the importance of historical memory in the dynamic processing of all performances, biocultural constraints and satisfactions will always shape spectatorial meanings. To expect otherwise is to yearn for audiences whose minds, bodies, and surrounds are "blank slates" at the start of a performance, awaiting meanings to be inscribed by producers and performers. But, of course, the realities of spectatorship and the dynamic emergence of meanings will never meet such unnatural conditions.

The audience response to *A Streetcar Named Desire* that I have outlined raises a chronic problem for all performance practitioners: How can the artists of performances ensure that spectators will ethically engage with their productions? The short answer to this question is simple: They cannot. Nonetheless, there are measures that can be taken. My next chapter, "A Deweyan Ethics for Performance Studies," will wrestle with some of the most important of them.

CHAPTER 5

A Deweyan ethics for performance studies

The recent rise of evolutionary and cognitive orientations in philosophy has stimulated ethical debates about altruism. As previously discussed, we *Homo sapiens* are more altruistic than any of our near relations among the other primates. This knowledge has led to a revival of the ethics of pragmatic naturalism, first suggested in the ideas of Charles Darwin and elaborated by John Dewey and other pragmatists. Philip Kitcher's *The Ethical Project* (2011) has recently emerged as one of the most encompassing and persuasive arguments for a pragmatic ethics based in Darwinian naturalism. I believe that Kitcher's notions of altruism and egalitarianism provide an appropriate and convincing standard for an ethics of biocultural performances.

My shift to first-person address in the last sentence is intended to signal a different rhetoric and intention for this final chapter of *Evolution, Cognition, and Performance*. Because Kitcher's approach is not the only ethical system compatible with the definition of performance I have developed in this book, I can hardly pretend that my endorsement of his work grows out of the same empirical and naturalistic orientation to the phenomena I have been examining thus far. Nonetheless, Kitcher's synthesis of solid science and sophisticated ethical thinking has convinced me of the validity of his approach. Consequently, I hope that my shift in rhetoric will help to convince you, "gentle readers," to consider adopting Kitcher's perspective as the basis for your own work in performance studies.

In the next section of this chapter, I will discuss Kitcher's ideas about the likely evolution of biocultural altruism and pair them, as appropriate, with examples from Tony Kushner's *Angels in America*, which – perhaps surprisingly – nicely exemplifies much of what Kitcher has to say. This will lead to a focus on institutional ethics and then on the devastations of neoliberalism, only partly countered by performances aimed at challenging its oppressions. Kitcher singles out the abolition of slavery in the West as a chief example of ethical progress in history. This prompts a final question that will conclude the chapter: Can progressives today muster the performative leverage and the long-term stamina that drove the Abolitionist performers of the nineteenth century in order to overcome the intertwined problems of climate change and international inequality in the twenty-first century? Kitcher's ethics speak directly to this already dire problem.

Ethics and enaction

Like all serious discussions of ethics, Philip Kitcher's *Ethical Project* begins with the assumption that humans have a degree of agency. Without positing some freedom of choice, the search for foundational principles of moral accountability is a fool's errand. Nietzsche's and Foucault's dismissal of human agency as movers of history backs ethics into just such an amoral corner. Naturalistic versions of ontology sometimes run into a similar problem at the other end of the human scale. Instead of discourse and other massive regimes of historical representation over-determining human actions, perhaps the synapses occurring among the one-and-a half billion neurons in our brains are leading us down a different garden path, all the while providing us with the illusion of a coherent self that has some control over human action. As Mark Johnson has noted, "This [kind of] problem has plagued all naturalistic accounts of mind, from David Hume to William James to Antonio Damasio." For this reason, Johnson adds, "We need a view of choice that is consistent with cognitive neuroscience and its insistence on the embodiment of mind and yet which doesn't make a shambles of our notions of moral responsibility" (Johnson 2007: 13).

Kitcher's *Project* works within Johnson's constraints. Deeply committed to moral responsibility, Kitcher also bases his approach on the best science available. Both of these concerns were evident in his critique of biologist Edwin O. Wilson's attempts to "biologicize" ethics, published in 1985 in *Vaulting Ambition: Sociobiology and the Quest for Human Nature*. Although Kitcher recognized the importance of human biology for any discussion of a possible ethics for humans, his book decried Wilson's confusions and leaps in logic. He continued his critique in 1993 with "Four Ways of 'Biologicizing' Ethics," an article, however, that also recognized that parts of Wilson's agenda, if separated from his other "ambitions," might actually be feasible. Kitcher pointed out that two of Wilson's "four ways" have long been understood by ethical philosophers as legitimate and important inquiries:

1. Sociobiology has the task of explaining how people have come to acquire ethical concepts, to make ethical judgments about themselves and others, and to formulate systems of ethical principles.
2. Sociobiology can teach us facts about human beings that, in conjunction with moral principles that we already accept, can be used to derive normative principles that we had not yet appreciated. (Kitcher 2003: 321–22)

Kitcher adds, "Human ethical practices have histories, and it is perfectly appropriate to inquire about the details of those histories. Presumably, if we could trace the history sufficiently far back into the past, we would discern the coevolution of genes and culture, the framing of social institutions, and the introduction of norms." He also notes, however, that it is "quite possible... that evolutionary biology would play only a very limited role in the story" (2003: 322). Evidently, Kitcher took his own advice; *The Ethical Project* tells the story of human ethical practices over time, from roughly four million years ago to the present, with some attention to the cultural and biological coevolution of altruism, but with a primary emphasis on the probable evolution of social norms and the institutions that derived from them.

Kitcher's *Project* continues a tradition of political and ethical thinking that dates to Hume in the eighteenth century and flourished in the work of John Dewey and the pragmatists in the early twentieth. Primarily in his *The Influence of Darwin on Philosophy and Other Essays* (1910), Dewey put together William James's psychology with Darwin's evolution to forge a practice-based ethics. Because Dewey understood that the mind had evolved to facilitate the survival of our species, he held that our body-minds worked best when trying to solve our own and others' practical problems. Recognizing our success when our bodies approached the fight against disease through a variety of approaches, for example, Dewey endorsed a similar pluralism for ameliorating social problems. This led the pragmatist to champion secular democracy, communities of scientific inquiry, and student-centered learning. Given historical change and the inevitable emergence of new problems for our species, however, Dewey also recognized that all solutions to society's problems must always be temporary. Drawing on Darwin, he understood that the only ethical stance possible was to begin with the recognition of change. With no final fix possible for human society, Dewey implicitly promised steady work for his pluralistic community of problem-solvers, which included artists as well as politicians, scientists, and educators. Further, he was optimistic that an informed public would chasten narrow-minded ideologues who refused to recognize the need to solve continuing problems through diverse means: "When democracy openly recognizes the existence of *problems* and of the need for approaching them *as* problems as its glory, it will relegate political groups that pride themselves on refusing to admit incompatible opinions to the obscurity which is already the fate of similar groups in science...," he believed (ital. in original) (Dewey 1939: 81). As we will see, Kitcher adopts Dewey's general approach to ethics, including his optimism, in *The Ethical Project*.

A more recent precedent for Kitcher's *Project* is Peter Singer's *A Darwinian Left*, published in 2000. Among his several insights, Singer pointed out that the findings of the evolutionary and cognitive sciences over the previous twenty years did not support neoliberal doctrines of competition and old-fashioned social Darwinism (which Darwin, by the way, scorned). Instead, said Singer, these sciences suggest that sociality and cooperation have been significant in our evolution and will continue to be relevant for our future success on this planet. Singer posited that a Darwinian Left would "promote structures that foster cooperation rather than competition, and attempt to channel competition into socially desirable ends; stand by the traditional values of the left by being on the side of the weak, poor, and oppressed, but think very carefully about what social and economic changes will really work to benefit them" (Singer 2000: 61–62). Since 2000, scholarly work in evolution and cognition has mostly confirmed and elaborated the science behind Singer's guarded optimism. In the midst of what remains an oppressive world economy perpetuated, in part, by reactionary political propaganda paid for by a neoliberal elite, Singer's fifteen-year old call-to-action is both more radical and more commonsensical now than when he wrote it.

So what about the possibility raised by Singer of channeling selfishness and competition toward more progressive ends? Behind Singer's hopes is the ongoing scientific work on human altruism, a partly inherited trait not found to the same extent in other species. Two recent books, David Sloan Wilson's *Does Altruism Exist: Culture, Genes, and the Welfare of Others* (2015) and Donald Pfaff's *The Altruistic Brain: How We Are Naturally Good* (2015), validate the existence of altruism and posit a neural mechanism for the reward of altruistic behavior. Kitcher's project, too, rests upon the biocultural foundations of altruism. He builds on archaeological knowledge and the mathematical modeling of possible evolutionary scenarios to argue that what he calls "psychological altruism" was the eventual key to ethical progress for our hunter-gatherer ancestors and may continue to help us today. Unlike "biological altruism," which has to do with the help that kin often provide to each other, or "behavioral altruism," which relates to satisfying the groupish desires of social others, "psychological altruism has everything to do with the intentions of the agent" and nothing to do with familial preferences or social anxieties (Kitcher 2011: 19).

Specifically, says Kitcher, "to be an altruist is to have a particular kind of relational structure in your psychological life – when you come to see that what you do will affect other people, the wants you have, the emotions you feel, the intentions you form change from what they would have been in the absence of that recognition" (2011: 20). The intention to act altruistically often begins interpersonally with perception, empathy, and emotion. Typically, the altruist takes the perspective of the other person, including an understanding of that person's emotions, **sympathizes** with what the other person is experiencing, changes her or his own emotions to assist the other, and then acts appropriately. Kitcher also insists that our altruistic proclivities can help us to establish norms and institutions that allow us to reach across racial, class, and other socially defined lines to eventually include all of humanity as our in-group. Kitcher, however, is no utopian, in the sense of supposing that all people can be taught to voluntarily give up their wealth and privilege for the benefit of humankind. Although he recognizes that utopian desires have played important roles in Abolitionism and other altruistic social movements in the past, his ethical project challenges humanity to work through the constraints of evolution and history, not around them, toward the satisfactions of a progressive future. That is, his ethics recognizes our bodily needs to avoid pain and maximize pleasure, the importance of our primary and secondary emotions, our tendency to groupishness in social behavior, and the changes to our situation as a species that history has effected and will continue to create. Consequently, Kitcher understands that progressive change will require the exercise of political and economic power to establish and maintain a social system that supports altruistic behaviors, norms, and institutions.

While most scientists would likely accept Kitcher's distinctions among different kinds of altruism, the evidence for how and why our species eventually evolved to include psychological, along with biological and behavioral, altruism is not yet complete. With most other anthropologists and evolutionary psychologists, Kitcher assumes that by roughly six million years ago, when our hominid ancestors had become a separate species, the social lives of our early kin were little different from those of the proto-chimpanzees and other primates of that era. That is, these hominids lived in small groups, mixed by age and sex, with much the same social psychology as present-day chimpanzees and gorillas. As occurs among chimps today, dominant males probably ruled the group, and our ancestors had to forage for themselves, with occasional help from mothers, for their young to survive. In Kitcher's terms, biological altruism probably flourished, but behavioral altruism often broke down, leading to a lack of group cooperation and frequent eruptions of violence, sometimes deadly. According to animal psychologists, the amount of time that present-day chimps and bonobos spend on grooming each other relates directly to the need to find allies and the struggle to keep the peace in the Hobbesian social world of our primate relatives. While contemporary humans also perform metaphorical acts of grooming, we can usually rely on a measure of cooperation and psychological altruism to ease our social problems – actions that are mostly beyond the abilities of other primates.

How, then, did our species get from where we were six million years ago to our present situation, where psychological altruism is at least a possibility in some areas of our social and ethical lives? Kitcher does not attempt to provide a detailed roadmap – given the skimpy evidence, no scientist could – but he does outline some probable steps. He speculates that our ancestors were probably able to build upon the fragile friendships and coalitions of early hominid life to move beyond the biological altruism of proto-chimps in order to sustain longer-term cooperation among members of the same band. Kitcher proposes that hominids had an advantage over other primates in this regard because of their emerging abilities to communicate their ideas and feelings more accurately through sounds and gestures, which gradually led hominid bands to reinforce and reshape their altruistic dispositions through what Kitcher calls "normative guidance" (2011: 74). Following the work of Sterelny and others, Kitcher demonstrates that dominant coalitions within bands likely enforced new norms regulating food sharing and restrictions on intra-group violence. Obeying the mandates of a dominant group would have led to an increase in behavioral altruism, the occasional sacrifice of one's own desires for the wishes of others.

While early normative guidance probably began with orders from dominant hominids, Kitcher supposes that later norms were likely "mediated by respect for the supposed commands of transcendent beings, respect tinged with hopes and fears" (2011: 84). Kitcher builds his assumptions concerning the importance of social norms on archaeological evidence about ritual religious practices. He draws on religious psychology to link religion to the adoption of a social conscience: "However it is formed, conscience is the internalization of the capacity for following orders...," he says.

"The commanding voice seems to come from within, initially and crudely as the expression of fears, later perhaps as the representation of membership in a particular social group" (2011: 94). Kitcher agrees with Hamlet's insight that conscience can make cowards of us all. But he adds, still following *Hamlet*, that it can also give rise to more complex social and psychological relations involving **guilt**, **shame**, **pride**, and hope. The emergence of an internal conscience regulating hominid social life, in other words, set the stage for the occasional blossoming of psychological altruism out of the behavioral kind.

While a demanding conscience reinforced through religious belief makes it appear that our hunter-gatherer ancestors must have been marching in lock-step to orders from authoritarian leaders and superstitious shamans, Kitcher is quick to dispel this image. Rather, he builds upon the insights of Christopher Boehm, Kim Sterelny, and others to argue that early *Homo sapiens* bands were generally egalitarian in social and economic organization. Given the pressures on group survival, each band gradually developed its own language, which fostered a give-and-take among adult speakers. Consequently, it appears that all had a say around the campfire, and most disputes were likely settled on the basis of traditional norms or through a new consensus. As previously discussed, our ancestors likely lived this way from 100,000 years ago until the gradual transition from hunter-gatherer tribes to an agricultural way of life, which began about 13,000 years ago. During these 87,000 years or so, a rough egalitarianism likely helped our species to survive, despite difficult ecological conditions. This means that culture worked with evolution, at both individual and group levels, to select for social and biological traits that emphasized psychological altruism. Egalitarian norms, in other words, supported the biocultural evolution of psychological altruism. I will further develop this side of Kitcher's ethics in the next section of the chapter.

More complex societies also expanded the possibilities for altruism, as humans began to aspire to richer notions of the good life. Kitcher terms the ancient agricultural-based tribes, societies, city-states, and empires that flourished before the common era "experiments of living" (2011: 104–37); all together, they explored a range of ethical practices that could sustain some of the aspirations of psychological altruism for various parts of their populations. Put another way, eating, copulating, and staying healthy and secure were no longer enough for our ancestors. Various agricultural societies encouraged the development of specialized talents, of individual contributions to religious and community life, and the legitimation and cultivation of particular kinds of social relationships that allowed for intimacy and trust. As Kitcher concludes, "By gradual steps, the ethical project could evolve, from the simple beginnings of socially embedded normative guidance to the ethical sensibilities we discern in ancient Greece" (2011: 137).

Ethics and *Angels*

Kushner's *Angels in America* can help us to explore the ramifications of Kitcher's ethical project. Examining the failures of psychological altruism evident in his two plays, *Millennium Approaches* and *Perestroika*, is an appropriate start. As Kitcher and others understand, all social systems built partly upon altruism must guard against bullies and free riders. Bullies take advantage of the expectation of trust that emerges when societies attempt to practice modes of cooperation through egalitarian norms and the internalization of altruistic values. While chimp bullies can effectively rule chimpanzee societies most of the time, humans usually appoint socially sanctioned enforcers of their norms to prevent the rise of gang leaders, Mafiosi, and other forms of bullying, or at least to relegate them to the sidelines of social activity. Roy Cohn is Kushner's representative bully in *Angels*, and his "clout" within the world of the play indicates the extent to which behavior based on cooperative norms has broken down in the 1980s.

Free riders, the second general problem for all societies that attempt to honor altruistic values, are people who benefit from egalitarian practices and values, but do not do the economic, social, and/or emotional work to ensure that the ethical norms and actions necessary for the practice of social harmony are maintained and continued. *Angels* features two prominent free riders, Joe Pitt and Louis Ironson. Joe wants to remain an officially married Mormon throughout the play, even after he recognizes his homosexual identity and sleeps with Louis. He is trying to "ride for free," both with his religion and with his wife, Harper. Paralleling Joe's free riding, Louis wants to remain Prior Walter's boyfriend, even after he ignores Prior's pleading and the advice from a Jewish rabbi about his abandonment of his boyfriend because of his fear of AIDS. In betraying the social and emotional trust of others to advance their selfish intentions, Joe and Lewis trash cultural and religious norms that work to ensure a level of mutual cooperation.

Near the opposite end of the continuum from bullying and free riding in *Angels* is Prior Walter, probably the most altruistic character in both parts of the play. Kitcher, in fact, has put together an "altruism profile" (2011: 31), which allows an ethicist to compare the possible psychological altruistic actions of all mammals and individuals (from a cow to Nelson Mandela, for example) by deploying the five factors of his profile. These are: "[T]he *intensity* of the animal's responses to others, the *range* of those to whom the animal is prepared to make an altruistic response, the *scope* of contexts in which the animal is disposed to respond, the animal's *discernment* in appreciating the consequences for others, and the animal's *empathetic skill* in identifying the desires others have or the predicaments in which they find themselves" (ital. in original) (Kitcher 2011: 31). Simply put, a species' or individual's possibility for ethical progress is a function of its altruism profile. Kitcher adds, by way of explanation, that animals must score positively in each of these five areas to be judged altruistic at all. Bullies, for example, "never respond to anyone else in any context: for the dimensions of intensity, range, and scope, they score 0, 0, and 0; their discernment and empathetic skill can be as you please, for these are never called into play" (2011: 31). From this perspective, Iago is probably Shakespeare's most empathetic character; his evident skill at identifying the desires and predicaments of others is excellent, but he has absolutely no interest in altruistic action within the world of *Othello*. Of course the parallel character in *Angels* is Roy Cohn, both for his massive egotism and for his ability to discern the fears and desires of his fellow characters.

Regarding *Angels*, however, the relevant question is Kushner's "altruism profile," not that of one of his characters. Although playwrights rarely dramatize their own moral perspective in any direct way, we can get a general notion of Kushner's ethics and, within that, his altruism profile, by examining Prior Walter and his narrative in both plays – both for their content and for the response that Kushner's rhetoric intends to call forth from audiences in performance. In addition, Kushner builds on the sympathetic appeal of Prior to accord him symbolic force and meaning in the world of *Angels*. Within this subjunctive world, which includes both fantastical and mundane levels, Kushner invites his audience to understand Prior both as a specific person struggling with significant problems and as a metaphor for larger ethical and trans-historical concerns. In particular, Kushner, like Kitcher, is interested in upholding the possibility of ethical progress for humankind and structures his two-part play to insist that humans must craft such progress for themselves and each other, even in the face of a Heaven committed to stasis and a universe bereft of ultimate purpose.

Most spectators would recognize Prior as both the most grounded and the most ethically ambitious figure in *Angels*. In terms of *intensity*, Prior cares deeply for Louis Ironson and even apologizes for his lover as his infections are worsening and Louis is preparing to abandon him. Prior's *range* of concern is immense; from Belize, his former lover, to his ancestors, the Prior Walters from the thirteenth and seventeenth centuries, to the Angel who visits him, to Little Sheba, his lost cat, Prior cares about living things in the past, the present, on earth and in heaven. This range also speaks to the *scope* of contexts in which Prior can express his concern for others. Despite his ongoing and worsening pain for most of the action, Prior never loses his ethical footing for long and manages to engage with others through humor and sympathy in hospital rooms, hallucinations, Heaven, and even at the Mormon Visitor Center. At the Center, he befriends Hannah, whose experience with angels helps Prior toward the insight that saves him from becoming the avatar of the Angels' commandment that humanity stop changing. Prior's *discernment*, in other words, leads to the major turning point of *Angels in America* and protects the possibility of human choice in history, albeit at the cost of future pain.

Prior's high-altruism profile effectively wins him the rhetorical legitimacy to talk directly to the audience in the Epilogue. A spokesperson for Hannah, Louis, and Belize, who have also gathered at the Bethesda Fountain in Central Park on a cold winter day, Prior tells us that it is now January 1990 and that he has survived AIDS for five years. Related primarily through their ties to Prior (and not through biological or behavioral altruism), the other survivors have helped and suffered for each other, even though they still share major disappointments and disagreements. In part for this reason, they look forward to bathing themselves "clean" when the renewed fountain of Bethesda flows again, but it is winter and the cleansing waters are frozen. Not surprisingly, Kushner gives Prior the last words of the play, which work as a kind of benediction for the audience:

> This disease will be the end of many of us, but not nearly all, and the dead will be commemorated and will struggle on with the living, and we are not going away. We won't die secret deaths anymore. The world only spins forward. We will be citizens.
>
> The time has come.
> Bye now.
> You are fabulous creatures, each and every one.
> And I bless you: *More life*.
> The Great Work Begins. (Kushner 1996: 146)

Kushner's ending acknowledges the building of a fragile foundation for "great work" that suggests the possibility of ethical growth in the future. His vision of a world inevitably spinning forward is reminiscent of the dynamic systems inherent in each living being that carry forward aging bodies and old learning even as they open to new options. Like Kitcher's narrative of painful ethical progress for humankind, *Angels* can only assert the possibility, never the inevitability of successfully working toward a more altruistic and just society.

Prior's final sentence in *Perestroika*, "The Great Work Begins," which repeats the Angel's words at the end of *Millennium Approaches*, also settles Kushner's mock theological conflict during the play. If there were ever any doubt, the only "angels in America" must be human ones, because only humans can begin the work of ethical cleansing and the building of an egalitarian future. In one sense, Kushner's two-part action pulls off a bait-and-switch operation. *Millennium Approaches* introduces the possibility that heavenly angels will intervene in human history to set things right. By the end of *Perestroika*, however, the Angels have been revealed as hapless bureaucrats stuck in the past and sick, suffering, secular humanity must fall back on itself to change the world. In another sense, though, the Angels in the play have made a difference. By wrestling with religion and rejecting angelic help, a few of the mere mortals in *Angels* learn that religious traditions offer resources that can help them in their struggle, even though they also come to realize that any ultimate salvation through observance or belief is not an option. In its general action, Kushner's *Angels* comes close to Kitcher's endorsement of Deweyan social problem-solving.

Kitcher arrives at a similar understanding of a possible role for the altruistic side of institutional religion, despite its past role as the enforcer of an autocratic conscience and its occasional contemporary embrace of murderous fanaticism. His *Ethical Project* distinguishes between faith-based commandments, which could only hobble progress toward an altruistic and egalitarian future by giving priests and mullahs more social power, and opportunities to use select religious traditions to help others toward more progressive secular ends. Similarly, Kushner facilitates the action of *Angels* to allow his characters to take opportunistic advantage of religion to further his own ethical project. By the end of *Perestroika*, religion retains some metaphorical power for psychological healing – the angel of Bethesda, after all, draws on Judaic mythology to proffer the possibility of ritual cleansing – but the ethical mandates of any institutional religion are not a part of the conversation among Kushner's survivors. Instead, the general action of the play shows major characters who must reject the constraints of their religious past in order to celebrate "more life."

Of the figures who must wrestle with their religious traditions, perhaps Harper Pitt, Louis Ironson, and Hannah Pitt take the longest journeys over

Ethics and Angels

the two parts of *Angels*. I will focus on Hannah, both because of her own trek away from Mormonism toward psychological altruism and because of Kushner's interest in Mormonism as a prototypically American faith. Like many white U.S. citizens, the Mormons suffered for their beliefs, pulled themselves up from their homes in the eastern part of the country, and migrated to the West during the nineteenth century. Despite this beginning in movement and progress, later generations of Mormons sought to "stay put" in the West (Kushner 1993: 82) – in the words of Sister Ella Chapter to Hannah Pitt early in *Millennium Approaches*. Hannah reverses this journey, however, when she flies to New York City to rescue her son Joe from what she takes to be his sinful embrace of homosexuality and to save his marriage to his wife, Harper. The Angels' commandment to stay put to ensure ethical stability and Prior's desire to keep moving toward possible ethical progress is a major conflict in the play and it structures much of the action, including Hannah's journey away from groupish loyalties and toward altruism.

The ethical problematics of moving forward or staying put are amply demonstrated in one of the diorama scenes at the Mormon Visitor Center, a comically grotesque bit of allegory that clearly links change of place to change in moral perspective. When Harper Pitt, who is struggling to move from **embarrassment** and **guilt** to moral perception, asks the wooden figure of the Mormon Mother in the diorama how people change, she replies:

> Well, it has something to do with God so it's not very nice. God splits the skin with a jagged thumbnail from throat to belly and then plunges a huge filthy hand in, he grabs hold of your bloody tubes and they slip to evade his grasp but he squeezes hard, he *insists*, he pulls and pulls till all your innards are yanked out and the pain! We can't even talk about that. And then he stuffs them back, dirty, tangled, and torn. It's up to you to do the stitching. (Kushner 1996: 77–78)

To which Harper, who recognizes herself in this description, replies, "And then get up. And walk around." "Just mangled guts pretending," adds the Mormon Mother (1996: 78). Like the Angel, the Mormon Mother is not recommending spatial and ethical movement or change.

"Mangled guts pretending" is also an apt description of Hannah's situation at the beginning of her journey to altruistic perception. We may chart her progress toward altruism through Evan Thompson's understanding of empathy. Recall that Thompson discerns four possible stages in a person's empathetic development, each one more reliant on conscious ethical awareness than the previous stage upon which it rests. As we mature, we gain the abilities to attune ourselves to others' feelings and intentions, to take the perspective of another person, to turn that perspective toward ourselves in order to reflect on our actions, and finally to see the other as a person who deserves concern and respect. Thompson is quick to add that these stages of empathy do not exhaust moral action, but they can provide a significant entry point into understanding and applying its complexities.

Initially **fearful** and confused when she arrives in New York, Hannah cannot understand the homeless person she talks with to get directions to her son's apartment; she is badly out of tune with that person in the social environment of the South Bronx. After moving in with Harper, Hannah grows increasingly frustrated when she finds that she can do nothing to avert the changes she is witnessing; she must struggle to take Harper's perspective on her marriage to her son, Joe. Despite these problems, Hannah begins to piece together a life for herself, in part by helping Harper through her drug problems and volunteering at the Mormon Visitor Center. While spectators can see that she has achieved a degree of empathy with regard to social attunement and perspective-taking, Hannah continues to balk at the hard, judgmental, and dry portrait of herself evident in the reiterated empathy that others are showing to her. Nonetheless, after Prior stumbles into the Center at a moment when AIDS is threatening his life, Hannah volunteers to take him to the hospital and becomes a kind of mother figure for him during his recovery. Knowing something about angels because of her Mormon past, she helps Prior to prevail over the Angel when they wrestle. By assisting Prior with his physical and psychological wounds, she effectively forgives her son, Joe, and also herself for her past misjudgments. Following Prior's victory, the Angel turns to Hannah and blesses her with what Kushner describes as "an enormous orgasm" (1996: 118). The mature ethical perspective that comes with reiterated empathy and moral perception in Hannah's case also has an embodied payoff; it momentarily transforms and softens her.

We know this, in part, because of one of the best comic lines in the two-part play. As she leaves the hospital temporarily to return home, Hannah corrects Prior's ironic homage to Blanche Dubois's, "I have always depended on the kindness of strangers," with, "Well that's a stupid thing to do" (1996: 137). Although arguably an extension of Hannah's past stoniness, the rejoinder is also correct – strangers are not often kind or empathetic. Still lacking in warmth, Hannah's version of psychological altruism nonetheless draws on her Mormon traditions of empathy and dependability. Significantly, Kitcher, like Kushner, does not typecast his altruists as sentimental optimists; his discussion allows for a wide range of altruistic psychologies. By extending her religiously based empathy to non-Mormon others in need, Hannah determines that she will try not to be a stranger to gay men requiring help, including her son. Her action demonstrates her ability to enlarge the range of her concerns beyond behavioral empathy toward members of her in-group to encompass outsiders that most Mormons in the 1980s viewed as sinners. Five years later when she joins the others at Bethesda Fountain, it is evident that she has moved further away from her religious past. According to the stage directions, the former Mormon mother from Utah "looks like a New Yorker and is reading the *New York Times*" (1996: 143). Nonetheless, Hannah, like the others at the fountain, still needs to be washed clean. Kitcher's ethics and Thompson's empathy do not insist that those who reach moral perception always show **compassion** and forgiveness, only that they have the capacity to do so. For all of Kitcher's and Kushner's progressive secularism, both want to preserve a place in their notion of ethical citizenship for altruistic versions of religious practice.

Institutional ethics

As discussed in previous chapters, all performances work at two levels of reality, the subjunctive and the actual. I have been discussing the subjunctive, fictional level of *Angels*, but it is important to keep in mind that the production had an actual history; financiers, lawyers, artistic teams, marketers, and others put together productions of Kushner's two-part play and brought it before various public audiences. The Mark Taper Forum in Los Angeles and the Eureka Theatre in San Francisco, two not-for-profit theaters, work-shopped and premiered early versions of *Millennium Approaches* and *Perestroika* in 1991 and 1992. After a West End theater in London successfully produced *Angels* in 1992 and 1993, a Broadway producer put together productions of both parts that ran sequentially in New York during 1994 and into 1995. George C. Wolfe directed both *Millennium Approaches* and *Perestroika* on Broadway, with a cast that included Steven Spinella as Prior Walter and Ron Leibman as Roy Cohn. When HBO Films decided to make a mini-series out of the play, they asked Kushner to do the adaptation and invited Mike Nichols to direct. Because HBO insisted on film stars, the new cast included Al Pacino and Meryl

Streep. As a theatrical and media success story, there was nothing odd about the movement of productions of *Angels* from not-for-profits, to profit-generating theaters in London and New York, to HBO Films in Hollywood, with changes in directing, casting, and marketing, etc. along the way. For the most part, this was show-business-as-usual for successful entertainment properties such as *Angels* in the 1990s.

But was it ethical? Kitcher's ethics invite us to ask questions about both actual and subjunctive realities when we investigate performances. Nearly all professional productions of sports, music, drama, and ritual these days are necessarily dependent upon institutional arrangements that are themselves caught up in legal, financial, and professional networks and structures and that rest within the larger cultural-cognitive ecosystems of the world. As anthropologist and evolutionary biologist Peter Turchin notes, "Institutions are systems of culturally acquired rules that govern behavior of individuals in specific contexts. Individuals internalize aspects of these rules, termed norms" (Turchin 2013: 67). Following the norms and institutions of theatrical and media production, those associated with *Angels* expected that the intellectual property rights of Kushner as a playwright would protect his financial interests during the various stages of the play's success, but that most others who had helped early productions of the play to flourish would not benefit financially as *Angels* grew in popular demand. Accepting these norms of theatrical and media production, the actors in the initial readings and productions of *Millennium Approaches* and *Perestroika* had no expectation of financial reward when *Angels* hit the big money as an HBO miniseries. But are such institutional arrangements and norms fair? Specifically, in relation to Kitcher's ethical values, are they egalitarian? While there are potentially several sides to debating this question, most would probably agree that the answer is "no."

While there is much more to say about the inegalitarian practices of show biz, I want to switch the subject to youth and school sports, primarily because sociologists, historians, psychologists, and anthropologists have studied the norms and institutions of sports much more rigorously and extensively than they have other genres of performance. In particular, I will draw on the work of sports sociologist Eric Anderson, whose *Sport, Theory, and Social Problems: A Critical Introduction* couches the results of over 250 empirical studies from the 1970s to 2010 within current theories of masculinity, cultural capital, sexism, adolescent conformity, cultural hegemony, and other approaches to mount a substantial critique of youth and school sports as they are currently practiced in the US and the UK. Although

Institutional ethics

Anderson's ideas do not take evolutionary psychology into account, his findings also offer no surprises to those who understand the ramifications of groupishness in our genetic and cultural past.

Rather than summarizing each of Anderson's major findings in a paragraph or so, I will list all seventeen of them, as he does in his conclusion, so that I can turn to his recommendations, which accord almost completely with Kitcher's ethical principles. At the start of his concluding chapter, Anderson states that his primary purpose has been "to put forth empirically supported, theoretically based arguments" concerning youth and school sports in order to demonstrate that:

1. Sport does not build character (at least not in the way we assume it does).
2. Sport does not promote substantial educational or socioeconomic attainment for the underprivileged.
3. Sport does not reduce prejudice.
4. Many types of competitive, organized sport not only fail to promote one's health but can also cause a great deal of injury, disease, and early death.
5. Sport is an arena in which youth are trained to follow the instructions of elders without thinking for themselves. This opens them up to emotional and physical abuse.
6. The structure of sport influences coaches to abuse their athletes (through too much training and risking their athletes' health) in order to win.
7. Sport teaches participants to sacrifice their health, education, and other life chances for the sake of moving up through its ranks.
8. In sport, we learn to commit violence not only against ourselves, but we learn to accept that violence committed against others is an acceptable 'part of the game.'
9. Because sport remains a socially valued institution (which nearly compels all youth to participate), they 'learn' that the sexes are not equal enough to compete together.
10. Men (particularly) learn the attitudinal positioning of homophobia, sexism, and anti-femininity.
11. Gender segregation in sports helps symbolically reproduce patriarchal privilege.
12. Gender segregation in sport also provides men with social capital and formal networks that help them (and not women) gain occupations within and outside of the sporting industry.

13. Sport reproduces a 'good old boys' network that privileges white, heterosexual, able-bodied men in many capacities.
14. Sport teaches us to hate our competitors, to view them as standing in the way of our success.
15. Sport discriminates against those who do not fit the athletic mold, and it sometimes (formally and informally) excludes those with disability or those who come out as sexual minorities.
16. Sport helps reproduce class inequality, particularly by offering false hope for those in economic disparity.
17. Sport is used to teach a modern (lower-class) workforce the requirements that employers wish of employees in a capitalist economy. In sport, these same youths are also being trained to value the attributes of soldiering. (Anderson 2010: 151–52)

In short, the institutions and norms of youth and school sports trap many of their participants in behaviors and attitudes that perpetuate massive social and economic inequalities, as well as inflicting individual physical and psychological harm.

Anderson, a school coach (in track and field) for many years before becoming a professor of sport studies, enumerates the failings of youth sports partly to advance his proposals for several major reforms. First, he urges that the way coaches are educated and evaluated must be upgraded and professionalized. Anderson wants to rein in the near-absolute power that coaches exercise over their young players, power that has led in numerous cases to emotional, physical, and sexual abuse. He believes that coaches, like other school teachers (and even community volunteers), must be monitored and evaluated on a regular basis. Second, Anderson also advocates integrating the genders in all sports activities, a reform that will require changing the rules of many games as well. Only when boys and girls are playing together and in manageable competition, he believes, will team sports move away from its "masculinized, homophobic, and sexist gender regime" (2010: 155). While Anderson does not go into detail about how this integration might be accomplished, he does suggest another book that gets specific: *Playing with the Boys: Why Separate Is Not Equal in Sport* (2008), by Eileen McDonagh and Laura Pappano. Third, Anderson puts forward ideas that will deemphasize team competition and the "us" versus "them" lust for victory. He imagines a Little League Baseball situation, for example, in which all the kids who sign up get to play, but they are not assigned to one team for the duration of the season. Instead, they play a couple of games per week with one team and coach and then are randomly assigned to a different team and coach for the second week, a new team and coach for the third week, and so on. "With my system," says Anderson, "no team emerges as the victor at the end of the season of play" (2010: 159).

Anderson also makes a strong case for disentangling competitive sports from school systems. Although socialized into sports in the US, he now favors the British system in which most sports are run by community organizations. He believes this structural shift could facilitate what sport sociologist Jay Coakley has termed the "pleasure and participation" model of sports activities, in which personal enjoyment, democratic decision-making, and sociality across teams are encouraged. Instead, says Coakley, the structure of U.S. school sports favors a "power and performance" model, which pushes student athletes to break records and strive for victory at all costs (cited in Anderson 2010: 162). In addition, the power and performance model of school sports, by expecting teens to play like the professional athletes they often revere, produces too many needless injuries. Anderson advocates changing the rules of American football to disallow the use of the head as a weapon. He also wants to ban the curve ball in youth baseball because it puts too much stress on teenage arms. Overall, Anderson is interested in altering sports to make them less competitive and more playful. Playing at soccer, he says, "still requires one to run back and forth for 90 minutes" and "is more likely to teach cooperation than when one competes at it" (2010: 163). Anderson believes that playing rather than competing at sports can be more fun, empathetic, and democratic.

While Kitcher does not discuss youth and school sports in *The Ethical Project*, he understands that all social norms and institutions have an immense role to play in the constraints and satisfactions available to all humans in various cultures. Kitcher critiques racism, sexism, classism, and all normative behaviors and social institutions at every level of the life cycle – from nurturing infants to the treatment of the dying – that might undercut egalitarian norms and practices. In this broad sense, Kitcher is proposing a normative ethics. Although most approaches to normative social standards emphasize the attainment of a static ethical vision, Kitcher's approach is dynamic and Deweyan. According to Kitcher, " . . . [A] normative ethics requires continuing efforts to decide how to live together in a common world. Each generation renews the project, going on from the point reached by its predecessors . . . The normative ethicist's role is not to offer the grand plan, but to help the coordination" (Kitcher 2011: 286). Working toward a better social ethics will usually involve two kinds of proposals, which Kitcher terms "diagnostic" (what's wrong now?) and "methodological" (how best can we fix it?). In terms of how to judge diagnostic and methodological proposals, Kitcher advocates a version of "consequentialism" initially advanced by John Stuart Mill, which simply states that the "rightness of actions depends on their consequences" (2011: 289). Rather than worrying about first principles or past traditions, consequentialism looks to intentional action to address problems and to more action when new problems crop up.

From his evolutionary and pragmatic perspective, Kitcher diagnoses the biggest immediate ethical problem in the world as a lack of material and social equity. "Contemporary societies have either abandoned the original emphasis on equality or spectacularly failed to achieve it . . . ," says Kitcher (2011: 294). Compared to our hunter-gatherer ancestors, who forged egalitarian arrangements to work together for survival in circumstances far more dire than our own, our failures of altruism are truly immense. Insofar as the consequences of the present norms and institutions of youth and school sports in the US and the UK inhibit the practice of altruism and the attainment of a more egalitarian society – and Anderson presents significant evidence that they do – Kitcher would oppose them and seek their reform, probably along many of the lines that Anderson suggests. Reforming the practices of youth and school sports may not seem to strike very directly at the general lack of material and social equity around the globe, but their reform could certainly help. It is clear from Anderson's diagnostic analysis and methodological proposals that most boys socialized through sports in the ways that he proposes would be less sexist, violent, classist, homophobic, domineering, and racist, plus more cooperative and egalitarian, than the average boys growing up in the US and the UK today. Altering the institutions and norms of youth sports should not be the only social reforms to attack the ongoing inegalitarian problems in which sports activities are embedded, but such reform would certainly count as ethical progress from Kitcher's perspective.

Egalitarian norms and nineteenth-century Abolitionism

One possible explanation (and excuse) for much of the world's indifference to the social and economic well-being of the poor, the migrant, and the socially marginalized is to assert that all social values are relative to specific cultures. From this perspective, it is impossible for a person embedded in one culture to judge the values and actions of those in another. Indeed, relativists like Nietzsche and Foucault hold that the attempt to discover and impose a general standard of ethics on all humanity is both foolish and counterproductive. Their position of ethical relativism is sometimes asserted to protect members of oppressed cultures, but it can also uphold the privileges of oppressors. On the basis of the same relativistic principles, it may be asserted that those who are not members of the economic elite should not oppose the culture of global capitalism because they do not share the neoliberal values of the super-rich. In contrast, Kitcher proposes that the expansion of psychological altruism and social egalitarianism over human evolution and history does constitute such an emerging ethical standard, even though assessing its successes and failures is often difficult. Nonetheless, Kitcher is clear that the period of rough egalitarianism among our ancestors during the High Paleolithic era provided early examples of such progressive change.

And Kitcher discusses three more: the advancement of human rights for girls and women, the abolition of chattel slavery in most of the world's societies, and, more recently, the shift among significant numbers of the earth's population from viewing homosexuality as a sin to understanding it in biocultural terms and extending human rights accordingly. Kitcher acknowledges that none of these progressive changes is complete or irreversible, but he celebrates them as significant. Indeed, the reversal in the last twenty-five years in social norms and laws in the US concerning homosexual marriage is one testament to the kind of ethical progress that Kitcher recognizes. Although (unsurprisingly) he says nothing in his book about *Angels in America*, it is clear that Kitcher would applaud theatrical performances of Kushner's play and similar dramatic productions for helping to alter the normative landscape concerning LGBTQ rights.

As Kitcher reports, the success of nineteenth-century Abolitionism in ending chattel slavery is perhaps the single most impressive piece of evidence for the possibility of ethical progress that is available in recent history. Because performance played such an important part in the Abolitionist movement, revisiting key parts of this history in the US can help us to think about how the eventual triumph of Abolitionism might be compared to what many believe is the next big battle for a more egalitarian future – the links connecting ecological disasters caused by climate change and the continuing neoliberal war on the working classes and poor of the world. These similarities and differences promise to reveal several significant problems that lie ahead for those of us who share Kitcher's ethics regarding the future of humanity and a liveable biosphere.

The consequences of climate change and neoliberalism are fast undermining any hope for a more just and egalitarian future for much of the world's population. If unimpeded in the next fifty years, the oil and gas oligarchs, with the cooperation of other neoliberals in many governments, will accumulate more wealth and power, undermine the stability of an increasingly precarious middle class, break up more unions, and cause ever more mass migrations and impoverishment across the globe. Stark images of this future already crowd into the imagined worlds of such dystopian novels and films as *Cloud Atlas* (novel, 2004; film, 2012), *The Hunger Games* (film, 2012), and *On Such a Full Sea* (novel by Chang-Rae Lee, 2014). All may be seen as warning signs that play out the social and cultural results of massive inequalities and irreversible ecological degradations that will shape the future if current trends continue. Economist Thomas Piketty's predictions, based in solid historical and mathematical understandings, have recently popped the bland excuses from both political parties in the US since the 1980s that the increasing wealth of Wall Street investors and the corporate elite would gradually raise incomes for all, narrow inequalities, and solve the problems of climate change. And Naomi Klein's *This Changes Everything: Capitalism vs. the Climate* (2014) details the extent of the disaster if the Carbon Neoliberals and Disaster Capitalists continue to exercise their hegemony.

Philip Kitcher raises the very real concern, first articulated by Thomas Malthus in the late eighteenth century, that the earth may not be able to sustain its rising population, especially if climate change and huge inequalities continue. *The Ethical Project* calls attention to the possibility of large-scale human degradation and even starvation in the future, and it challenges Kitcher's readers for solutions. As the novels, films, and political realities noted above suggest, we seem to be slipping toward a world in which the elite will be able to carve out and defend ecologically safe niches for themselves that drain human and material resources from most of the rest of the earth, leaving much of the population to scrounge for survival or perish in an increasingly depleted, violent, and **fear**-ridden world. Yet, each of the films and novels above that depict such a Hobbesian future also feature characters and incidents in which the fundamentals of human equality and respect still matter and where acts of altruism shape crucial moments in their narratives. In asking how the Abolitionists eventually accomplished their goals, Kitcher, with his focus on empathy and psychological altruism, states that Abolitionism began by tearing down "the distortions allowing Europeans to view Africans as utensils rather than people" (2011: 158). From Kitcher's perspective, creating and enforcing international norms and laws reliant on our evolutionary proclivities for empathy and altruism toward the poor and marginal so that they do not become even more expendable must be a major component in the present and future fight for a more egalitarian world.

Defending the scientific justification for taking steps to limit climate change is somewhat akin to the theological justification that the Abolitionists needed before they could mobilize U.S. citizens against what they called the Slavocracy. Kitcher recognizes that before their emotional appeal to end slavery could have an effect, they had to demonstrate that the Christian god of their culture cared about the souls of black folk. Quakers and other Christians began to challenge the Bible's apparent support for slavery in the eighteenth century by pointing out that the suffering of slaves was similar to that of other outcasts in the Bible that had excited the **sympathy** of Jesus. In addition to theological-emotional concerns about Christian duty, several Christians who interacted with slaves on a regular basis also began to empathize with them as near equals – as people with emotions and aspirations similar to their own. Finally, says Kitcher, as a result of these experiences, the budding Abolitionists realized that "the men and women routinely bought and sold are no longer anonymous... but fully, individually, and equally human" (2011: 162). In the more secular twenty-first century, however, a religious justification for protecting the weak carries much less credibility – among most radicals as well as the neoliberal elite. Twenty-first-century progressives need to articulate and publicize a different justification that is as compelling and unifying as Christian belief was for the Abolitionists in the nineteenth.

Another major difference between then and now is that U.S. Abolitionists at mid-century could also count on some support for their goals from the most powerful nation on the planet. Great Britain had ended the slave trade in 1807 and finally abolished slavery altogether at home and in their colonies in 1833. The British navy patrolled the coast of Africa to arrest slavers, and British abolitionists supported their U.S. counterparts in several ways (including helping to secure legal freedom for Frederick Douglass). In contrast, neoliberal oligarchs and corrupt Communist politicians set the policy parameters on economics and energy for the two most powerful nation-states today. Despite their recent agreement on greenhouse gases, there is little political will to reverse our slide into greater economic disparity and ecological disaster in either the US or China today.

Although U.S. Abolitionists had little national political success until the middle of the Civil War, the movement did win some organizational, strategic, and rhetorical victories. In 1830, the Abolitionists broke with the gradualists and colonizers in the American Colonization Society, up to that point the major institution in the U.S. crusade against slavery, to form the biracial American Antislavery Society. Instead of gradually shipping former slaves back to Africa, the new organization aimed to "abolish" slavery all at once. With support from wealthy patrons like Lewis Tappan and the fiery journalism of Abolitionist William Lloyd Garrison, the American Antislavery Society was able to take advantage of Nat Turner's slave rebellion in Virginia in 1831 to underline the hypocrisy in the South's position that painted slavery as a benevolent institution. Through numerous antislavery sermons from Northern pulpits, the ongoing institutional support of a few Protestant denominations, testimonials from runaway slaves, and the dangerous work of helping slaves to freedom, the Abolitionists began to stir the consciences of anxious Christians in the North during the 1830s. In contrast, the campaign to prevent the degradation of humanity (if we can call it that) remains in disarray in 2015, with few strong alliances joining environmental groups to robust progressive institutions aimed at empowering workers and the poor. No one calls the energy barons the "Czars of Carbon" or "Pushers of Petroleum" in public discourse – perhaps rough equivalents to "Lords of the Lash," one of several scurrilous names given to the slave owners by the Abolitionists. Instead, these despoilers are celebrated as international ambassadors of trade, generous philanthropists, and job creators. In terms of comparing these two groups of past and present progressives, most of the current groups have not gotten past the American Colonization Society phase of their opposition.

Unlike many environmentalists, American Abolitionists learned to make the most of opportunities to publicize their cause. When a slave revolt on board the *Amistad* in 1839 led to the arrest of the Africans that had seized the schooner, their jailing in New Haven and public appearances in the next two years created several opportunities for the U.S. Abolitionists to puncture stereotypes about the Africans and to promote them as heroes in the fight for freedom. Performance played an important role in the Abolitionists' ability to publicize the plight of the *Amistad* captives and, by extension, of all slaves in America. By the time of their Supreme Court trial in 1841, the *Amistad* Africans had appeared five times in American courts. Former President John Quincy Adams successfully defended the right of the rebels to freedom, a huge national victory for the Abolitionists as well as the Africans.

Before their return to Africa, the Abolitionist committee that had helped them during their time in the US organized several performances of the former slaves in New York, Philadelphia, Boston, and several mid-sized New England towns, where they appeared to large crowds and supportive publicity. Most of the press coverage commented on their American dress, their muscular physical presence, and their knowledge of Christianity. The two-hour program began with comments on their culture from the translator who had learned their Mende language well enough to teach some English to the Africans and to aid in their legal defense. Then he invited a few of the fastest learners to read some passages from the Bible, sing a church hymn, perform a couple of their own songs, and also answer some questions from the audience in English. The high point of the evening was invariably their leader's reenactment of the *Amistad* rebellion. Although speaking in Mende, the handsome Cinque spoke with such passion and mimed his actions on board the schooner with such clarity that most in the audience easily followed the outline of his performance and shared in his emotions. The empathy and **sympathy** created by his action-filled narrative typically left many spectators in tears. Noting that the Abolitionists certainly achieved their goal of demonstrating that the Africans were capable of becoming "civilized" Christians, historian of the Amistad rebellion, Marcus Rediker, adds that they also achieved "something more important" – seeing "a sovereign political entity called the 'Mendi people' in action" (Rediker 2012: 199).

There is a rough parallel between the kind of emotions and publicity generated by the Mende Africans and their Abolitionist supporters and the ordinary people, political activists, and filmmakers in the contemporary anti-fracking movement across the US. This is one of the few hopeful signs in the otherwise bleak prospects for environmental and economic justice in the US. In such documentary films as *Gasland I* and *Gasland II*, interviewers have gone onto people's farms and into their homes to talk with ranchers, housewives, retirees, and others forced to abandon their residences because of leaking chemicals from the fracking process. Director Josh Fox caught several instances of people turning on their kitchen or bathroom water faucets, holding a match to the spigot, and jumping back in amazement as the methane in the water caught fire. These and similar events have spurred an online network of citizens in western Pennsylvania, where I live, to oppose the incursion of fracking under public parks in Allegheny County and other public lands; the coalition lost the first round in May 2014, but further actions lie ahead. As a member of the network, I can report a growing awareness of the links connecting these events to reports of the increasing number of wildfires in California, the widespread rejection of fracking in the UK and elsewhere (including neighboring New York), and the gradual sinking of the Maldives in the Indian Ocean. Despite the general failure of mainstream media to connect these dots, most of my neighbors in this movement have done so, and the result has been the gradual radicalization of this local movement. In the end, the grassroots desire to protect home, neighborhood, and friends cannot succeed on the local level, as they know, but such family-oriented and groupish beginnings are already connecting these citizens to international allies through self-interest, as well as empathy and altruism.

The success of the exhibitions featuring the *Amistad* Africans helped to spur more local-level action among the Abolitionists. Antislavery fairs, which had emerged in New England in the 1830s, became a more appealing means of publicizing abolitionism than sermons. Featuring music, dancing, occasional performances of amateur plays, sales of baked goods and handicrafts, the fairs were organized by churches to involve their local communities in activities that mixed political protest with Protestant fun. Several of the larger fairs in towns and cities also invited prominent antislavery speakers, such as Angelina Grimke, William Lloyd Garrison, and Henry "Box" Brown, who had escaped from the slave South by securing himself inside a box with breathing holes and effectively mailing himself North. As more slaves made their way to freedom, the Abolitionists encouraged some to testify at antislavery fairs about the conditions they had witnessed and managed to escape. Many Abolitionists understood that meeting with and listening to former slaves was a powerful empathetic tool for their cause. They also knew that arousing white **fears** about rape – specifically, the rape of a female slave by her male owner – was a sure way of gaining passionate converts.

Realizing that such stories evoked strong emotions, the Reverend Henry Ward Beecher held "slave auctions" featuring mostly young mulatto women and children at his church in Brooklyn, New York. He had begun by encouraging his congregation to purchase actual slaves for sale in the South in order to secure their freedom, and this practice led to his staging of auctions in his church. According to performance historian Heather Nathans, "As the slave stood on the church platform, Beecher called upon his congregation to contribute money to redeem the captive. Beecher then paid the slave's owner and the slave was formally freed by the congregation" (Nathans 2009: 193). These popular spectacles evidently played upon several emotional responses from the spectators that crowded his church to overflowing, including **sympathy**, **lust**, **guilt**, and **play**. According to Beecher's wife, the Reverend had watched an auctioneer sell slaves in Kentucky, and his New York spectators appreciated his performance (2009: 196).

Some Abolitionists criticized Beecher for what we would now call the eroticization of slavery, but others cheered him on. Arguably, Beecher's effectiveness as a charismatic Abolitionist leader depended upon the dynamics of blending. For the public, here was a man of the cloth obviously pretending to be a greedy and lascivious auctioneer. Because his audience believed that Beecher was devout in his beliefs, they could understand his role-playing as a feigned mask – in cognitive terms, as a temporary conceptual integration – even as they thrilled to the unruly emotions that his acting rucked up. Recall that Kitcher's primary yardstick for ethical judgment is consequentialism; what consequences did the action lead to? Following Kitcher, the historian of Beecher's slave auctions would need to look very carefully at the consequences of these performances for all concerned, including the female slaves and the Abolitionists in the movement, before arriving at a conclusion about the ethics of such strategies.

Beecher's role-playing certainly invites contemporary performance studies activists to consider similar interventions with regard to specific human tragedies caused, in part, by the oil and gas campaign to dehumanize poverty-bound "losers" around the world when they cannot silence them. Ironically, perhaps, the U.S. Department of Defense has already underlined the causal links among climate change, the world-wide depletion of resources for farming, and civil unrest, rebellion, and war. There are many reasons for the ongoing warfare in Syria, for example, but one of the important ones is the increasing desertification of Syrian land. Media coverage in the US tends to CONTAIN events such as the degradation and destruction of the Syrian people in a box marked international politics, but such containers are no longer adequate when the causes range from authoritarianism to patriarchy, religious fundamentalism, oil and gas producers, the colonial past, and probably several other reasons as well. Performers may not need real female victims from Syria to grab public attention, as Beecher seems to have believed he needed real slaves for his performances, but the rhetoric of sexual sensationalism to oppose the exploitation of humanity should not be altogether ruled out. The question of the consequences of such performances pertains here as well.

Abolitionist and women's rights advocate Lucretia Mott mixed empathy with logic in her speeches denouncing slavery. A Quaker guided by the "inner light within," Mott traveled widely, to parts of the South as well as England, to denounce the U.S. Constitution for upholding slavery and to preach the universality of human rights for all. Theater historian Gay Gibson Cima connects her actions to the ethics of British philosopher Kwame Anthony Appiah's "rooted cosmopolitanism," which shares significant similarities with Kitcher's pragmatic egalitarianism. Like Kitcher, Appiah advocates bridge-building based in commonalities of judgment among different ideological constituencies in movements such as Abolitionism. According to Appiah,

> What we learn from efforts at actual intercultural dialogue – what we learn from travel, but also from poems or novels or films from other places – is that we can identify points of agreement that are much more local and contingent... We can agree, in fact, with many moments of judgment, even if we do not share the [cultural] framework within which those judgments are made. (Appiah 2005: 253)

Kitcher would add that such agreements are possible because we all share strong biocultural predilections for altruism and egalitarianism. Prompted by her inner light, Mott used these predilections to argue that Abolitionists did not need to abandon their own particular religious or political beliefs to arrive at provisional, pragmatic steps to end slavery. Not all agreed with her, of course, but the clarity and forcefulness of her speeches did help to provide some unity of purpose to a movement that was always in danger of breaking apart into strong-willed factions. Mott's modest success provides a rough example for environmental and egalitarian advocates today. Present-day Motts, of course, have several more performance media than public speaking to choose from, including rap songs, animated blogs, and filmmaking.

The next wave of Abolitionist success occurred after the passage of the Fugitive Slave Act in 1850, which obligated northerners to cooperate in the capture and return of runaway slaves to the South. Harriet Beecher Stowe (Henry's sister) wrote *Uncle Tom's Cabin* (1851) in response to the Act, and it sold over 300,000 copies in its first year and a half, a testament, in part, to the ways in which the Act directly implicated northern citizens in perpetuating the South's "peculiar institution." As noted in Chapter 4, Stowe made heroes of George and Eliza, her light-skinned slave characters who escape to the North. Theater-going Americans in the mid 1850s, however, saw two very different adaptations of *Uncle Tom* after it reached the stage in 1852. While the Aiken/Howard version kept most of Stowe's sentimental crusade against slavery, the H.J. Conway adaptation gutted Stowe's antislavery intentions, especially her invitation to empathize and **sympathize** with George, Eliza, and their Abolitionist allies. Instead of celebrating their escape to the North, for example, the Conway version allows the couple to reunite on Simon Legree's planation, where Uncle Tom, rather than being whipped to death as in the novel, also rejoins friends from earlier days. Conway's version, however, called the "Compromise Uncle Tom" by contemporaries, was much more popular than the adaptation done by Aiken for Howard's troupe. Historian of dramatic adaptations of Stowe's novel John W. Frick notes that "once the antiabolition *Uncle Tom's Cabin* was created, it gained momentum as subsequent

Tom Troupes continued to purge any radical messages from the drama" (Frick 2012: 106).

One of the primary reasons that theatrical entrepreneurs turned stage versions of *Uncle Tom's Cabin* against Abolitionism was the popularity of black-faced minstrelsy on northern, working-class stages after the mid-1840s. By the 1850s, minstrel troupes had settled on an idealized version of the southern plantation as a welcome site for white enjoyment; its sentimental Old-Folks-at-Home masters and humorous black folks – from sly tricksters to Earth Mother mammies, "yaller girls," and foolish Jim Crows – could provide a soothing contrast to the violence, crowding, and confusion of northern city life. Not surprisingly, mid-century minstrelsy parodied the Aiken/Howard version of *Uncle Tom's Cabin*. One skit, entitled "Happy Uncle Tom," depicted Stowe's exemplar of self-sacrificing morality and vigorous spirituality as a decrepit old uncle meant to be laughed at for his grotesque jigs and foolish speeches. Minstrel plantation skits and musical numbers avoided the realities of slavery in the deep South – exhausting work, the forced separation of families, and physical torture to increase cotton production – to deliver its audience to a never-never land of domestic warmth, buffoonish slaves, and easy power in which whiteness provided entitlement to security and fun. By 1860, on the eve of the Civil War, the popularity of degrading images of blacks in minstrelsy had spread from urban working-class audiences into middle-class parlors, in part through the success of Stephen Foster's playful and sentimental minstrel tunes with northern auditors.

Regarding the possibilities of empathizing with black characters and endorsing the goals of Abolitionism, the widening success of minstrelsy with all theater audiences kept commercial theater on a short leash in the years before the war. Minstrel skits allowed whites to feel some **pity** and **affection** for the "yaller girls" of plantation life, even though these mulattos were performed (as were all minstrel figures) by white males in blackface. Similarly, a few sentimental melodramas allowed white audiences to **sympathize** with white actresses playing mulatto slaves who were about to be sold to wicked masters or ensnared by slave catchers and returned to imagined rape in the South. Dion Boucicault's *The Octoroon* (1859) Wrung **fear** and **panic** from northern spectators for the first situation, and John Trowbridge's *Neighbor Jackwood* (1857) appealed to similar emotions for the second. In both, a kindly father figure from the North attempts to save the young women from their impending fate; both melodramas allowed spectators to imagine individual acts of salvation for worthy, white-skinned slaves but ruled out wholesale structural change to the system. Nonetheless, *Neighbor Jackwood*, the more radical of the two, did work toward a resolution that pits an entire Vermont town against the Federal Government's Fugitive Slave Act. Still, despite some surface similarities, both productions asked much less from their audiences than Henry Ward Beecher's slave auctions or Lucretia Mott's cosmopolitan abolitionism.

By the late 1850s, the most effective spokespeople for the Abolitionist cause were not well-meaning whites but articulate, escaped slaves. "Immediatist" black abolitionists, such as William Wells Brown and Frederick Douglass, urged their white allies in the movement to keep their focus on the terrible consequences of the system for enslaved bodies and minds. In his public speeches, Douglass frequently drew from his own autobiography, which was replete with horrific images of whippings and degradations, but also demonstrated his own courage and perseverance in the face of overwhelming odds. His very presence at any lectern in the 1850s was a living rebuke to moderate Abolitionists who counseled patience and compromise. Historian Nathans argues that Douglass as a writer and speaker was able to position himself rhetorically as both a witness to and an unwilling participant in the evils of slavery. She gives as an example Douglass's description of the whipping of his Aunt Hester, a part of his autobiography that occurred when he was a boy, which he also used in several of his speeches. By noting that such an experience "was all new to me" (Nathans 2009: 208), Douglass was able to appeal directly to his white auditors, for whom the violence of slavery was also frighteningly eye-opening.

Nathans also draws on the scholarship of John Stauffer, whose *The Black Hearts of Men: Radical Abolitionism and the Transformation of Race* (2002) argues that several Abolitionist radicals on both sides of the racial divide, including John Brown as well as Douglass, created black or white "performative selves" that both "subverted and traversed" conventional racial boundaries (2009: 169). From a cognitive and evolutionary perspective, empathy, blending, and the opportunities opened up by durative events made such performances possible and potentially transformative. Once their auditors understood that such Abolitionists could move freely among several such temporary identities, Douglass, Beecher, and other radicals could and did immerse their spectators' imaginations in the horrors of chattel slavery. One takeaway for "immediatists" fighting Big Oil today is the need to encourage and empower those contemporaries who have directly suffered degradation to increase their rhetorical sophistication and their popular appeal through a range of performative media.

Likewise, as in the 1850s, we should not expect mainstream entertainment institutions and performers seeking stardom in the US today to endorse any radical challenges to the gradual degradation of much of humanity. As May Joseph, the Director of an environmental theater in New York City, notes, "Actors trained in drama schools are already inducted into the neoliberal agenda of profits and celebrity status... An environmental theatre requires a whole different set of skills of which long hours in harsh weather, and the possibility of having no audience, are regular features" (Joseph 2012: 274–75). Joseph is one of many ecologically minded theater artists working to inspire opposition to the degraders of the earth. Her theater, Harmattan, involves its spectators in opposing neoliberalism through experiencing part of the ecological history of the island of Manhattan. Other ecological and egalitarian theaters include the Otesha Project in Ottawa, Canada, and Stan's Café, a European company with a home base in England. Otesha sends small youth groups on bicycle and performance tours around Canada. According to Meg O'Shea, the Otesha traveling company "performs a play about climate-conscious consumer choices for diverse audiences and leads an interactive game designed to draw commitments from audience members to live more sustainably" (O'Shea 2012: 139). Stan's Café performer/facilitators for "Of All the People in All the World," nicknamed "The Rice Show," weigh and measure out carefully calculated piles of rice – each grain representing one person – and place them in public spaces to identify various demographic statistics detailing contrasts between countries, continents, and rich and poor populations. Cognitive scholar Nicola Shaughnessy states that this "cartographic dramaturgy" provides a critique of "cultural homogeneity and corporate capitalism (we are all but grains of rice and McDonald's is a feature of almost every urban environment) as well as emphasizing cultural differences visually and cognitively" (Shaughnessy 2012: 117). Each of these theaters join democratic and ecological concerns to oppose the neoliberal world order.

While these kinds of theatrical productions are certainly an improvement over *The Octoroon* and *Neighbor Jackwood* in the 1850s with regard to the causes that concern them, it is necessary to ask whether live performance events are the best way to engage average spectators in the push for humanitarian and ecological justice. Reversing the degradation of the earth and its peoples requires major institutional and systemic reforms across many nation-states. Given this global reality, Kitcher's criteria of consequentialism require a range and scope for ethical, economic, and political actions that are beyond the ability of live theater to deliver. Live events, however, can certainly provide hope and camaraderie for those activists in the front lines of the struggle, much as local church events provided similar groupish support for the Abolitionists. These events can also help to recruit more activists among the committed.

As we learned from the Occupy Wall Street and Arab Spring uprisings, twenty-first-century radicals eager to stir up mass opposition to the status quo can do this more quickly through smart phones and the Internet than through live performances. Both groups of activists soon realized, however, that Internet **anger** could bring demonstrators to the streets but seemed to be an insufficient tool for changing institutional power. The Internet, however, offers other possibilities. In her book, *Reality Is Broken,* game designer and executive Jane McGonigal proposes that we start to use what we know about designing and playing games to fix actual-world problems. She offers as an example the game *Evoke*, which puts gamers to work on the problems of poverty and climate change. I am not recommending that we follow all of McGonigal's specific ideas for addressing human and ecological degradation, but the general strategy of deploying video games to help solve social and economic problems makes a lot of (Deweyan) sense. Subjunctive possibilities must be explored before actual solutions can be offered, and massive multiplayer games may be a more egalitarian way than current arrangements of decision-making for arriving at just ends. I have already noted the success of *Waking Mars*, an environmentalist game that encourages players to explore possibilities for ecological balance; many more such games already exist and could be put to more radical purposes. Exploring, tweeting, and publicizing such options could put pressure on the oligarchs to open up their system to more democratic processes. In the future, these kinds of performances may help to convince a few nation-states to give up some of their sovereignty to begin a global government, an idea already put forward by Frank Biermann in his *Earth System Governance: World Politics in the Anthropocene* (2014).

As I noted in Chapter 2, historian Marshall T. Poe explores the constraints and satisfactions of historical media networks in his *History of Communications*. Because much of humanity has only recently entered the Internet era and the Internet itself can be manipulated and controlled by the powerful, it is too early to predict if Internet modes of communication may be effective against the Carbon Czars. Poe, however, does provide some hope in his contrast between the social practices that tended to be encouraged by twentieth-century media and those practices that may be more easily advanced in the Internet era. In the place of "hierarchicalized," "centralized," and "professionalized" social practices resulting from three of the network attributes of the previous dominant media, networks reliant on the Internet encourage "equalized," "democratized," and "amateurized" practices (Poe 2011: 152–250). Of course no one flicked a switch and moved all world biocultures from the Hollywood-neoliberal-consumer norms and institutions of the late twentieth century into a more egalitarian world around the year 2000; history never happens that quickly. Nonetheless, the constraints and satisfactions of the Internet era are beginning to change social practices and expectations in ways that may be beneficial for those eager to mount new kinds of performances to challenge the hegemony of the oligarchs. It is easier now than it has ever been to mock the powerful before an audience of millions and to begin to close the vast disparities of power that divide ordinary folks from the neoliberal elite.

This is not to suppose that the fight will be easy. It took a Civil War and a constitutional amendment to ensure the end of slavery in the United States. The Abolitionists remained an embattled minority in the North when the fighting began; only a few northerners joined the Union Army to free the slaves. Even after his famous Proclamation, Lincoln resisted full emancipation, and blackface minstrelsy, an unfortunately accurate gauge of urban sentiment in much of the North, continued to mock the aspirations of freed black men for citizenship and a chance to serve in the Union Army. Nonetheless, the logic of Abolitionism gained traction during the war as deaths and casualties mounted and black refugees sought safety behind Union lines, leading to more hatred of the South, more stories about the horrors of slavery, and greater political leverage for the abolitionists and Radical Republicans. In the move from subjunctive possibility to actual power, many of the Abolitionists transformed themselves from utopian crusaders into political operatives, just as adept at mudslinging and groupish strategies as their opponents in the war-torn North. It is worth noting that Kitcher's ethics do not flinch from the possibility of practicing these necessary measures.

How and whether slavery in the US might have ended without a war cannot be known, but the main impediment to abolition before 1861 had always been the sanctity of private property. As long as slaves were held as property by U.S. citizens, most believed that the only legal way to free them was through monetary compensation, which had been the method used by Great Britain. By 1860, however, there was more capital tied up in slaves and the business of slave trading than in all of the other enterprises in the United States combined; manumission through compensation was not financially feasible. And even if it had been, many capitalists in the

North and South who profited directly or indirectly from slavery would have opposed the measure. Recent historical research and several significant books have made it clear that the rapid growth of capitalism in the US and Great Britain before the U.S. Civil War was based primarily on slavery and cotton. By 1850, British cotton mills imported 72 percent of their cotton from the US, and the global empire of cotton manufacturing, which depended upon slave labor, fueled the Industrial Revolution. While the rise of industrial capitalism in the West has been traditionally linked to private property rights and the rule of law, Sven Beckert's *Empire of Cotton: A Global History* underlines the fact that it was also characterized by the conquest and confiscation of land for growing cotton (both in the US and India) and the violence and coercion of slavery.

Part of the boldness of the Abolitionist campaign in the US was to deny that capitalist property rights should trump human rights where slavery was concerned. Their radical stand, of course, also made it difficult for many Northern and British capitalists to endorse the Abolitionist cause. Lincoln's Emancipation Proclamation, which freed slaves in the Confederacy but not the border states, used the war as an excuse to ignore what had been the property rights of Southern slave holders. But without the bitterness that many in the North felt toward the South for starting the war, it is difficult to believe that Northern capitalists and a minstrelized public would have approved Lincoln's eventual decision to free all the slaves and make them citizens. Lincoln sensed the reluctance of white voters to make this commitment and knew that he had to get the House of Representatives to approve his Thirteenth Amendment before the fighting was over. We can thank the recent film *Lincoln* (2012), scripted by Tony Kushner and starring Daniel Day-Lewis (both of whom combine fierce idealism with savvy politics), for a fairly accurate depiction of the difficult history behind the passage of that amendment.

The problem of slaves as private property and its wartime solution are directly relevant to the current problems of inequality and ecology facing the world today. On the basis of substantial scientific evidence, radical environmentalists like Greenpeace and Bill McKibben, arguably the William Lloyd Garrison of environmentalists, have demanded that the Carbon Oligarchs of the world leave most of their coal, oil, and gas in the ground; to drill, mine, and market it would eventually send the earth past the tipping point into an ecological nightmare, the dynamics of which no one can predict (www.billmckibben.com). McKibben and his activists won a temporary reprieve from the Obama administration on extending the Keystone XL pipeline, but their world-saving demand is nearly beyond the power of any nation-state to enact. It contradicts current property rights and laws as they are defined and enforced around the globe. Further, the decision to leave such resources in the ground would eliminate billions of dollars in assets at a stroke and seriously undermine the future viability of the corporations and governments who control these carbon-based resources. Not surprisingly, Big Oil is ignoring this environmentalist demand and has told the U.S. media that it will extract and sell all of its usable carbon resources and continue to hunt for more (Cohan 2014: 20–24). The economic parallel to the property rights of slaveholders on the eve of the Civil War is inescapable and it raises the same kind of question: How might it be possible to move the world away from the burning of oil and methane without a war to justify such a massive appropriation of property from the likes of Exxon, BP, and Gazprom?

This is bad but not unexpected news for those of us advocating substantial reforms to curb continuing human and ecological degradation. In a recent speech, an influential political consultant to the U.S. oil and gas industry vowed "an endless war" against the environmentalists that he said could only be won by appealing to people's "fear and anger" (Cohan 2014: 22). This is the kind of rhetoric that southern "fire-eaters" used on the eve of the Civil War, when they feared that the North might restrict the expansion of slavery into the West. But, of course, the consultant's speech was also cognitively opportunistic; **fear** and **anger** have worked before in many media campaigns. My citation of this provocation is not meant to predict actual armed conflict, but it should be a wake-up call to those of us who believe that the subjunctive possibilities of our performances can meet and overcome the **fear**-inducing performances paid for by the Czars of Carbon. Can we build stronger alliances, help to raise the necessary funds, and find performative strategies – perhaps through new ways of deploying Internet communication – that are commensurate with the global threat we face? Perhaps, but we'll need to start right away. May Kitcher's substantial evidence of past ethical progress for humanity give us hope and stamina.

Bibliography

Ambady, Nalini, Joan Y. Chiao, and Patricia Deldin. 2006. "Race and Emotion: Insights from a Social Neuroscientific Perspective." In *Social Neuroscience: People Thinking About People*, eds. John T. Cacioppo, Penny Visser, and Cynthia L. Pickett, 209–27. Cambridge, MA: Massachusetts Institute of Technology Press.

Ames, Daniel R. 2005. "Everyday Solutions to the Problem of Other Minds: Which Tools Are Used When." In *Other Minds: How Humans Bridge the Divide Between Self and Others*, eds. Bertram R. Malle and Sara D. Hodges, 158–73. New York: Guilford Press.

Anderson, Eric. 2010. *Sport, Theory, and Social Problems: A Critical Introduction*. New York: Routledge.

Anscombe, G.E.M. 1956. "Intention." *Proceedings of the Aristotelian Society*. 57 (1 January), 321–32.

Appiah, Kwame Anthony. 2005. *The Ethics of Identity*. Princeton University Press.

Asma, Stephen T. 2011. "Gauging Gender." *The Chronicle of Higher Education*. 58 (4 November), B7–B9.

Atran, Scott. 2002. *In Gods We Trust: The Evolutionary Landscape of Religion*. New York: Oxford University Press.

Audi, Robert. 2013. *Moral Perception*. Princeton University Press.

Auslander, Philip. 2008. *Liveness: Performance in a Mediatized Culture*, 2nd edition. London: Routledge.

Austin, J.L. 1961. *Philosophical Papers*. Oxford: Clarendon Press.

Barish, Jonas. 1981. *The Antitheatrical Prejudice*. Berkeley, CA: University of California Press.

Barkow, John, Leda Cosmides, and John Tooby, eds. 1992. *The Adapted Mind: Evolutionary Psychology and the Generation of Culture*. New York: Oxford University Press.

Barrett, Justin L. 2007. "Gods." In *Religion, Anthropology, and Cognitive Science*, eds. H. Whitehouse and James Laidlaw, 105–32. Durham, NC: Carolina Academic Press.

Barsalou, Lawrence W. 2009. "Situating Concepts." In *Cambridge Handbook of Situated Cognition*, eds. Philip Robbins and Murat Aydede, 236–63. Cambridge University Press.

Bateson, Gregory. 1973. "The Message 'This is Play'." In *Steps Toward an Ecology of Mind: Collected Essays in Anthropology, Evolution, and Epistemology*. 236–63. San Francisco: Chandler.

Batson, C. Daniel. 2009. "These Things Called Empathy: Eight Related but Distinct Phenomena." In *The Social Neuroscience of Empathy*, eds. Jean Decety and William Ickes, 3–15. Cambridge, MA: Massachusetts Institute of Technology Press.

Beckert, Sven. 2014. *Empire of Cotton: A Global History*. New York: Alfred A. Knopf.

Benjamin, Walter. (1936) 1986. "The Work of Art in the Age of Mechanical Reproduction." In *Video Culture: A Critical Investigation*, trans. Harry Zohn, eds. John G. Hanhardt, 27–52. Layton, UT: Peregrine Smith Books.

Bering, Jesse M. and David E. Bjorklund. 2007. "The Serpent's Gift: Evolutionary Psychology and Consciousness." In *The Cambridge Handbook of Consciousness*, eds. Philip David Zelazo, Morris Moscovitch, and Evan Thompson, 597–630. Cambridge University Press.

Biermann, Frank. 2014. *Earth System Governance: World Politics in the Anthropocene*. Cambridge, MA: Massachusetts Institute of Technology Press.

Blair, Rhonda. 2008. *The Actor, Image, and Action: Acting and Cognitive Neuroscience*. London: Routledge.

Bleeker, Maaike and Isis Germano. 2014. "Perceiving and Believing: An Enactive Approach to Spectatorship." *Theatre Journal* 66 (October), 363–83.

Bluedorn, Allen C. 2002. *The Human Organization of Time: Temporal Realities and Experience*. Stanford Business Books.

Boehm, Christopher. 1999. *Hierarchy in the Forest: The Evolution of Egalitarian Behavior*. Cambridge, MA: Harvard University Press.

Bogdan, Radu. 2013. *Mindvaults: Sociocultural Grounds for Pretending and Imagining*. Cambridge, MA: Massachusetts Institute of Technology Press.

Bordwell, David and Noel Carroll, eds. 1996. *Post-Theory: Reconstructing Film Studies*. Madison, WI: University of Wisconsin Press.

Bottineau, Didier. 2010. "Language and Enaction." In *Enaction: Toward a New Paradigm for Cognitive Science*, eds. John Stewart, Olivier Gapenne, and Ezequiel A. DiPaolo, 267–306. Cambridge, MA: Massachusetts Institute of Technology Press.

Bourdieu, Pierre. 1984. *Distinction: A Social Critique of the Judgment of Taste*, trans. Richard Nice. Cambridge, MA: Harvard University Press.

——— 1996. *The Rules of Art: Genesis and Structure of the Literary Field*, trans. Susan Emanuel. Stanford University Press.

Boyd, Brian. 2005. "Evolutionary Theories of Art." In *The Literary Animal: Evolution and the Nature of Narrative*, eds. Jonathan Gottschall and David Sloan Wilson, 149–78. Evanston, IL: Northwestern University Press.

——— 2009. *On the Origin of Stories: Evolution, Cognition, and Fiction*. Cambridge, MA: Belknap Press.

Boyer, Pascal. 2001. *Religion Explained: The Evolutionary Origins of Religious Thought*. New York: Basic Books.

Bustamante, Nao. 2002. *Performance of America, The Beautiful*. www.naobustamante.com/art_america.html. Accessed July 27, 2014.
Carlson, Marvin. 2001. *The Haunted Stage: The Theatre as Memory Machine*. Ann Arbor, MI: University of Michigan Press.
  2004. *Performance: A Critical Introduction*, 2nd edition. New York: Routledge.
Carroll, Joseph. 1995. *Evolution and Literary Theory*. Columbia, MO: University of Missouri Press.
Carroll, Joseph, Jonathan Gottschall, John A. Johnson, and Daniel J. Kruger. 2012. *Graphing Jane Austen: The Evolutionary Basis of Literary Meaning*. Cognitive Studies in Literature and Performance. New York: Palgrave Macmillan.
Cash, W.J. 1941. *The Mind of the South*. New York: Knopf.
Cima, Gay G. 2014. *Performing Anti-Slavery: Activist Women on Antebellum Stages*. Cambridge University Press.
Ciompi, Luc and Jaak Panksepp. 2005. "Energetic Effects of Emotions on Cognitions: Complementary Psychobiological and Psychosocial Findings." In *Consciousness and Emotion: Agency, Conscious Choice, and Selective Perception*, eds. Ralph D. Ellis and Natika Newton, 23–56. Amsterdam: John Benjamins Publishing.
Clark, Andy. 2001. *Mindware: An Introduction to the Philosophy of Cognitive Science*. Oxford University Press.
Clark, Bruce and Mark B.N. Hansen, eds. 2009. *Emergence and Embodiment: New Essays on Second-Order Systems Theory*. Durham, NC: Duke University Press.
Clayton, Martin, Rebecca Sager, and Udo Will. 2004. "In Time with the Music: The Concept of Entrainment and Its Significance for Ethnomusicology." *ESM Counterpoint*. 1, 1–45.
Coffin, Rachel, ed. 1948. *New York Theatre Critics' Reviews*. 8. New York: Critics' Theatre Reviews, 1947. 249–52.
Cohan, Steven. 1997. *Masked Men: Masculinity and the Movies in the Fifties*. Bloomington, IN: Indiana University Press.
Cohan, William D. 2014. "Big Oil Wants to Burn It All," *The Nation*. 299, no. 26 (29 December), 20–24.
Colombetti, Giovanna. 2010. "Enaction, Sense-Making, and Emotion." In *Enaction: Towards a New Paradigm for Cognitive Science*, eds. John Stewart, Olivier Gapenne, and Ezequiel A. Di Paolo, 145–64. Cambridge, MA: Massachusetts Institute of Technology Press.
  2013. *The Feeling Body: Affective Science Meets the Enactive Mind*. Cambridge, MA: Massachusetts Institute of Technology Press.
Cook, Amy E. 2007. "Interplay: The Method and Potential of a Cognitive Scientific Approach to Theatre." *Theatre Journal* 4, no. 3 (December), 587–91.
  2010. *Shakespearean Neuroplay: Reinvigorating the Study of Dramatic Texts and Performance Through Cognitive Science*. Cognitive Studies in Literature and Performance. New York: Palgrave Macmillan.
Cook, Patrick J. 2011. *Cinematic Hamlet: The Films of Olivier, Zeffirelli, Branagh, and Almereyda*. Athens, OH: Ohio University Press.

Cosmides, Leda and John Tooby. 2000. "Consider the Source: The Evolution of Adaptations for Decoupling and Metarepresentations." In *Metarepresentations: A Multidisciplinary Perspective*, ed. Dan Sperber, 53–116. New York: Oxford University Press.

Damasio, Antonio. 1999. *The Feeling of What Happens: Body and Emotion in the Making of Consciousness*. New York: Harcourt Brace.

  2003. *Looking for Spinoza: Joy, Sorrow, and the Feeling Brain*. New York: Harcourt Brace.

Davidson, Donald. 2001. *Essays on Actions and Events*. Oxford: Clarendon Press.

Decety, Jean and Philip L. Jackson. 2006. "A Social-Neuroscience Perspective on Empathy." *Current Directions in Psychological Science* 15, no. 2, 54–58.

Dewey, John. 1910. *The Influence of Darwin on Philosophy and Other Essays*. New York: Henry Holt.

  1939. *Freedom and Culture*. New York: Putnam.

  (1938) 1991. *Logic: The Theory of Inquiry in the Later Works*, Volume 12, ed. Jo Ann Boydston. Carbondale, IL: Southern Illinois University Press.

Dickinson, Peter. 2010. *World Stages, Local Audiences: Essays on Performance, Place, and Politics*. Manchester University Press.

Di Paolo, Ezequiel A., Marieke Rohde, and Hanne DeJaegher. 2010. "Horizons for the Enactive Mind, Social Interaction, and Play." In *Enaction: Toward a New Paradigm for Cognitive Science*, eds. John Stewart, Olivier Gapenne, and Ezequiel A. DiPaolo, 33–88. Cambridge, MA: Massachusetts Institute of Technology Press.

Dolan, Jill. 2005. *Utopia in Performance: Finding Hope at the Theatre*. Ann Arbor, MI: University of Michigan Press.

Donald, Merlin. 2001. *A Mind So Rare: The Evolution of Human Consciousness*. New York: Norton.

  2006. "Art and Cognitive Evolution." In *The Artful Mind: Cognitive Science and the Riddle of Human Creativity*, ed. Mark Turner, 3–20. New York: Oxford University Press.

Doxtader, Erik. 2009. *With Faith in the Works of Words: The Beginnings of Reconciliation in South Africa, 1985–1995*. East Lansing, MI: Michigan State University Press.

Edelman, Gerald. 1987. *Neural Darwinism: The Theory of Neuronal Group Selection*. New York: Basic Books.

  1992. *Bright Air, Brilliant Fire: On the Matter of the Mind*. New York: Basic Books.

  2004. *Wider than the Sky: The Phenomenal Gift of Consciousness*. New Haven, CT: Yale University Press.

Edelman, Gerald and Guilio Tononi. 2000. *A Universe of Consciousness: How Matter Becomes Imagination*. New York: Basic Books.

Eibl-Ebesfeldt, Irenaus. 1970. *Ethology: The Biology of Behavior*. New York: Holt, Rinehart and Winston.

Ekman, Paul. 2003. *Emotions Revealed: Recognizing Faces and Feelings to Improve Communication and Emotional Life*. New York: Henry Holt.

Ellis, Michael. 1973. *Why People Play*. Englewood Cliffs, NJ: Prentice-Hall.
Engel, Andreas K. 2010. "Directive Minds: How Dynamics Shapes Cognition." In *Enaction: Toward a New Paradigm for Cognitive Science*, eds. John Stewart, Olivier Gapenne, and Ezequiel A. DiPaolo, 219–43. Cambridge, MA: Massachusetts Institute of Technology Press.
Eversmann, Peter. 2004. "The Experience of the Theatrical Event." In *Theatrical Events: Borders, Dynamics, Frames*, eds. Vicky Ann Cremona, Peter Eversmann, Hans van Maanen, Willmar Sauter, and John Tulloch, 139–74. Amsterdam: Rodopi.
Fagen, Robert. 1995. "Animal Play, Games of Angels: Biology and Brain." In *The Future of Play Theory: A Multidisciplinary Inquiry into the Contributions of Brian Sutton-Smith*, ed. Anthony D. Pellegrini, 23–34. Albany, NY: State University of New York Press.
Farber, Manny. 1951. ["Review of *A Streetcar Named Desire*"], *Nation*. 173 (20 October), 27.
Fauconnier, Gilles. 2005. "Compression and Emergent Structure." *Language and Linguistics*. 6, no. 4, 523–38.
Fauconnier, Gilles and Mark Turner. 2002. *The Way We Think: Conceptual Blending and the Mind's Hidden Complexities*. New York: Basic Books.
Fiske, Edward B, ed. 1999. *Champions of Change: The Impact of the Arts on Learning*. Washington, DC: Arts Education Partnership.
Flanagan, Mary and Helen Nissenbaum. 2014. *Values at Play in Digital Games*. Cambridge, MA: Massachusetts Institute of Technology Press.
Flanagan, Owen. 2007. *The Really Hard Problem: Meaning in a Material World*. Cambridge, MA: Massachusetts Institute of Technology Press.
Fowler, Bridget. 1997. *Pierre Bourdieu and Cultural Theory: Critical Investigations*. London: Sage.
Freeman, Walter J. 2000. *How Brains Make Up Their Minds*. New York: Columbia University Press.
Frick, John W. 2012. *Uncle Tom's Cabin on the American Stage and Screen*. New York: Palgrave Macmillan.
Fromm, Harold. 2009. *Nature of Being Human: From Environmentalism to Consciousness*. Baltimore, MD: Johns Hopkins University Press.
Gallagher, Shaun. 2005. *How the Body Shapes the Mind*. Oxford: Clarendon Press.
Gallese, Vittorio. 2001. "The 'Shared Manifold' Hypothesis: From Mirror Neurons to Empathy." *Journal of Consciousness Studies*. 8, 33–50.
Gallese, Vittorio, Christian Keysers, and Giacomo Rizzolatti. 2004. "A Unifying View of the Basis of Social Cognition." *Trends in Cognitive Sciences*. 8, 1–8.
Gapenne, Olivier. 2010. "Kinesthesia and the Construction of Perceptual Objects." In *Enaction: Toward a New Paradigm for Cognitive Science*, eds. John Stewart, Olivier Gapenne, and Ezequiel DiPaolo, 183–218. Cambridge, MA: Massachusetts Institute of Technology Press.
Gazzaniga, Michael. 2008a. *Learning, Arts, and the Brain: The Dana Consortium Report on Arts and Cognition*, eds. Carolyn Asbury and Barbara Rich. New York: Dana Press.

2008b. *Human: The Science Behind What Makes Us Unique*. New York: Harper Collins.

Gibbs, Raymond W., Jr. 2006. *Embodiment and Cognitive Science*. Cambridge University Press.

Gibson, James J. 1979. *The Ecological Approach to Visual Perception*. Boston, MA: Houghton Mifflin.

Gobert, R. Darren. 2012. "Cognitive Catharsis in *The Caucasian Chalk Circle*." In *Reading Modern Drama*, ed. Alan Ackerman, 217–45. University of Toronto Press.

Godfrey-Smith, Peter. 2003. *Theory and Reality: An Introduction to the Philosophy of Science*. Chicago: University of Chicago Press.

Goffman, Erving. 1959. *The Presentation of Self in Everyday Life*. Garden City, NJ: Doubleday.

1974. *Frame Analysis: An Essay on the Organization of Experience*. New York: Harper & Row.

Gregg, Melissa and Gregory J. Seigworth. 2010. *The Affect Theory Reader*. Durham, NC: Duke University Press.

Grodal, Torben. 2009. *Embodied Visions: Evolution, Emotion, Culture, and Film*. New York: Oxford University Press.

Guthrie, Stewart Elliott. 2007. "Anthropology and Anthropomorphism in Religion." In *Religion, Anthropology, and Cognitive Science*, eds. H. Whitehouse and James Laidlaw, 37–62. Durham, NC: Carolina Academic Press.

Haidt, Jonathan. 2012. *The Righteous Mind: Why Good People Are Divided by Politics and Religion*. New York: Random House.

Harris, Paul. 2000. *The Work of Imagination*. Oxford: Blackwell.

Hartung, Philip. 1951. ["Review of *A Streetcar Named Desire*"], *The Commonwealth*. 54 (28 September), 596–97.

Harvey, David. 2005. *A Brief History of Neoliberalism*. Oxford University Press.

Hines, Melissa. 2004. *Brain Gender*. Oxford University Press.

Hogan, Patrick Colm. 2003. *Cognitive Science, Literature, and the Arts: A Guide for Humanists*. New York: Routledge.

2010. "Literary Universals." In *Introduction to Cognitive Cultural Studies*, ed. Lisa Zunshine, 37-60. Baltimore, MD: Johns Hopkins University Press.

Hutchins, Edwin. 1995. *Cognition in the Wild*. Cambridge, MA: Massachusetts Institute of Technology Press.

2010. "Enaction, Imagination, and Insight." In *Toward a New Paradigm for Cognitive Science*, eds. John Stewart, Olivier Gapenne, and Ezequiel A. DiPaolo, 423–50. Cambridge, MA: Massachusetts Institute of Technology Press.

2014. "The Cultural Ecosystem of Human Cognition." *Philosophical Psychology*. 27, 34–49.

Ingold, Tim. 2000. "Evolving Skills." In *Alas, Poor Darwin: Arguments Against Evolutionary Psychology*, ed. Steven Rose, 273–97. Westminster, MD: Harmony Books.

Jacob, Pierre and Marc Jeannerod. 2003. *Ways of Seeing: The Scope and Limits of Visual Cognition*. Oxford University Press.

Johnson, Mark. 1987. *The Body in the Mind: The Bodily Basis of Meaning, Imagination, and Reason*. Chicago University Press.
    1993. *Moral Imagination: Implications of Cognitive Science for Ethics*. University of Chicago Press.
    2007. *The Meaning of the Body: Aesthetics of Human Understanding*. University of Chicago Press.
Johnston, J.C., R.S. McVann, and R.W. Remington. 1995. "Chronometric Evidence for Two Types of Attention." *Psychological Science*. 6, 365–69.
Joseph, May. 2012. "Aquatopia: Harmattan Theater, Neoliberal Provisionality, and the Future of Water." In *Neoliberalism and Global Theatres: Performance Permutations*, eds. Lara D. Nielsen and Patricia Ybarra, 266–76. Basingstoke, UK: Palgrave Macmillan.
Kazan, Elia. 1988. *Elia Kazan: A Life*. New York: Knopf.
Kelso, J.A. Scott. 1995. *Dynamic Patterns: The Self-Organization of Brain and Behavior*. Cambridge, MA: Massachusetts Institute of Technology Press.
Kemp, Rick. 2012. *Embodied Acting: What Neuroscience Tells Us About Performance*. New York: Routledge.
Kitcher, Philip. 2003. *In Mendel's Mirror: Philosophical Reflections on Biology*. Oxford University Press.
    2011. *The Ethical Project*. Cambridge, MA: Harvard University Press.
    2013. "Battling the Undead: How (and How Not) to Resist Genetic Determinism." In *Arguing About Human Nature: Contemporary Debates*, eds. Stephen M. Downes and Edouard Machery, 160–73. New York: Routledge.
Kittleson, Roger. 2014. *The Country of Football: Soccer and the Making of Modern Brazil*. Los Angeles: University of California Press.
Klein, Naomi. 2014. *This Changes Everything: Capitalism vs the Climate*. New York: Simon & Schuster.
Koch, Sabine C., Thomas Fuchs, and Michela Summa, eds. 2012. *Body Memory, Metaphor, and Movement*. Amsterdam: John Benjamins Publishing Company.
Kögler, Hans-Herbert and Karsten R. Stueber, eds. 2000. *Empathy and Agency: The Problem of Understanding in the Human Sciences*. Boulder, CO: Westview Press.
Kolin, Philip C. 2000. *Williams: A Streetcar Named Desire*. Plays in Production. Cambridge University Press.
Krasner, David and David Z. Saltz, eds. 2006. *Staging Philosophy: Intersections of Theater, Performance, and Philosophy*. Ann Arbor, MI: University of Michigan Press.
Kretchmar, R. Scott. 2007. "The Normative Heights and Depths of Play." *Journal of the Philosophy of Sport*. 34, 2–12.
Kushner, Tony. 1993. *Angels in America, Part I: Millennium Approaches*. New York: Theatre Communications Group.
    1996. *Angels in America, Part II: Perestroika*. New York: Theatre Communications Group.

Lakoff, George. 1987. *Women, Fire, and Dangerous Things: What Categories Reveal About the Mind*. University of Chicago Press.

Lakoff, George and Mark Johnson. 1980. *Metaphors We Live By*. University of Chicago Press.

1999. *Philosophy in the Flesh: The Embodied Mind and Its Challenge to Western Thought*. New York: Basic Books.

Lanman, Jonathan A. 2007. "How 'Natives' Don't Think: The Apotheosis of Overinterpretation." In *Religion, Anthropology and Cognitive Science*, eds. Harvey Whitehouse and James Laidlaw, 105–32. Durham, NC: Carolina Academic Press.

Larson, Steve. 2012. *Musical Forces: Motion, Metaphor, and Meaning in Music*. Musical Meaning & Interpretation, ed. Robert S. Hatton. Bloomington, IN: Indiana University Press.

Latta, Robert L. 1999. *The Basic Humor Process: A Cognitive-Shift Theory and the Case Against Incongruity*. Berlin: Mouton de Gruyter.

Lee, D.N. 1993. "Body-Environment Coupling." In *The Perceived Self: Ecological and Interpersonal Sources of Self-Knowledge*, ed. U. Neisser, 43–67. Cambridge University Press.

Lorenz, Konrad. 1966. *On Aggression*. New York: Harcourt, Brace, & World.

Lutterbie, John. 2011. *Toward a General Theory of Acting: Cognitive Science and Performance*. Cognitive Studies in Literature and Performance. New York: Palgrave Macmillan.

Machery, Edouard. 2013. "A Plea for Human Nature." In *Arguing About Human Nature: Contemporary Debates*, eds. Stephen M. Downes and Edouard Machery, 64–70. New York: Routledge.

Mahar, William J. 1999. *Behind the Burnt Cork Mask: Early Blackface Minstrelsy and Antebellum Popular Culture*. Chicago University Press.

Malle, Bertram F. 2005. "Three Puzzles of Mindreading." In *Other Minds: How Humans Bridge the Divide Between Self and Others*, eds. Bertram R. Malle and Sara De. Hodges, 26–43. New York: Guilford Press.

Mandela, Nelson. 2003. "State of the Nation Address to Parliament." In *Nelson Mandela in His Own Words*, eds. Kader Asmal, David Chidester, and Wilmont James, 148–51. New York: Little Brown.

Mantzavinos, C. 2005. *Naturalistic Hermeneutics*, trans. Darrell Arnold. Cambridge University Press.

Marcus, Gary, Adam Marblestone, and Jeremy Freeman. 2014. "Brain Theory: The Future of Neuroscience," *The Chronicle of Higher Education*. 61, (21 November), B10–B12.

Mason, David V. 2009. *Theatre and Religion on Krishna's Stage: Performing in Vrindavan*. New York: Palgrave Macmillan.

May, Elaine Tyler. 1988. *Homeward Bound: American Families in the Cold War Era*. New York: Basic Books.

McConachie, Bruce. 1992. *Melodramatic Formations: American Theatre and Society, 1820–1870*. Iowa City, IA: University of Iowa Press.

2001. "Doing Things with Image Schemas: The Cognitive Turn in Theatre Studies and the Problem of Experience for Historians." *Theatre Journal.* 53 (December), 569–94.

2003. *American Theater in the Culture of the Cold War: Producing and Contesting Containment.* Iowa City, IA: Iowa University Press.

2006. "A Cognitive Approach to Brechtian Theatre." *Theatre Symposium.* 14, 9–24.

2007. "Falsifiable Theories for Theatre and Performance Studies." *Theatre Journal.* 59 (December), 553–77.

2008. *Engaging Audiences: A Cognitive Approach to Spectating in the Theatre.* New York: Palgrave Macmillan.

2010. "Towards a Cognitive Cultural Hegemony." In *An Introduction to Cognitive Cultural Studies,* ed. Lisa Zunshine, 134–50. Baltimore, MD: Johns Hopkins University Press.

2011. "An Evolutionary Perspective on Play, Performance, and Ritual." *TDR: The Journal of Performance Studies.* 55 (Winter), 33–50.

2012a. "Ethics, Evolution, Ecology, and Performance." In *Readings in Performance and Ecology,* eds. Wendy Arons and Theresa J. May, 91–100. New York: Palgrave Macmillan.

2012b. "Moving Spectators Toward Progressive Politics by Combining Brechtian Theory with Cognitive Science." In *Playing with Theory in Theatre Practice,* eds. Megan Alrutz, Julia Listengarten, and M. Van Duyn Wood, 148–60. New York: Palgrave Macmillan.

2013. *Theatre and Mind.* Houndmills: Palgrave Macmillan

2014a. "All in the Timing: The Meanings of Streetcar in 1947 and 1951." In *The Theatre of Tennessee Williams,* ed. Brenda Murphy, 181–205. New York: Bloomsbury.

2014b. "Chapter 25: Empathetic Engagement." In *Performance Studies: Key Words, Concepts, and Theories,* ed. Bryan Reynolds, 227–33. New York: Palgrave Macmillan.

McConachie, Bruce and F. Elizabeth Hart, eds. 2006. *Performance and Cognition: Theatre Studies and the Cognitive Turn.* London: Routledge.

McDonagh, Eileen and Laura Pappano. 2008. *Playing with the Boys: Why Separate Is Not Equal in Sport.* Oxford University Press.

McGonigal, Jane. 2011. *Reality Is Broken: Why Games Make Us Better and How They Can Change the World.* New York: Penguin.

McKibben, Bill. *Bill McKibben: Author, Educator, Environmentalist.* October 28, 2014. www.billmckibben.com/index.html.

McNeill, David. 2005. *Gesture and Thought.* University of Chicago Press.

Michaels, Lloyd. 1985. *Elia Kazan: A Guide to References and Resources* (Reference Publication in Film). Boston, MA: GK Hall.

Miell, Dorothy, Raymond MacDonald, and David J. Hargreaves, eds. 2005. *Musical Communication.* Oxford University Press.

Miller, A. 2006. *Collected Plays, 1944–1961,* ed. Tony Kushner. New York: Library of America.

Muñoz, José Esteban. 2009. *Cruising Utopia: The Then and There of Queer Futurity.* New York University Press.
Nathans, Heather S. 2009. *Slavery and Sentiment on the American Stage, 1787–1861.* Cambridge University Press.
Neisser, Ulric. 1976. *Cognition and Reality: Principles and Implications of Cognitive Psychology.* San Francisco: W.H. Freeman.
Nellhaus, Tobin. 2010. *Theater, Communication, Critical Realism.* New York: Palgrave Macmillan.
Nereson, Ariel. 2014. "Feeling History: Emotion, Performance, and Meaning-Making in Bill T. Jones/Arnie Zane Dance Company," Ph.D. thesis, University of Pittsburgh.
  1951. ["Review of A Streetcar Named Desire"], *Newsweek.* 38 (October 1), 87.
Noë, Alva. 2004. *Action in Perception.* Cambridge, MA: Massachusetts Institute of Technology Press.
Nussbaum, Martha. 2001. *Upheavals of Thought: The Intelligence of Emotions.* Cambridge University Press.
  2013. *Political Emotions: Why Love Matters for Justice.* Cambridge, MA: Harvard University Press.
Oatley, Keith. 2011. *Such Stuff as Dreams: The Psychology of Fiction.* Chichester: Wiley-Blackwell.
O'Connor, Flannery. 1961. "Some Aspects of the Grotesque in Southern Fiction." In *Mystery and Manners: Occasional Prose,* eds. Sally Fitzgerald and Robert Fitzgerald, 36–50. New York: Farrar, Stras and Giroux.
O'Shea, Meg. 2012. "Bikes, Choices, Action! Embodied Performances of Sustainability by a Traveling Theater Group." In *Readings in Performance and Ecology,* eds. Wendy Arons and Theresa J. May, 137–46. New York: Palgrave Macmillan.
Ott, Ulrich. 2007. "States of Absorption: In Search of Neurological Foundations." In *Hypnosis and Conscious States: The Cognitive Neuroscience Perspective,* ed. Graham A. Jamieson, 257–70. Oxford University Press.
Paavolainen, Teemu. 2012. *Theatre/Ecology/Cognition: Theorizing Performer-Object Interaction in Grotowski, Kantor, and Meyerhold.* Cognitive Studies in Literature and Performance. New York: Palgrave Macmillan.
Pagel, Mark. 2012. *Wired for Culture: Origins of the Human Social Mind.* New York: W.W. Norton & Co.
Palmer, David. 2012. "Tragedy, Integrity, Guilt, and Shame: Understanding John Proctor." *The Arthur Miller Journal.* 7 (Fall), 23–41.
Panksepp, Jaak. 1998. *Affective Neuroscience: The Foundations of Human and Animal Emotions.* New York: Oxford University Press.
Panksepp, Jaak and Lucy Biven. 2012. *The Archaeology of Mind: Neuroevolutionary Origins of Human Emotions.* New York: W.W. Norton & Co.
Petit, Philippe. *To Reach the Clouds: My High Wire Walk Between the Twin Towers.* www.amazon.com/To-Reach-Clouds-Philippe-Petit. Accessed December 22, 2014.

Pfaff, Donald W. 2015. *The Altruistic Brain: How We Are Naturally Good*. New York: Oxford University Press.
Phelan, Peggy. 1993. *Unmarked: The Politics of Performance*. London: Routledge.
  1998. "Introduction." In *The Ends of Performance*, eds. Peggy Phelan and Jill Lane, 1–19. New York University.
  n.d. "Philippe Petit." *Wikipedia*, http://en.wikipedia.org/wiki/Philippe_Petit. Accessed July 26, 2014.
Piketty, Thomas. 2014. *Capital in the Twenty-First Century*, trans. Arthur Goldhammer. Cambridge, MA: Belknap Press.
Plantinga, Carl. 2009. *Moving Viewers: American Film and the Spectator's Experience*. Berkeley, CA: University of California Press.
Plotkin, Henry. 2003. *The Imagined World Made Real: Towards a Natural Science of Culture*. New Brunswick, NJ: Rutgers University Press.
Poe, Marshall T. 2011. *A History of Communications: Media and Society from the Evolution of Speech to the Internet*. Cambridge University Press.
Port, Robert and Timothy van Gelder, eds. 1995. *Mind as Motion: Explorations in the Dynamics of Cognition*. Cambridge, MA: Massachusetts Institute of Technology Press.
Provine, Robert R. 2000. *Laughter: A Scientific Investigation*. New York: Viking.
Pryor, Richard. 1979. *Richard Pryor: Live in Concert* [Recorded 1978]. Long Beach, CA.
Ray, William J. 2007. "The Exercise of Agency and Hypnosis from an Evolutionary Perspective." In *Hypnosis and Conscious States: The Cognitive Neuroscience Perspective*, ed. Graham A. Jamieson, 223–40. Oxford University Press.
Read, Stephan J. and Lynne C. Miller. 2005. "Explanatory Coherence and Goal-Based Knowledge Structures in Making Dispositional Inferences." In *Other Minds: How Human Beings Bridge the Divide Between Self and Others*, eds. Bertram R. Malle and Sara D. Hodges, 124–39. New York: Guilford Press.
Rediker, Marcus. 2012. *The Amistad Rebellion: An Odyssey of Slavery and Freedom*. New York: Viking.
Reed, John Shelton. 2003. *Minding the South*. Columbia, MO: University of Missouri Press.
Richerson, Peter J., and Robert Boyd. 2005. *Not By Genes Alone: How Culture Transformed Human Evolution*. University of Chicago Press.
Rilling, James K. 2008. "Neuroscientific Approaches and Applications Within Anthropology." *Yearbook of Physical Anthropology*. 51, 2–32.
Roberts, Robert C. 2003. *Emotions: An Essay in Aid of Moral Psychology*. Cambridge University Press.
Salazar, Philippe-Joseph. 2002. *An African Athens: Rhetoric and the Shaping of Democracy in South Africa*. Mahwah, NJ: Lawrence Erlbaum Associates.
Savran, David. 2014. "Trafficking in Transnational Brands: The New 'Broadway Style' Musical." *Theatre Survey*. 55, 3, 318–42.
Schechner, Richard. 1993. *The Future of Ritual*. London: Routledge.
  2003. *Performance Theory*. London: Routledge.
  2006. *Performance Studies: An Introduction*, 2nd edition. London: Routledge.

Scott, Robert A. 2006. "Making Relics Work." In *The Artful Mind: Cognitive Science and the Riddle of Human Creativity*, ed. Mark Turner, 211–24. Oxford University Press.

Shamay-Tsoory, Simone. 2009. "Empathetic Processing: Its Cognitive and Affective Dimensions and Neuroanatomical Basis." In *The Social Neuroscience of Empathy*, eds. Jean Decety and William Ickes, 215–32. Cambridge, MA: Massachusetts Institute of Technology Press.

Shanon, Benny. 2010. "Toward a Phenomenological Psychology of the Conscious." In *Enaction: Toward a New Paradigm for Cognitive Science*, eds. John Stewart, Olivier Gapenne, and Ezequiel A. DiPaolo, 387–424. Cambridge, MA: Massachusetts Institute of Technology Press.

Shaughnessy, Nicola. 2012. *Applying Performance: Live Art, Socially Engaged Theatre, and Affective Practice*. Basingstoke, UK: Palgrave Macmillan.

Singer, Peter. 2000. *A Darwinian Left: Politics, Evolution, and Cooperation*. New Haven, CT: Yale University Press.

Snow, C.P. 1969. *The Two Cultures: and A Second Look: An Expanded Version of the Two Cultures and the Scientific Revolution*. Cambridge University Press.

Solis, Felipe, Roberto V. Alonso, and Roberto Rochin. 2010. *Ulama: El Juego de la Vida y la Muerte/The Game of Life and Death*. Sinaloa Autonomous University.

Spector, Susan. 1989. "Alternative Visions of Blanche DuBois: Uta Hagen and Jessica Tandy in A Streetcar Named Desire." *Modern Drama*. 32, 545–60.

Spence, J.E., ed. 1994. *Change in South Africa*. London: Pinter Publishers.

Spolsky, Ellen. 2001. "Darwin and Derrida: Cognitive Literary Theory as a Species of Post-Structuralism," *Poetics Today*. 23, 43–62.

Stanyek, Jason and Benjamin Piekut. 2010. "Deadness: Technologies of the Intermundane." *The Drama Review*. 54 (Spring), 12–38.

Stauffer, John. 2002. *The Black Hearts of Men: Radical Abolitionists and the Transformation of Race*. Cambridge, MA: Harvard University Press.

Steinbock, Anthony J. 2014. *Moral Emotions: Reclaiming the Evidence of the Heart*. Chicago: Northwestern University Press.

Sterelny, Kim. 2012. *The Evolved Apprentice: How Evolution Made Humans Unique*. Cambridge, MA: Massachusetts Institute of Technology Press.

Stern, Daniel N. 1985. *The Interpersonal World of the Infant: A View from Psychoanalysis and Developmental Psychology*. New York: Basic Books.

Stewart, John. (1951) 1993. *A Streetcar Named Desire*, dir. Elia Kazan (Film). Burbank, CA: Warner Brothers.

——— 2010. "Foundational Issues in Enaction as a Paradigm for Cognitive Science." In *Enaction: Toward a New Paradigm for Cognitive Science*, eds. John Stewart, Olivier Gapenne, and Ezequiel A. DiPaolo, 1–31. Cambridge, MA: Massachusetts Institute of Technology Press.

Stromberg, Peter G. 2009. *Caught in Play: How Entertainment Works on You*. Stanford University Press.

Stoutland, Frederick. 2011. "Introduction: Anscombe's *Intention* in Context." In *Essays on Anscombe's Intention*, eds. Anton Ford, Jennifer Hornsby, and Fredderick Stoutland, 1–22. Cambridge, MA: Harvard University Press.

Stowe, Harriet Beecher. 1852. *Uncle Tom's Cabin, or, Life Among the Lowly*. Boston, MA: John P. Jewett & Co.
Sutton-Smith, Brian. 1997. *The Ambiguity of Play*. Cambridge, MA: Harvard University Press.
Sutton-Smith, Brian, John Gerstmyer, and Alice Meckley. 1988. "Playfighting as Folkplay Amongst Preschool Children," *Western Folklore*. 47, 3, 161–76.
Thompson, Evan. 2007. *Mind in Life: Biology, Phenomenology, and the Sciences of the Mind*. Cambridge, MA: Belknap Press.
Tomasello, Michael. 1999. *The Cultural Origins of Human Cognition*. Cambridge, MA: Harvard University Press.
   2008. *Origins of Human Communication*. Cambridge, MA: Massachusetts Institute of Technology Press.
   2009. *Why We Cooperate*. Cambridge, MA: Massachusetts Institute of Technology Press.
Tomlinson, Gary. 2015. *A Million Years of Music: The Emergence of Human Modernity*. New York: Zone Books.
Tribble, Evelyn B. 2011. *Cognition in the Globe: Attention and Memory in Shakespeare's Theatre*. Cognitive Studies in Literature and Performance. New York: Palgrave Macmillan.
Turchin, Peter. 2013. "The Puzzle of Human Ultrasociality: How Did Large-Scale Complex Societies Evolve?" In *Cultural Evolution: Society, Technology, Language, and Religion*, eds. Peter Richerson and Morten H. Christiansen, 61–74. Cambridge, MA: Massachusetts Institute of Technology Press.
Turner, Mark. 2006. "The Art of Compression." In *The Artful Mind: Cognitive Science and the Riddle of Human Creativity*, ed. Mark Turner, 93–114. Oxford University Press.
Turner, Victor. 1988. *The Anthropology of Performance*. New York: PAJ.
Van Gelder, Timothy and Robert F. Port. 1995. "It's About Time: An Overview of the Dynamical Approach to Cognition." In *Mind as Motion: Explorations in the Dynamics of Cognition*, eds. Robert F. Port and Timothy van Gelder, 1–43. Cambridge, MA: Massachusetts Institute of Technology Press.
Varela, Francisco J., Evan Thompson, and Eleanor Rosch. 1991. The Embodied Mind: Cognitive Science and Human Experience. Cambridge, MA: Massachusetts Institute of Technology Press.
Vincs, Kim. 2013. "Structure and Aesthetics in Audience Responses to Dance." In *The Audience Experience: A Critical Analysis of Audiences in the Performing Arts*, eds. Jennifer Radbourne, Hilary Glow, and Katya Johanson, 129–42. Bristol: Intellect.
Ward, Lawrence M. 2002. *Dynamical Cognitive Science*. Cambridge, MA: Massachusetts Institute of Technology Press.
Werry, Margaret. 2013. "Interdisciplinary Objects, Oceanic Insights: Performance and the New Materialism." In *Theater Historiography: Critical Interventions*, eds. Henry Bial and Scott Magelssen, 221–34. Ann Arbor, MI: University of Michigan Press.

Whitehouse, Harvey. 2007. "Towards an Integration of Ethnography, History, and the Cognitive Science of Religion." In *Religion, Anthropology, and Cognitive Science*, eds. H. Whitehouse and James Laidlaw, 247–80. Durham, NC: Carolina Academic Press.

Williams, Tennessee. (1951) 1975. *A Streetcar Named Desire*. New York: Penguin Putnam.

Wilson, David Sloan. 2015. *Does Altruism Exist: Culture, Genes, and the Welfare of Others*. New Haven, CT: Yale University Press.

Wilson, Elizabeth. 1998. *Neural Geographies: Feminism and the Microstructure of Cognition*. New York: Routledge.

Winner, Ellen, Thalia R. Goldstein, and Stéphan Vincent-Lancrin. 2012. *Art for Art's Sake? The Impact of Arts Education*. OECD Publishing. http://dx.doi.org/10.1787/9789264180789-en.

Wittgenstein, L. 1980. *Remarks on the Philosophy of Psychology*, Volume 2, trans. C.G. Lukhardt and M.A.E. Aue. Oxford: Blackwell.

Woody, Erik and Henry Szechtman. 2007. "To See Feelingly: Emotion, Motivation, and Hypnosis." In *Hypnosis and Conscious States: The Cognitive Neuroscience Perspective*, ed. Graham A. Jamieson, 241–56. Oxford University Press.

Wright, David J. 2015. "The Philosophy of Action in Live Performance Interaction Design: Aligning Flows of Intentionality," Ph.D. Dissertation. University of Pittsburgh.

Zarrilli, Philip B., Bruce McConachie, Gary J. Williams, and Carol F. Sorgenfrei. 2010. *Theatre Histories: An Introduction*, 2nd edn. New York and London: Routledge.

Zbikowski, Lawrence M. 2002. *Conceptualizing Music: Cognitive Structure, Theory, and Analysis*. Oxford University Press.

  2006. "The Cognitive Tango." In *The Artful Mind: Cognitive Science and the Riddle of Human Creativity*, ed. Mark Turner, 115–32. Oxford University Press.

Zlatev, Jordan, Timothy P. Racine, Chris Sinha, and Esa Itkonen, eds. 2008. *The Shared Mind: Perspectives on Intersubjectivity*. Amsterdam: John Benjamins B.V.

Zunshine, Lisa. 2006. *Why We Read Fiction: Theory of Mind and the Novel*. Columbus, OH: Ohio State University Press.

Zunshine, Lisa, ed. 2010. *Introduction to Cognitive Cultural Studies*. Baltimore, MD: Johns Hopkins University Press.

Index

Abolitionism, 196, 199–200
  and Christian belief, 189–91
  Beecher, Reverand Henry Ward, 192
  Brown, William Wells, 196
  Douglass, Frederick, 196
  Mott, Lucretia, 193
action, 29, 32–33, 59, 65, 95, 105, 129, 140, 169
  agency, 76–78
  intentionality, 29, 43, 54, 77
    flows of, 32, 79, 87, 152, 153
  perception-action system, 104, 131, 137, 140–41, 149
  subjunctive, 46, 53, 59, 63, 66–67, 75, 109, 181
affect, 98, 103–104, 107, 108, 140. *See also* emotion
affordances, 132
altruism, 41, 44, 100–101, 168, 171, 172–75, 188, 192
  altruism profile, 175–77
Ambady, Nalini, 148
America, The Beautiful, 112
Ames, Daniel, 165
Amistad slave revolt, 191
Anderson, Eric, 182–85, 186
Angels in America, 168, 175–82
  Millennium Approaches, 175–79
  Perestroika, 175, 178–82
animal performance, 63
Anscombe, Elizabeth, 32–33
Appiah, Kwame Anthony, 193
Aristotle, 13, 32–33, 110
Asma, Stephen, 12
Atkinson, Brooks, 156
Atran, Scott, 69, 70
Auslander, Philip, 73
Austin, J.L., 128
autopoiesis, 31, 63, 140, 142

Barish, Jonas, 130
Barkow, John, 9
Barnes, Howard, 155
Barnes, Richard, 156
Barsalou, Lawrence, 49–51
Batson, C. Daniel, 120
behaviorism, 16, 17, 142
Benjamin, Walter, 73
  aura, 73–74, 91
Bill T. Jones/Arnie Zane Dance Company, 116–19
bioculture, 28, 29, 59, 65, 78, 95–97, 105, 154, 157, 160, 166, 187, 194, 199
Biven, Lucy, 133, 134
Bluedorn, A.C., 135
body-environment coupling, 83, 139. *See also* empathy, sensorimotor coupling
Boehm, Christopher, 92, 174
Bogdan, Radu, 45
Bottineau, Didier, 20
Boucicault, Dion, 195
Boyd, Brian, 36–39, 70, 99
Boyer, Pascal, 68
Branagh, Kenneth, 61
Brando, Marlon, 155
Brecht, Bertolt, 101, 102, 120
  verfremdungseffekt, 10, 101
Burke, Kenneth, 28
Bustamante, Nao, 112

Cameron, James, 109–11, 136
capitalism, 94, 187, 197, 199
Carlson, Marvin, 14–16
Cash, W.J., 157
Chapman, John, 155
Clark, Andy, 93
class, 94, 95, 172, 184, 188, 195
cognitive networks, 93, 95–97
Cold War, 158–60
Cole, Nat "King", 76–77
Cole, Natalie, 76–77
Coleman, Robert, 155
Colombetti, Giovanna, 104, 107, 140–41

216

Index

concepts
  as simulations, 49–51
  conceptual blending, 45–49, 53, 59, 61, 84
    spectator blending, 62, 109
  conceptual integration. *See* conceptual blending
conditional, subjunctive, 44. *See also* action, subjunctive
connectionism. *See* theories of cognition
Conquergood, Dwight, 18, 28
consciousness, 34
  higher-order, 34, 41, 63, 121
  primary, 33, 34
Cook, Amy E., 62
cultural-cognitive ecosystem, 65, 93–97, 119, 131–32, 152, 154, 182

Damasio, Antonio, 104, 105, 107, 141, 169
dance, 116–19, 150–51
Darwin, Charles, 19, 170
Davidson, Donald, 32
deconstructionism, 14
Derrida, Jacques, 10, 72
Dewey, John, 19, 34, 81, 170
Dickinson, Peter, 128
discourse theory, 14
Dolan, Jill, 28
Donald, Merlin, 47, 56

Edelman, Gerald, 33–34, 41
Ekman, Paul, 61, 102–103
emotion, 3, 98–100, 101–19, 140, 157
  anger, 100, 116, 148, 156, 198, 201
  primary emotions, 40, 103
  production emotion, 109
  seven distinct neurobiological emotion systems, 104
  social/secondary emotions, 41, 105, 108
    antipathy, 100, 102, 105, 108
    contempt, 105
    embarrassment, 105, 109, 113, 122, 179
    guilt, 55, 105, 122, 143, 174, 179, 192
    humiliation, 105
    pride, 105, 108, 109, 119, 126, 174
    shame, 41, 55, 105, 124, 126, 174
    sympathy, 100, 102, 105–106, 108, 114, 120, 122, 126, 144, 145, 146, 156, 163, 166, 172, 176, 177, 189, 191, 192
empathy, 22, 40, 102, 119–23, 145, 148, 149, 162, 163, 179, 180, 181, 188, 191, 192
  affective, 120
  cognitive, 120
  imaginary transposition, 122
  reiterated empathy, 122, 126–27

sensorimotor coupling, 121, 124, 134–37, 142
enaction. *See* theories of cognition
Enlightenment, 3, 8
entrainment, 135–37, 142, 151
environmentalism, 187, 188, 190, 191, 193, 200
  Big Oil, 196–201
  McKibben, Bill, 200
  Otesha Project, 197
  Stan's Café, 197
epistemology, 6–8, 10, 14, 17–18, 25–26, 51, 71
  naturalism, 19
ethics, 167
  consequentialism, 186, 193, 197
  morality, 107
  relativism, 186
  virtue ethics, 101
event, 46–48
evolution, 14, 17, 18, 29, 33–53, 56, 62, 174
  continuity theory, 17
  cultural, 93–97

Farber, Manny, 156
Fauconnier, Giles, 45, 48, 109
feminism, 11, 15
film, 60–62, 74–77, 107–11, 156–57
Flanagan, Mary, 90
Foucault, Michel, 9, 11, 14, 28, 169, 186
Freeman, Walter J., 139–42, 149
Freud, Sigmund, 160

Gallese, Vittorio, 60, 121
games, 198
  computer, 45, 77, 86, 89–90
  sports, 83–86, 95, 136, 138, 182–86
Gasland I and II, 191
Gazzaniga, Michael, 1–2, 3–6
Geertz, Clifford, 15, 28
gender, 11–12, 157, 159, 183–84
genre, 78, 94, 96, 130, 132
Gerstmyer, John, 42
Gibbs, Raymond, 152
Gibson, James J., 132
Godfrey-Smith, Peter, 19, 25
Goffman, Erving, 9, 15, 28
Grodal, Torben, 74–75, 110
groupishness, 54, 69, 96, 100, 101, 172, 183

Hartung, Philip T., 156
Hawkins, William, 155
Hogan, Patrick Colm, 13
Huizinga, Johan, 15
Hume, David, 106, 110, 170
Hutchins, Edwin, 93–97, 152

Hypersensitive Agency Detection Device (HADD), 68, 74

image schemas, 52, 65, 81–82, 84–90, 152, 153
James, William, 170
Johnson, Mark, 3, 34–35, 46, 51, 52, 59, 81, 85, 169
Jonker, Ingrid, 124–26
Joseph, May, 197

Kant, Immanuel, 3
Kazan, Elia, 155, 156, 166
Kelso, J.A. Scott, 142
Kemp, Richard J., 60, 138
Kindertotenleider, 113–16
Kitcher, Philip, 168–75, 185–88
knowledge. *See* epistemology
Kretchmar, R. Scott, 84
Kronenberger, Louis, 155
Kushner, Tony, 168, 175–82, 200

Lacan, Jacques, 28
Lakoff, George, 46, 52, 59, 85
language, 20, 31, 33, 35, 36, 41, 44, 49, 51–52, 53–54, 58, 73, 93, 115, 129, 153
  literacy, 78–79
  performative, 128
Latta, Robert, 147
Lee, D.N., 83
Leigh, Vivien, 155–58
Locke, John, 3, 15
Lord Krishna, 71
Louppe, Laurence, 150

MacAloon, John, 28
Machery, Edouard, 13–14
machine performance, 63
Magelson, Scott, 28
magic "if", 45
Mahler, Gustav, 113–16
Mandela, Nelson, 123–27
Marx, 96. *See also* Marxism
Marxism, 15
McGonigal, Jane, 198
McLuhan, Marshall, 28
meaning, 30
memory, 2, 20, 49, 154, 157, 160, 166
  procedural memory, 49
  semantic memory, 49, 50
mental projecting, 44
metaphor, 52, 85–87
Mill, John Stuart, 186
Miller, Lynn, 162
minstrelsy, 195, 196
mirror neurons, 22, 39–40, 60, 121
morality, 10, 121, 122, 126

Morehouse, Ward, 155
Muñoz, Josè, 28
music, 86–89, 113–16, 136
  jazz, 76–77, 88, 99
  John Lennon, "Hey, Jude", 88
  musicking, 56
  vitality affects, 87, 115
musical comedy, 94–95

narrative, 27, 38, 41, 56, 60, 74, 79, 84, 88, 91, 92, 94, 106, 108, 110, 111–13, 134, 144, 146, 147, 162, 164, 165, 176, 178, 191
Nathans, Heather, 192, 196
nature and nurture, 9–14
Neighbor Jackwood, 195, 197
Neoliberalism, 187
Nereson, Ariel, 117–19
networks. *See* cognitive networks
Nietzsche, Friedrich, 169, 186
Nissenbaum, Helen, 90
Nussbaum, Martha, 101, 106, 116, 119

O'Connor, Flannery, 157
O'Shea, Meg, 197
object performance, 26
Octoroon, The, 195, 197
Olivier, Laurence, 61
Ong, Walter, 28

Pagel, Mark, 100–101
Panksepp, Jaak, 103–105, 133, 134
Petit, Philippe, 79–83
Pfaff, Donald, 171
Phelan, Peggy, 72
phenomenology, 8, 10, 21
Piekut, Benjamin, 77
Plantinga, Carl, 107–11
Plato, 130
  The Republic, 130
play, 36–39, 44, 65, 67, 78, 133–34
Plotkin, Henry, 127
Poe, Marshall T., 96, 198
Port, Robert F., 138
poststructuralism, 7, 52, 72, 103, 150, 151
Pryor, Richard, 142–49

race, 101, 148, 149. *See also* abolitionism
ras lila. See Lord Krishna
Read, Stephen, 162
Reason, Matthew, 150
Rediker, Marcus, 191
Reed, John Shelton, 157
religious belief, 175, 178–79, 181, 189, 193, 194
Richard Pryor: Live in Concert, 142–49
ritual, 71

animal, 35
City Dionysia, 90–91
religious, 66–71, 90–91, 134, 173
Roach, Joseph, 28
role-play, 44, 48, 53, 63, 89–90
Rosch, Eleanor, 8, 21
Rousseau, Jean-Jacques, 130

Salazer, Philippe-Joseph, 124
Saussure, Ferdinand de, 10, 28
Schechner, Richard, 6, 18, 28, 35, 65, 91
Schechner, William, 16
Scott, Robert A., 68
semiotics, 10, 14, 153
Sessions, Roger, 87–88
Shakespeare, William, 58–62
  Hamlet, 58–62
Shamay-Tsoory, Simone G., 120
Shaughnessy, Nicola, 197
Singer, Peter, 171
slavery. *See* Abolitionism
social constructivism, 12–15
spectating system, 131, 137, 139–41, 142, 144, 147, 149, 153
Sprinkle, Annie, 128–29
Stanislavsky, Konstantin, 44
Stanyek, Jason, 77
Stauffer, John, 196
Stein, Edith, 122
Stephens, Elizabeth, 128–29
Sterelny, Kim, 106, 173–74
Stern, Daniel, 87, 115
Stewart, John, 21, 33
Stoutland, Frederick, 32
Stowe, Harriet Beecher, 194
Stravinsky, Igor, 88
Stromberg, Peter G., 66, 89
Sutton-Smith, Brian, 39

Tandy, Jessica, 155–58
Thelen, Esther, 139
theories of cognition
  computational theory of mind (CTM), 21, 120
  connectionism, 16, 21
  distributed cognition, 93, 128
  dynamic systems theory (DST), 16, 131, 142, 149, 151, 162, 165
    attractors, 142, 144–47, 151, 163, 165
    boundary conditions, 142, 143–44, 145–46, 147, 151, 160
    perturbations, 142, 146–47, 151
    phase shift, 142, 145–46, 147
  embodiment, 27, 29–31, 71, 73, 76, 89, 169
  enaction, 8, 16, 17, 21–26, 29–33, 99, 101, 131, 139
  The Shared Mind, 103
  representationalism, 21
  situated cognition, 16
  Theory of Mind (ToM), 102
Thompson, Evan, 8, 21, 30, 106, 121–23
Titanic, film, 109–11, 136
Tomasello, Michael, 43, 47, 106
Tomlinson, Gary, 55, 56
Tooby, John, 9
tools, 33, 44, 48, 74, 94
Trowbridge, John, 195
Turchin, Peter, 182
Turner, Mark, 45, 48, 109
Turner, Victor, 9, 15, 28, 91

Uncle Tom's Cabin, 116–19, 194–95
  Aiken/Howard, 194
  Conway, H.J., 194

van Gelder, Timothy, 138
van Gennep, Arnold, 91
Varela, Francisco J., 8, 21
video game. *See also* games, computer
Vincs, Kim, 150–52

Watts, Richard, 155
Williams, Tennessee, 156, 162–63, 166
  Streetcar Named Desire, 154–67
willing suspension of disbelief, 10, 75
Wilson, David Sloan, 171
Wilson, Edwin O., 169
Wittgenstein, Ludwig, 102

Zbikowski, Lawrence, 88